# DODGE SCAT PACK
# PLYMOUTH R TRANSIT SYS

Chrysler's Muscle Car Marketing Programs 1968–1972

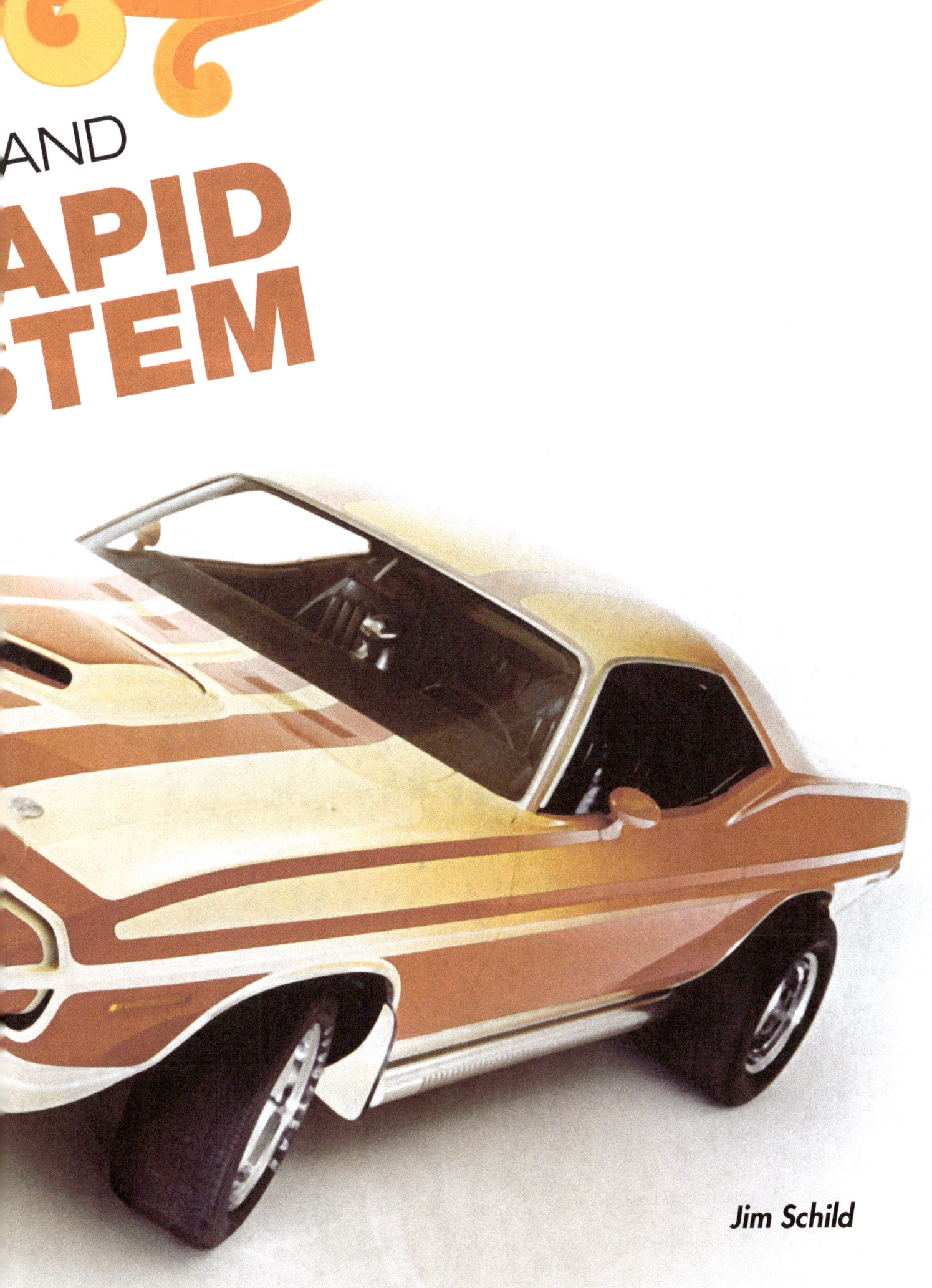

Jim Schild

# CarTech®

CarTech®, Inc.
6118 Main Street
North Branch, MN 55056
Phone: 651-277-1200 or 800-551-4754
Fax: 651-277-1203
www.cartechbooks.com

© 2018 by Jim Schild

All rights reserved. No part of this publication may be reproduced or utilized in any form or by any means, electronic or mechanical, including photocopying, recording, or by any information storage and retrieval system, without prior permission from the Publisher. All text, photographs, and artwork are the property of the Author unless otherwise noted or credited.

The information in this work is true and complete to the best of our knowledge. However, all information is presented without any guarantee on the part of the Author or Publisher, who also disclaim any liability incurred in connection with the use of the information and any implied warranties of merchantability or fitness for a particular purpose. Readers are responsible for taking suitable and appropriate safety measures when performing any of the operations or activities described in this work.

All trademarks, trade names, model names and numbers, and other product designations referred to herein are the property of their respective owners and are used solely for identification purposes. This work is a publication of CarTech, Inc., and has not been licensed, approved, sponsored, or endorsed by any other person or entity. The Publisher is not associated with any product, service, or vendor mentioned in this book, and does not endorse the products or services of any vendor mentioned in this book.

Edit by Wes Eisenschenk
Layout by Connie DeFlorin

ISBN 978-1-61325-879-8
Item No. CT597C

Library of Congress Cataloging-in-Publication Data
Names: Schild, James J., author.
Title: Dodge Scat Pack and Plymouth Rapid Transit System : Chrysler's muscle car marketing programs 1968-1972 / Jim Schild.
Description: Forest Lake, MN : CarTech, [2018] |
Identifiers: LCCN 2017028057 | ISBN 9781613253434
Subjects: LCSH: Dodge automobile. | Dodge automobile--History. | Plymouth automobile. | Plymouth automobile--History. | Muscle cars--History.
Classification: LCC TL215.D6 S34 2018 | DDC 338.7/629222097309046--dc23
LC record available at https://lccn.loc.gov/2017028057

Written, edited, designed and printed in the U.S.A.

**Front Cover:** *Illustrator George Trosley recreates a stylistic impression of the advertising artwork seen within the Rapid Transit System marketing program. (Artwork Courtesy George Trosley)*

**Frontispiece:** *The 1971 Plymouth Sport Fury GT was arguably the most unusual of the Rapid Transit System cars. The large C-Body was not generally thought of as a high-performance vehicle, but the promotional materials and shows strongly presented that image to the buying public. (Curtiss Lichty Photo)*

**Title Page:** *Very little changed aesthetically from the 1970 rendition. The front fascia, mirrors, shaker assembly and sidepipes returned for 1971. One clear addition was a dash-mounted tachometer. (Photo Courtesy Promotions, Inc.)*

**Back Cover Photos**

**Top:** *A full-page magazine period ad shows the three optional engines used in the 1968 Dodge Scat Pack performance cars. The 426 Hemi and 440 V-8 were used for the Coronet R/T while the 340 was used in the Dart GTS. (Dodge, Plymouth and the AMC designs are registered trademarks of FCA US LLC.)*

**Middle:** *One of the displays set up for the 1970 sales season with visitors checking out the special customized 1970 Plymouth Road Runner built especially for the events.*

**Bottom:** *The passenger-side front view of a blue 2015 Charger R/T 392 Hemi Scat Pack from Charger's online brochure and information site. The Scat Pack Charger is equipped with 20 x 9–inch forged aluminum wheels and performance tires as well as a hood scoop. (Dodge, Plymouth and the AMC designs are registered trademarks of FCA US LLC.)*

# TABLE OF CONTENTS

Acknowledgments ..................................................6

### Chapter 1: 1966–1967: Precursors to the Scat Pack and Rapid Transit System ...................7
The Performance Image Begins ............................7
The Charger Arrives .............................................11
Charger Advertising ..............................................14
Plymouth's Performance Offering .........................14
Plymouth Performance Ad Campaigns ..................15
New A-Body Lines.................................................18
Dodge Dart.............................................................18
Plymouth Valiant and Barracuda ...........................21

### Chapter 2: 1968: Dodge Scat Pack Program .............26
Birth of the Scat Pack ............................................27
First Scat Pack Show Car: Daroo I .........................30
Scat Pack Trademark Battle ....................................30
Scat Pack Lineup for 1968 .....................................31
1968 Dodge Charger R/T .......................................31
1968 Dodge Coronet R/T .......................................34
1968 Dodge Dart GTSport .....................................36
First Marketing Appearance of the Scat Pack.........40
1968 Dodge Coronet Super Bee.............................40
Scat Pack Dealership Advertising ...........................43

### Chapter 3: 1969: Dodge Scat Pack Program .............45
Scat Pack Lineup for 1969 .....................................45
1969 Dodge Charger R/T .......................................46
1969 Dodge Charger 500 .......................................48
1969 Charger Daytona............................................49
1969 Dodge Coronet R/T .......................................53
1969 Dodge Coronet Super Bee .............................55
1969½ Super Bee A12 ............................................57
1969 Dart GTS.......................................................60
1969 Dart Swinger 340 ..........................................60

### Chapter 4: 1970: The Scat Pack Continues ...............67
Dodge Announces Scat City ..................................69
Scat Pack Lineup for 1970 .....................................72
The Challenger ......................................................74
Charger R/T ...........................................................74
1970 Dodge Coronet R/T .......................................77
1970 Coronet Super Bee ........................................79
1970 Dodge Challenger ..........................................83
1970 Dodge Challenger R/T ...................................84
1970 Challenger T/A ..............................................86
1970 Dodge Dart Swinger 340 ...............................89
Winding Down the 1970 Model Year .....................92

### Chapter 5: 1971: Bold New Designs ........................93
Scat Pack Lineup for 1971 .....................................94
1971 Dodge Charger R/T and Super Bee................95
1971 Dodge Challenger R/T .................................103
1971 Dodge Demon 340 ......................................106
The End of the Scat Pack.....................................108

### Chapter 6: 1968–1969: Toward the Plymouth Rapid Transit System .................................109
Plymouth Performance for 1968..........................109
1969 High-Performance Plymouths.....................114
The Slot Car World ..............................................117

### Chapter 7: The Rapid Transit System Is Born .......119
1970 Rapid Transit System Lineup ......................120
1970 GTX .............................................................121
1970 Plymouth Road Runner and Road Runner Superbird .......................................123
1970 Plymouth Barracuda ....................................126
1970 Plymouth `Cuda ...........................................127
1970 Plymouth `Cuda AAR ..................................130
1970 Plymouth Duster..........................................131
1970 Fury .............................................................134

### Chapter 8: Rapid Transit System for 1971 .............148
1971 Model Overview..........................................149
1971 Road Runner and GTX ................................149
1971 `Cuda ...........................................................156
1971 Plymouth Duster 340...................................159
1971 Sport Fury GT..............................................160

### Chapter 9: Rapid Transit System for 1972 .............166
1972 Rapid Transit System Lineup ......................166
1972 Road Runner................................................167
1972 Plymouth `Cuda ...........................................169
1972 Plymouth Duster 340...................................171
The End of the High-Performance Era.................172

### Chapter 10: 2014 and Beyond: Scat Pack Version 2.0 ..173
The Hemi Returns................................................173
2014: Chrysler Markets Directly to the Muscle Car Era ..........................................174
2015 Dodge Scat Pack ..........................................179
2016 Scat Pack Lineup .........................................183
2017 Scat Pack Program.......................................188
2018 Scat Pack Program.......................................191

# ACKNOWLEDGMENTS

No book of this type could be completed without the help and generosity of a number of people who contribute their knowledge and photos or allow their cars to be photographed so that an author can offer the most accurate information. I have to thank those enthusiasts, photographers, advertising agencies, and, of course, FCA Chrysler and Dodge automobiles without which I could not have finished this work.

First and foremost, Chrysler Corporation, Dodge and Plymouth Divisions, and more recently FCA Chrysler and Dodge must be recognized for their creative and artistic advertising and marketing programs that made the Scat Pack and Rapid Transit System story one of the most successful in the history of automobile marketing.

It is impossible to list all of the talented people who made these programs possible but some of the most important were the artists, designers, and advertising executives, including Bob Osborn, David Bradesku, Paul Williams, Harvey J. Winn, Diran Yazejian, N. Dale Dalton, Jack Smith, Andy Agosta, and many more too numerous to name.

Most important to me was the cooperation of the owners of these wonderful automobiles who allowed me to create and use images of their cars to illustrate this book. These generous owners include but are not limited to: Richard Heidbreder, Tim Kues, Tim Wellborn, Michele and Craig Dozeman, Howard Tony Crull, Ken Mosier of Final Details Restoration, Greg Hernandez, Tim Ranch, Arthur Idler, Joel Johnson, Paul McGhee, Mike Boswell, Reggie Key, Kathy and Greg Mosley, Jerry Brown, Paul Veney, Joseph Gershenov, Steve Southwell, Andy Markiewicz, Roger Schmeling, Paul R. Sanborn, Dan Printz, Denny Guest, Art Idler, and Tom Lembeck.

Thanks must go to those who contributed their own special photography and information, including Tim Costello, Mark Rozman, Kori Alexander, Diego Rosenberg, Jim Stodolka, and David Zatz of AllPar.com. Most important, I must recognize and thank Steve Juliano for all of his efforts in collecting and preserving the history of the Scat Pack and Rapid Transit System cars, documents, and memorabilia. Without his work, much of this history might be lost. Other images and advertising are courtesy of Chrysler Corporation, Fiat Chrysler Automobiles, and *Mopar* magazine, produced and published by J. R. Thompson Company.

Last, but certainly not least, I must thank my editor, Wes Eisenschenk, for his vision and unfaltering attention to detail and quality. Without his work, this book would not exist.

---

**Publisher's Note:** *In reporting history, the images required to tell the tale will vary greatly in quality, especially by modern photographic standards. While some images in this volume are not up to those digital standards, we have included them, as we feel they are an important element in telling the story.*

---

# 1966–1967

## Precursors to the Scat Pack and Rapid Transit System

*"Names such as Sox & Martin, Dick Landy, The Ramchargers, and The Golden Commandos were emblazoned in print and burned into the minds."*

Chrysler Corporation was anything but a newcomer to performance-related advertising and publicity campaigns in the late 1960s. As early as 1963 Dodge and Plymouth magazine advertising featured the winning Max Wedges of the Ramchargers and The Lawman, Al Eckstrand. After the dramatic win at the 1962 NHRA Nationals, Chrysler's advertising staff used the concept of "Win on Sunday, Sell on Monday" more than any other manufacturer to promote the power and reliability of their engine and chassis combinations to let the performance-minded public know that these were the *only* new cars to own. Their full-page magazine ad titled "Some days you win, some days you lose" with Max Wedge 1963 Dodges in both pictures made it clear that you always win with Dodge.

By 1965, full-page ads featuring Hemi engines with altered-wheelbase hardtops filled the pages of enthusiast publications, including *Hot Rod, Car Craft, Super Stock & Drag Illustrated,* and others. Names such as Sox & Martin, Dick Landy, The Ramchargers, and The Golden Commandos were emblazoned in print and burned into the minds of ready young readers and potential new car buyers. The popular and creative ads featured not only the Dodge and Plymouth styling, but also detailed close-up views of the 426 race Hemi engines that pushed those cars to the winner's circle. The public learned quickly that if they wanted to win on the street or the dragstrip, Chrysler products were the way to serve their purpose.

### The Performance Image Begins

By 1966, Chrysler began to shift advertising agencies around to find the right people to direct their new campaigns in print and other media. Dodge and Dodge trucks had been depending on Batten, Barton, Durstine & Osborn (BBD&O) Advertising since 1960, and this experienced company did a

*A 1967 Dodge Rebellion ad shows the entire lineup. It includes the Charger, Coronet, Dart, and the full-size Polara. All were available with a full line of engine and drivetrain options. (Dodge, Plymouth, and the AMC design are registered trademarks of FCA US LLC)*

Plymouth combined the announcement of the 1967 Belvedere GTX with Plymouth's "Out to Win You Over" slogan used in 1967. The red GTX is featured with the standard 440-ci V-8 and optional racing stripes on the hood in this ad from *Hot Rod* in November 1966. (Dodge, Plymouth, and the AMC design are registered trademarks of FCA US LLC)

great job for the market. In 1966, Plymouth moved its $30 million account from the old guard N. W. Ayer to the Young & Rubicam Group, which was already handling the Chrysler Corporate and Imperial lines. The company came out of the gate in 1967 with its "Plymouth is Out to Win You Over" marketing phrase for the 1967 model year. This campaign included the red heart logo in all of its print and TV ads. Dodge and BBD&O opened 1966 with the "Dodge Rebellion" theme in 1966 and carried it over for 1967.

By the end of the 1966 selling season, the climate of the performance and racing world shifted from the ultra-high-performance altered-wheelbase Funny Cars, Factory Experimental, and Super Stock sedans to stock class drag racing machines that were closer to actual production automobiles similar to those that the public drove on the street. Even the Dodge and Plymouth drag racing support moved from the Super Stock and Funny Cars to NHRA stock classes to promote sales of real daily driver models that were available to the public. Factory-backed drag racers were told they would have to change to stock vehicles for 1967. Dodge and Plymouth leadership knew that they did not sell a lot of funny cars or top fuel dragsters the previous year, so they had to focus their advertising and publicity programs on stock vehicles.

### RO23 and WO23

This dramatic change did not mean that Dodge and Plymouth would not supply race cars to their teams and independent drivers. Early in 1967, the Hemi-powered RO23 Plymouths and WO23 Dodges were delivered to the racers. These new competitors were based on the popular Dodge 440 two-door hardtop and Plymouth Belvedere II two-door hardtop rather than the base lightweight Maximum Performance sedans of 1964 and 1965. The RO/WO cars were available in white only and had a lightweight hood scoop,

This original, unrestored 1966 Dodge Coronet two-door sedan has a 426 Hemi engine and 4-speed transmission. The model year 1966 was unique in that the 426 Hemi was available in any Dodge or Plymouth B-Body model except the station wagon.

similar to those used in 1965. Although the RO/WO Hemi hardtops were not just cars that customers would drive on the street, they represented a normal passenger car to enthusiast buyers who saw one like theirs winning on the dragstrip on the weekends.

A significant mechanical and model change for the 1967 model year for both Dodge and Plymouth was the more limited availability of the 426 Street Hemi engine package. For 1966, the Hemi was available in any B-Body model and body type, except the station wagon; customers could have the powerful street beast in anything they desired, including base two-door and four-door sedans. In addition, none of the Coronet and Belvedere based models had any type of performance badging that identified them as something special on the street.

### 440 Super Commando and Magnum

For 1967, the availability of the 426 Street Hemi and the introduction of the monster 440-ci high-performance engines were limited to only the Plymouth Belvedere GTX and the Dodge Coronet R/T models. These models were uniquely badged not only for the 426 Hemi engine, but included special badging and trim for the specific models. The R/T received a special badge on the grille and decorative hood louvers, while the GTX had unique badging plus twin nonfunctional scoops on the hood that immediately caught the attention of the public and especially the youthful performance-minded buyers. Dropping the availability of these high-performance powerplants from the low, high, and premium line series models had an intention that would become even more obvious and important for the 1968 model year lineup.

The 1967 Dodge Coronet R/T and its Plymouth Belvedere GTX stablemate were the first B-Body Chrysler products badged and identified as high-performance cars. The R/T was identified by its VIN prefix of WS23 or WS27 for Dodge Sport two-door hardtop or convertible. The name of the R/T stood for Road and Track and the car featured a red-trimmed metal badge on the driver-side end of the grille, the distinctive rear deck panel, and on each of the rear-side quarter panels. The hood of the 1967 Dodge Coronet R/T had four nonfunctional

*This white 1967 Dodge Coronet R/T two-door hardtop was Dodge's first attempt to give a high-performance model an identity, a unique appearance and a name. R/T stood for Road and Track and only two high-performance engines were available.*

*The 1967 Plymouth GTX had a standard Super Commando 440 engine that produced 375 hp at 4,600 rpm. The chrome valvecovers, unique air cleaner plate and red battery caps are correct for this one-owner RR-1 Yellow Plymouth.*

*The 1967 Dodge Coronet R/T interior was a high line style in vinyl. This R/T is equipped with a Dark Red pleated vinyl interior trim scheme with bucket seats and a steering column–mounted shifter for the TorqueFlite transmission.*

*This white 1967 Dodge Coronet R/T is equipped with a 425-hp 426 Hemi. The large chrome-plated air cleaner housing sits atop a pair of Carter AFB 4-barrel carburetors.*

*One of the first images of the new Dodge Fever girl was in this ad from late 1967. She encouraged prospective buyers to "Join the fun. Catch Dodge Fever." The outfit, a white miniskirt and high white boots, was a sign of the styles in that era. (Dodge, Plymouth, and the AMC design are registered trademarks of FCA US LLC)*

louvers at the rear center of the hood panel. The R/T grille still had four headlights but differed from the standard 1966 Coronet grille by its fine vertical bars and lack of the 1966-only vertical center bar. Its design was similar to that of the new Charger, but without the Charger's retractable headlights. When so equipped, a 426 Hemi badge identifying the engine was placed on the center rear of the front fenders. The R/T had no horizontal bright trim. A total of 10,109 Coronet R/T hardtops and 628 R/T convertibles were built.

### Dodge Rebellion Operation 67

Advertising for both Dodge and Plymouth advanced along with the performance-oriented models. For Dodge, the BBD&O program continued with the "Dodge Rebellion Operation 67," a theme that began in 1966. Among the most popular and successful parts of Dodge's ad programs during that era were the print and TV ads featuring the beautiful, long-legged, and blonde-haired Pamela Austin.

Nebraska-born Austin (real name Pamela J. Akert) was an experienced actress and dancer who was already well known for her appearances in TV shows of the time such as *Surfside 6*, *The Twilight Zone*, and *The Wild Wild West*. She also appeared in Elvis Presley films, including *Kissing Cousins* and *Blue Hawaii*. Even with this caliber of work behind her, she quickly became best known as the Dodge Girl in the Dodge Rebellion ads. Usually dressed in white knee-high boots, tight mini-skirts, or bright white sports pants, her youthful and attractive look was sure to draw the attention of the younger market, especially the young men who were likely to buy a new high-performance Dodge.

One of the more interesting magazine ads for Dodge was the full-page ad displayed in the May 1967 issue of *Motor Trend*. The ad featured a red 1967 Dodge Coronet R/T, "The newest hot one from Dodge," with a black vinyl roof and mag-type wheel covers. The text below the nine color pictures touted the optional 426 Hemi, tachometer, long-duration cam, and high-performance red streak tires. The interesting part of the ad was the large white words spread top and bottom that read "Road Runner." Of course, at this point few knew about the Plymouth Road Runner that would be offered later that year on the 1968 models, but to see it being used on a Dodge advertisement was unique. Obviously, the Dodge ad agency did not know what the Plymouth ad agency was doing at the time.

*This interesting full color, full-page ad was featured in* Road & Track *magazine in 1967. Dodge advertising chose to use "Road Runner" in this ad, making one believe they were not aware of Plymouth's plans to use this name for its new performance car in the 1968 model year. (Dodge, Plymouth, and the AMC design are registered trademarks of FCA US LLC)*

a name taken from a number of special 1964 and 1965 show cars, was a totally new design that incorporated the basic sculptured layout of the Coronet with a distinctive fastback body design. In place of the normal B-pillar, the Charger's roofline swept back to the end of the rear deck. The rear wheel openings were more rounded and the side windows closely followed the lines of the roof. The 1965 Charger II prototype was clearly based on the design concepts of the 1964 Barracuda, but it was longer and wider.

Most of the development of the 1966 Coronet was already under way in the Dodge Design studio under the direction of manager John Schwarz. A team led by product planner Chuck Kelly; his boss, Burt Bouwkamp; and Dodge chief designer Bill Brownlie was charged with making the proposed fastback as distinctive as possible while keeping the list price under $3,500. The principal exterior stylist responsible for the Charger was Carl "Cam" Cameron, who had retired from his position as manager of Chrysler's Product Identity Studio several years earlier. Cameron went to Chrysler in 1962 from Ford and the Detroit-based industrial design firm of Sundberg-Ferar.

In Cameron's July 1963 formative sketch, he designed around the Coronet cowl, windshield, A-pillar, and hardtop door. The fastback roofline took shape, with the side window opening drawn back to end in a vertical drop just forward of

### The Charger Arrives

On January 1, 1966, coinciding with the introduction of the 426 Street Hemi, a derivative of the advertised 117-inch-wheelbase (actually 116-1/2 inches) Dodge Coronet was introduced with great fanfare. The 1966 Dodge Charger,

*This studio shot was prepared for use in 1966 Charger advertising campaigns. The Charger was an entirely new model and new concept for 1967 and it employed the first use of fastback roof styling in a larger B-Body car. (Dodge, Plymouth, and the AMC design are registered trademarks of FCA US LLC)*

*The 1966 Charger advertising and sales brochures showed the distinctive features and accessories available exclusively with the Charger. The new electroluminescent instrument panel was unique to the Charger. An inside hood release was considered special in 1966. (Dodge, Plymouth, and the AMC design are registered trademarks of FCA US LLC)*

*A January 1966 ad for the new Charger identifies it as "The Leader of the Dodge Rebellion." This silver Charger with red interior was used in most of the introductory Charger ads. (Dodge, Plymouth, and the AMC design are registered trademarks of FCA US LLC)*

Dodge Scat Pack and Plymouth Rapid Transit System

*The Dodge Fever girl was the centerpiece model for many Dodge and Charger ads in 1967. Here she illustrates the active youth culture the Charger wants to attract. The clothes she is wearing are typical of the times. (Dodge, Plymouth, and the AMC design are registered trademarks of FCA US LLC)*

the rear wheels. The hardtop style was chosen, even though it meant adding reinforcing panels in the C-pillars and across the upper deck panel, the boxed-in construction of which doubled as a rigid support for the deck lid. This support also served as a plenum chamber for venting air from the passenger compartment through two large rubber-covered vents. The Charger front-end treatment featured hidden electrically operated retractable quad headlights in the grille.

The Charger was the first glimpse of Dodge's "Rebellion" (as it was called in ads) toward a new, unique and identifiable performance image that came with a name. It was obvious that younger, performance-minded buyers were the market and Charger's styling made that very clear.

The interior of the 1966 Charger was among its most unique features; it included front and rear stylish bucket seats and a full-length bright metal-trimmed floor console. The carpet-backed rear seats could be folded down individually to provide more than 7 feet of cargo storage through the rear deck area. A 1,421-square-inch, gently curved backlight provided more than adequate rear vision. The instrument panel was also unique and had four round instrument clusters, which included a 6,000-rpm tachometer and a 150-mph speedometer. The instruments were lighted by an electroluminescent system powered by an under-dash transformer.

The Charger's standard engine was the 318-ci polysphere-head V-8; it made 230 hp and used a 2-barrel carburetor. The 318 was not a track burner but adequate for the compromise of street power and economy. The lineup included a 265-hp B-block 361, a 325-hp 4-barrel-equipped 383, and the top-of-the-line 426 Hemi that produced an advertised 425 hp. All but the 318 were offered with optional 4-speed manual or 3-speed TorqueFlite automatic transmissions. A 3-speed manual was available only with the 318.

The Charger continued for the 1967 model year with few changes, although a new 375-hp 440 RB V-8 was also made available. Cosmetically, the only immediately noticeable change in appearance was the addition of small chrome-plated turn signal indicators on the top of each front fender. The indicators were connected to the full-length bright moldings on the top crease of the body. The interior was changed a bit by removing the full-length console and replacing it with an optional front console and a center armrest for the rear seats. A standard full-width front bench seat was now

*This restored 1966 Dodge Charger has a 426 Hemi engine and a 4-speed manual transmission. It is finished in Silver and has a red interior trim, exactly like the Charger used in many of the ads when it was introduced in January 1966.*

Chapter 1: 1966–1967    13

available. The same engine and transmission choices were still on the docket but, of course, the polysphere 318 was replaced with the new LA-series 318 engine.

The 1966 and 1967 Dodge Charger fastback body styling seemed to lend itself very well to winning on the long NASCAR tracks. Initial runs on the high-banked ovals at speed showed handling to be tricky, but later in the season Dodge engineers developed a small and rather crude bolt-on rear spoiler that corrected the problem. The spoiler was available to the public as a dealer-installed accessory and is rare today. The fix must have worked because Dodge increased its win record from two in 1965 to eighteen by the end of 1966. Dodge also took the Manufacturer's Championship for 1966, followed by Plymouth with sixteen wins. Of course, these wins at the tracks transferred to sales at the showrooms around the country. A total of 37,344 Chargers were built in 1966 and 15,788 for 1967.

### Charger Advertising

The 1966 and 1967 Chargers were included as part of BBD&O and Dodge's "Dodge Rebellion" theme, but a number of the Charger ads maintained their own theme that represented the new design and direction of the Charger. The 1966 Charger was a mid-model year introduction in January 1966, so the character of Charger advertising did not exactly follow that of the rest of the Dodge line.

The initial January 1966 ads for the new Charger consistently featured a striking silver Charger with red interior equipped with a 426 Hemi engine. It was clear that Dodge had great expectations for the Charger, identified as "The leader of the Dodge Rebellion." Of course, the Charger was included as part of the pack with Dodge girl Pamela Austin accompanying it in many of the ads.

One of the introductory ads for the Charger featured Pamela in a blue outfit and boots sitting on the bottom half of the advertisement below the silver Charger holding an antique pistol. She was saying, "Put down undersized and under-equipped personal cars . . . go Charger." Another showed her in a multi-photo two-page layout with a small bomb in her hand next to the same silver Charger. The text read, "Charger, The leader of the Dodge Rebellion." Dodge was hitting hard to push all of the exciting new features of the Charger.

### Racing Chargers

Additional publicity was provided by Chargers used as race cars both in NASCAR and NHRA drag racing competition. Drivers Sam McQuagg (number 98) and David Pearson (number 6) ran 1966 Chargers with reduced displacement 405-ci Hemi engines to satisfy NASCAR rules for that year. Famed Indy driver Mario Andretti drove a white Charger under number 5 for Cotton Owens at the July 4, 1966, Firecracker 400 but finished only 31st. The unique styling and sloping roof were still enough to attract the attention of fans.

Not too many Chargers were used on the dragstrip; the additional weight of the body was a hindrance and the perceived aerodynamics was not advantageous at drag racing speeds. A few notable exceptions were the *Color-Me-Gone* Dodge funny car of Roger Lindamood, the *Stardust* funny car of Don Schumacher, and the *Tickle Me Pink* funny car of Al Graeber. Veteran Super Stock Driver "Lawman" Al Ekstrand drove his 426 Hemi-powered blue and white 1966 Charger in Super Stock. All of this exposure added to the already aggressive Charger performance advertising produced by Dodge in 1966 and 1967.

### Plymouth's Performance Offering

The performance-oriented 1967 Plymouth Belvedere GTX was Plymouth's answer to the Coronet R/T. The GTX was identified by its VIN as either an RS23 two-door hardtop or RS27 two-door convertible. The GTX name was probably a takeoff of the popular Pontiac GTO (Gran Turismo Omologato), but Plymouth did not have the actual meaning possessed by the Pontiac. The GTX was based on the Belvedere but had no bright body trim as did the Satellite and Belvedere II, giving it a clean and sporty appearance.

Its identifying features included Belvedere and GTX badges on the front side of each front fender, a distinctive GTX badge on the passen-

*This restored 1967 Charger is finished in KK-1 Medium Turquoise Poly, one of the standard colors for 1967. The identifying feature of the 1967 Charger is the chrome fender-mounted turn signal indicators.*

*This red 1966 Plymouth Belvedere I two-door sedan is equipped with the 425-hp 426 Hemi engine and a TorqueFlite automatic transmission. The low-line sedan with the highest-performance Hemi engine was only available in 1966.*

ger side of the rear deck, and a pair of unique nonfunctional scoops on the hood. Optional wide, dual longitudinal contrasting vinyl stripes were available that intersected under the hood scoops and finished on the rear deck of the body. The driver-side rear quarter of the GTX housed a distinctive chrome-plated, racing-type, quick-fill fuel filler cap. A vertical medallion on the front center of the hood identified the engine.

Like the Coronet R/T, the Belvedere GTX offered a standard 375-hp 440-ci big block wedge V-8. The 440 had a single 4-barrel carburetor and dual exhausts. The only optional engine was the 426-ci Hemi V-8 rated conservatively at 425 hp. The Hemi had an impressive pair of Carter AFB 4-barrel carburetors mounted between its wide Hemi heads. Either an A833 4-speed manual or a 3-speed TorqueFlite automatic would be available to transmit power to the rear axle. A heavy-duty Dana 60 rear axle with a 9¾-inch ring gear was supplied when the Hemi was ordered with the manual transmission. A total of 12,010 1967 Belvedere GTX hardtops and 680 convertibles were built.

### Plymouth Performance Ad Campaigns

Plymouth performance advertising was not ignored and their ads, produced by Young & Rubicam took every opportunity to use their "Plymouth Is Out to Win You Over" program slogan. The May issue of *Motor Trend* carried a full-page color ad that showed a split view of the front of a 1967 GTX with a pretty young blond model leaning on the hood. On the left she is dressed as a racing driver and the car is lettered. On the right she is in a dress and looking sporty. The lead line says, "Goldilocks and the two Bears," referring to the street and strip capabilities of the standard 440 and optional Hemi GTX.

*This ad from* **Popular Hot Rodding** *is from August 1967 and shows a blue Plymouth GTX with wide slicks and a helmeted driver heating up the tires. "They don't call it King Kong for nothing," the text reminds us. (Dodge, Plymouth, and the AMC design are registered trademarks of FCA US LLC)*

*Goldilocks and the two Bears in this ad represent the two possibilities of the 1967 Plymouth GTX. One is an already fast and powerful standard version. The other has been modified for supervised acceleration trials, as they were known in the industry. The GTX satisfied both needs well. (Dodge, Plymouth, and the AMC design are registered trademarks of FCA US LLC)*

*This* Car Life *ad from December 1966 fills the reader in on all of the performance-oriented features and engineering of the new GTX. From the 375- and 425-hp engines to the red streak tires and 4-speed transmission, every aspect of this powerful offering from Plymouth is well detailed. (Dodge, Plymouth, and the AMC design are registered trademarks of FCA US LLC)*

In July 1967, both *Hot Rod* and *Car Life* carried a full-page color ad with Sox & Martin's 1967 Plymouth Hemi GTX featured prominently under the question, "Caught our Strip Show yet?" Three pictures showed Ronnie Sox, Buddy Martin, and Jake King talking with young fans at a dealership during one of their Supercar Clinics. A picture on the left showed Ronnie in the driver's seat of the Hemi GTX demonstrating how he shifts the Hurst 4-speed lever. Across the top was an action shot of the rear of the Plymouth as it charged off the line at a local dragstrip. The text mentioned Plymouth's Pop Stock Eliminator contest, which offered the chance for a local personality to race against "The Boss" on the track.

In August 1967, *Popular Hot Rodding* displayed a full-page ad for the 1967 GTX. A blue GTX with yellow racing stripes and wide slicks was seen from the front, charging off the line

*This RR-1 Yellow 1967 Plymouth Belvedere GTX is a fine example of a modern high-quality restoration of one of the iconic high-performance vehicles produced by Plymouth in 1967. It's equipped with the standard 440-ci V-8. The red streak tires were standard.*

*The color of this BB-1 black 1967 Belvedere GTX adds a sinister look to an already exciting example of Plymouth's growing efforts to promote the high-performance image of its products. This GTX has the optional Magnum 500 styled wheels and standard red streak tires.*

Plymouth advertising did not miss the chance to promote its winningest drag racing team, Sox & Martin. This ad describes not only the drag racing successes but also the popular Performance Clinics held at Plymouth dealers around the country. (Dodge, Plymouth, and the AMC design are registered trademarks of FCA US LLC)

This end-of-the-year ad, although of poor quality, describes both the mystic and engineering qualities of the famous and powerful 426 Hemi engine. For the 1967 model year, the Hemi was only available in the high-performance image models such as the GTX, but in 1968 that would change. (Dodge, Plymouth, and the AMC design are registered trademarks of FCA US LLC)

Chapter 1: 1966–1967     17

with the headline text stating, "They don't call it King Kong for nothing." The text further pointed out that it turned 11-second ETs and won Top Stock Eliminator at the 1966 Springnationals, Summernationals, and World Championship finals. Plymouth was taking every opportunity to exploit the power and performance of the Belvedere and the engines it offered.

Plymouth's advertising year ended with a full-page black-and-white ad in the December 1967 issue of *Car Life* showing a larger image of the 426 Hemi engine close up. The headline beneath the Hemi simply said, "Beat it." The text pointed out that, "In the case of Plymouth's Hemi that is a tall order." The ad ended with "It's gotta be voodoo, baby!"

### New A-Body Lines

New to both the Dodge and Plymouth performance lineup for 1967 were the redesigned A-Body offerings. The new third-generation Dodge Dart was based on a 111-inch wheelbase and was considered a "senior compact," competing in the market with the Ford Falcon and Chevrolet Nova. Plymouth's offering was the also-redesigned Valiant. It was accompanied by its sporty Barracuda stablemate, both on a shorter 106-inch wheelbase. Both the Dart and the Valiant had been available since 1963 and 1964. The 1964 Barracuda was announced just a short few weeks prior to the Ford Mustang, which although later, quickly took over in the popularity and publicity departments, giving birth to the "Pony Car" classification.

### Dodge Dart

When the 111-inch-wheelbase Dodge Dart compact was first introduced in 1963 it was considered a low price model that was economical to own and operate. It was not considered a replacement for its predecessor, the larger, midsized Dodge Dart.

### 1964

At its introduction, the 1963 Dart was offered only with 170- and 225-ci Slant Six engines, but in early 1964 a new 273-ci, 180-hp 2-barrel V-8 was introduced. This began the progression of performance-based powerplants for the previously economically equipped A-Body cars. The Dart introduced its GT model in 1964 but even that European-sounding title and the 273 4-barrel equipped engine did not present an image of performance to a buyer. Only small GT letters on the hood, the sides of the convertible roof, and the roof pillars of the hardtop identified the 1964 Dart GT, or Gran Turismo.

*A factory publicity photo shows the design of the 1964 Dart that follows the two-headlight theme of the larger 1963 and 1964 Dodges. The Dart was considered a compact car because of its shorter 111-inch wheelbase. A 273-ci V-8 was the highest power engine and became available for the first time in 1964. (Dodge, Plymouth, and the AMC design are registered trademarks of FCA US LLC)*

### 1965

For 1965, the Dart lost its GT badges and replaced them with three horizontal bright pseudo vents just above the rocker panel and behind the front wheel openings. An optional longitudinal contrasting racing stripe was available that went from the front top of the hood to the rear of the body on the

driver's side only. Of course, the sporty interior featured premium pleated and diamond-tufted bucket seats and chrome trim. The base engine was still two versions of the Slant Six but a new optional 4-barrel 235-hp version of the 273 was added. This was still not close to real high-performance, with a quarter-mile elapsed time (ET) of 16.4 seconds and a 0-60–mph time of 9.3 seconds.

### 1966

The body styling of the Dart did not change much for 1966 but the fake vents were gone, replaced by bright trim on the rocker panels and a unique GT medallion just in front of the Dart script on the rear quarter panels. A new optional center console and redesigned bucket seat trim finished up the redesign for that model year. Bucket seats were standard on the GT hardtop, but a bench seat was standard on the convertible. Engine and drivetrain options remained the same as 1965.

*A period ad photo of a white 1966 Dart GT convertible shows off its sporty gold vinyl interior, bucket seats, and GT badge on the rear quarters. (Dodge, Plymouth, and the AMC design are registered trademarks of FCA US LLC)*

### 1967

A total restyling announced the new 1967 Dodge Dart body and its lines were now straighter and flatter on the sides and more square and vertical at the front and rear fascias. A completely new roofline profile with wide rear pillars gave a more solid look to the body. A medallion on the rear of the front fenders identified the performance-directed GT and a special badge was placed at the front of the fender to identify the optional 273 V-8. There were still four engines available in the GT from the standard 170-ci Slant Six to the 235-hp 273 V-8.

Other performance options on the 1967 Dart GT included heavy-duty shock absorbers, a faster 16:1 manual steering gear ratio, front disc brakes, and D70x14 Red Streak tires mounted on 5.5J steel wheels. A new Dart Rallye package was also available that included the above-mentioned items plus heavier rear springs, heavy-duty torsion bars, and an anti-sway bar. The styling of the 1967 Dart carried over into the 1968 and 1969 models. It was mostly unchanged except for the sidelight design and grille. The 1967 had no sidelights.

New for 1967 was the introduction of the Dart GT Sport, or GTS, late in the model year.

*A factory publicity photo of a Dart GT convertible shows that the 1966 Dart styling was beginning to change its character with a more square appearance. Its look was becoming more solid, preparing for its next generation. (Dodge, Plymouth, and the AMC design are registered trademarks of FCA US LLC)*

*By the 1965 model year, the Dart was evolving into what Dodge called "Funsize" referring to its compact size and sporty powerplants. It had not yet had the opportunity to offer real performance levels, but it was on its way. (Dodge, Plymouth, and the AMC design are registered trademarks of FCA US LLC)*

The Dodge Rebellion "Operation 67" promoted Dodge's new styling for the 1967 model year. This introduced what would be the definitive appearance for the Dart for a number of years and evolved into newer models using the same basic concept. (Dodge, Plymouth, and the AMC design are registered trademarks of FCA US LLC)

The 1967 Dart GTS magazine ads put the Dart a step closer to becoming a real high-performance car with the announcement of the B-block 383 V-8. It took some engineering changes to make this work, and this was only the beginning. (Dodge, Plymouth, and the AMC design are registered trademarks of FCA US LLC)

This ad and its red 1967 Dart GTS told us to, "Revolt against Kiddy car compacts. Go '67 Dart." The rest of the text noted the ever-growing list of options and drivetrain choices available on the new Dart. (Dodge, Plymouth, and the AMC design are registered trademarks of FCA US LLC)

The GTS was a huge jump in power and performance with a standard 383 Magnum B-block with a 4-barrel carburetor producing 280 hp and 400 ft-lbs of torque. The 383 was not available with power steering due to lack of space in the engine compartment. It was the only engine available in the 1967 GTS. The 383 was available with either a 4-speed manual or a 3-speed TorqueFlite automatic transmission. The 383 was identified by a "383 4-barrel" badge on the front fenders.

### Advertising

The 1966 and 1967 A-Body Dodge Darts were not conceived as performance cars and were designed with the intention of marketing them as compact economy commute vehicles. By the late 1960s that concept had to be broadened because the perfor-

One of the Dodge girls poses happily with the new 1967 Dodge Dart GTS. This Dart was the beginning of a horsepower race that Dodge was sure to win. The Dart would improve performance options for the next three years, including the quickest factory race cars ever built in 1968. (Dodge, Plymouth, and the AMC design are registered trademarks of FCA US LLC)

20   Dodge Scat Pack and Plymouth Rapid Transit System

mance and the youth market became the key to sales. Every manufacturer wanted to have fastest and quickest in their class. For the Dart, this meant that performance was based on the GT model.

Although the 1966 version of the 235-hp 273-ci V-8 had adequate street performance, it was not until 1967 that the program was stepped up significantly with the introduction of the Dart GTS late in the model year. The most important piece was a full-page black-and-white *Car and Driver* ad showing a photo of the Dart with the large text reading, "GT + 383 = New Dart GTS." Smaller photos showed the 383 4-barrel badge, a view of the engine compartment, and the bright GTS badge.

**Plymouth Valiant and Barracuda**

The 106-inch-wheelbase Plymouth Valiant was not marketed as a performance car, but when the Valiant-based Barracuda fastback was introduced in May 1964, it was immediately evident that it held the potential for just that purpose. Although the body from the firewall forward was clearly a Valiant, the striking and unusual design of the rear half was different from anything offered by the competition at that time. Ford's Falcon-based Mustang did not offer a fastback version until August of that year, and its more conservative rear glass was not as expansive as that of the Barracuda.

The sporty fastback Barracuda roof was an integral part of the car's basic design, and Plymouth worked closely with Pittsburgh Plate Glass Company to develop what was the largest rear window ever installed in a production automobile at that time. The 14.4 square feet of glass wrapped completely around the sides and down to the upper fender line of the body.

The fastback roof and rear window were not only sporty, they were functional and provided considerably more rear visibility, which was a safety factor. An added advantage to the Barracuda interior was the increased storage area provided when the rear seat backs were folded forward and the carpeted rear security panel was lowered. The Barracuda owner was then offered a 7-foot-long, full-width carpeted floor, long enough to carry skis, luggage, lumber, or other long cargo that was inserted through the deck opening. Of course, the huge glass area contributed to a hotter interior on sunny days.

*1964*

Like the Dart, the 1964 Barracuda was available with three engines. A 170-ci Slant Six was standard, and optional extra-cost powerplants were offered up

*A 1964 Barracuda ad announced to the public all of the reasons the new sporty and practical Barracuda was the car for you. With a base price under $2,500, it was a bargain. The Barracuda beat the more publicized Ford Mustang to the market. (Dodge, Plymouth, and the AMC design are registered trademarks of FCA US LLC)*

*Although the fastback styling of the new 1964 Barracuda was a big plus, its under-$2,500 price and seating capacity were always mentioned in its advertising presentations. (Dodge, Plymouth, and the AMC design are registered trademarks of FCA US LLC)*

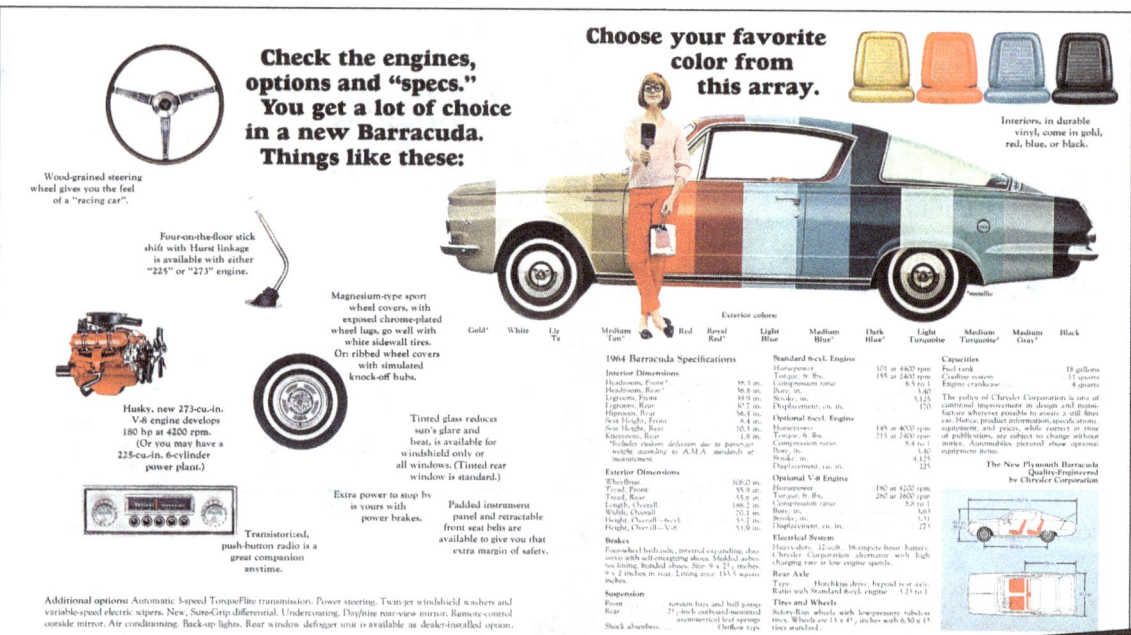

What better way to promote all of the colors, trim, and options available on the 1964 Barracuda than to spread them across two magazine pages? The new 273-ci engine was the center point of its performance capabilities. (Dodge, Plymouth, and the AMC design are registered trademarks of FCA US LLC)

to a 180-hp 273-ci V-8. Both the larger 225-ci six and the V-8 were available with an optional Chrysler-designed A833 4-speed manual transmission or 3-speed TorqueFlite automatic. Chrysler's new Sure Grip limited-slip differential was an option. Safety-rim 13-inch wheels were standard, along with 6.50x13 tires.

Options such as magnesium-style sport wheel covers with chrome-plated fake lug nuts, ribbed wheel covers with simulated knock-off hubs, and a wood-grained sport steering wheel helped to foster the sport and performance image in a subtle way.

The 1964 Barracuda was identified as a Valiant derivative by the chrome script deck lid badge, but for the 1965 model year, this family connection was dropped and it was known simply as a Barracuda. The styling was subtle and cosmetic only. Standard base engines included the 145-hp Slant Six and the 273-ci V-8 at no extra cost. The Commando 273 was now available with a 4-barrel carburetor and made 235 hp. Rallye Pack Suspension was offered and included heavier rear springs, heavier torsion bars and shock absorbers, and a hefty .82-inch-diameter front stabilizer bar.

### 1965

For the first time, a true performance identity was created with the optional 1965 Barracuda Formula S package. The Formula S included the Commando 273 V-8, the Rallye Suspension Package, wide-rim wheels with 6.95 x 14–inch Goodyear Blue Streak tires, simulated bolt-on wheel covers, and a 6,000-rpm tachometer. A distinctive Formula S badge on the

The overhead view of this bright red Barracuda Formula S captured the performance potential of the package to potential buyers in 1965. Notice the special white-letter blue streak performance tires that were part of the Formula S package. (Dodge, Plymouth, and the AMC design are registered trademarks of FCA US LLC)

This two-page magazine ad promotes the cargo and passenger space offered in the 1965 Barracuda. Although in the same market, the Ford Mustang did not offer this much room. The sporty performance-oriented instrument panel was an impressive part of the deal. (Dodge, Plymouth, and the AMC design are registered trademarks of FCA US LLC)

front fenders identified the car's image to the public. A racing stripe was optional and was applied down the center of the car. The Formula S was priced at $3,169, which was $669 more than the base Barracuda.

## 1966

The Barracuda received a facelift for 1966 and this was reflected in details such as a new die-cast metal grille and a new medallion featuring a real Barracuda fish on the grille divider and also at the base of the rear window. Fender-mounted turn signal indicators were added and the taillights were redesigned. Inside, new shell-type buckets seats replaced the old design and a new instrument panel was adopted. Engine and drivetrain options and specifications were essentially the same, except for an unsilenced air cleaner on the 273 V-8.

Many of the Barracuda images in 1965 advertising showed an overhead view to emphasize the lines of the fastback roof. The large rear window was a difficult and expensive feature to design and produce, but it added a great deal to the unique appearance. (Dodge, Plymouth, and the AMC design are registered trademarks of FCA US LLC)

The black-and-white factory publicity photo shows well the redesigned front grille and fascia appearance of the 1966 Barracuda. The Barracuda nameplate and model badge always appeared on the front fender. (Dodge, Plymouth, and the AMC design are registered trademarks of FCA US LLC)

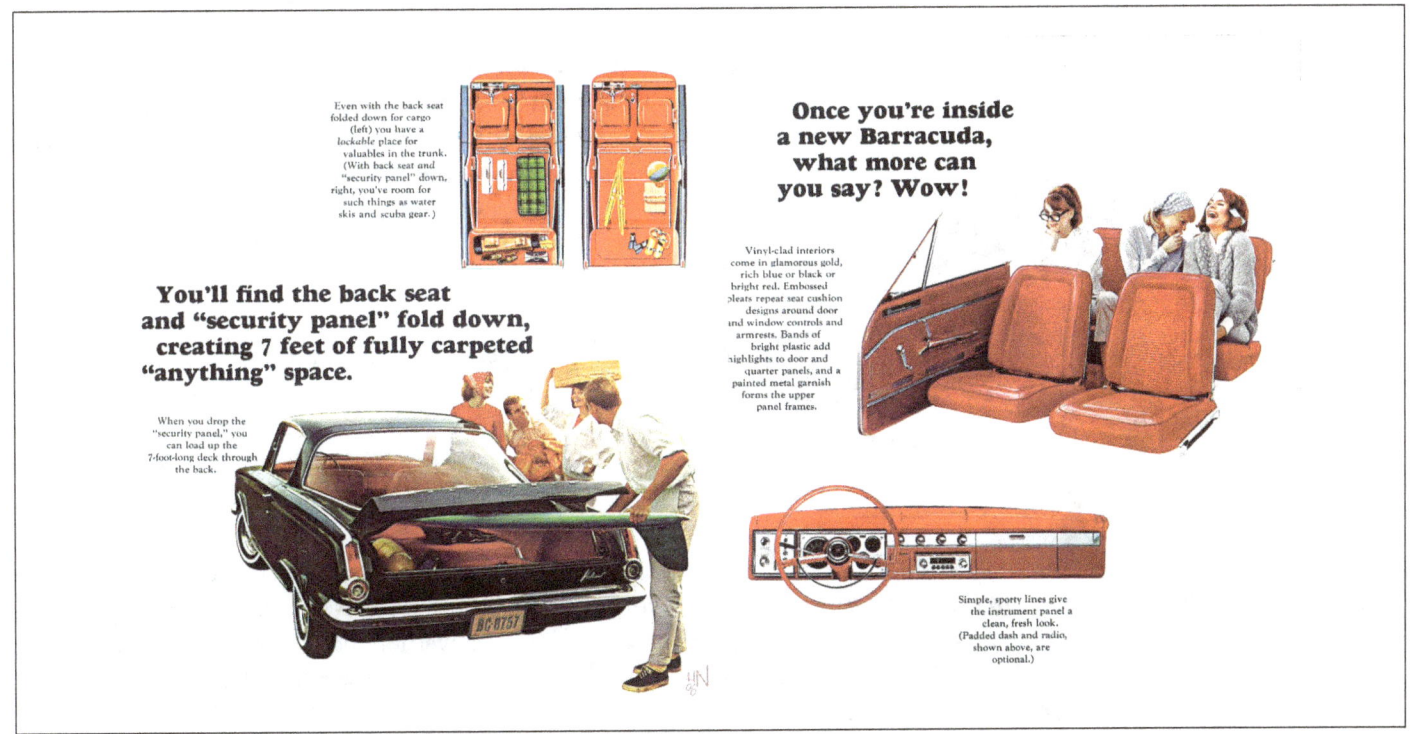

This Gold Poly 1966 Barracuda ad refers to the "fish" connection with the name. The features of the Formula S package are mentioned clearly to promote the performance image that was becoming more important each year. (Dodge, Plymouth, and the AMC design are registered trademarks of FCA US LLC)

The Gold Poly 1966 Barracuda from the previous ad was also used for other advertising purposes during the model year. The dual longitudinal black racing stripes were optional. (Dodge, Plymouth, and the AMC design are registered trademarks of FCA US LLC)

### Barracuda Styling for 1967

Like the 1967 Dart, the second-generation Plymouth Barracuda, styled chiefly by John E. Herlitz and John Samsen, introduced a completely redesigned body structure that was clearly directed toward the younger, performance-oriented market. Rather than the straighter, squarer concept used for the Dart, the new Barracuda came with a smoother and more aerodynamic shape for 1967. Plymouth's new Young & Rubicam Group–directed advertising campaign led with a slogan of "Plymouth is out to win you over" accompanied by a red heart and upturned arrow that appeared in all ads.

The 1967 Barracuda had a wheelbase of 108 inches, extended 2 inches from 1966. Front track width was increased from 55.9 to 57.4 inches and the overall width grew from 70.1 to 71.6 inches. The overall length increased from 188.2 to 192.8 inches, giving the car a decidedly larger appearance. The large fastback rear window idea was retained, but the design was flatter and did not wrap around the rear pillar, as did the earlier design. The rear quarter panels had a distinct upturn over the more rounded wheel openings. The design concept for the Barracuda was intended to be more European, reflecting the feeling of a Ferrari Lusso or a Maserati Mistral.

The grille of the new 1967 Barracuda retained the distinctive wide split in the center but surrounded it with wide rectangular openings for the headlights and parking lights. They were designed to appear similar to European driving lights. A narrow chrome bumper greatly added an air of lightness to the front view and was identical to the rear bumper in design. The driver-side rear quarter of the Barracuda housed the chrome racing style flip-open fuel filler cap. The 1967 Barracuda design incorporated a conventional trunk and deck lid.

The interior of the new Barracuda still had styled individual bucket seats as an option, but a sports front bench seat was standard. The rear seat back folded and had a new type of latch that was more convenient to lock or release the seat. The Sports Barracuda also kept the security panel feature used on the 1966 model to hide the contents of the rear compartment from the eye of the public. All Barracuda models had full instrumentation with the large, round 120-mph speedometer on the left and a round cluster with the fuel gauge, temperature gauge, oil pressure gauge, and ammeter on the right. A front console was an option when the 4-speed manual transmission was ordered.

New for 1967 were the optional convertible and hardtop models. The hardtop did not have the fastback and could be considered a coupe design. The convertible had a power-operated roof and a real glass rear window. The convertible was a sports model and had standard front bucket seats.

Engine choices were similar to those in 1966 with the 225-ci Slant Six still standard. The V-8 options began with the 180-hp 273 V-8 with 2-barrel carburetor, followed by the 235-hp version with a 4-barrel with a low-restriction single exhaust system. A new option, available only in the Barracuda Formula S model, was the 383-ci B-block V-8 with a 4-barrel carburetor producing 280 hp and 400 ft-lbs of torque. The 383 had standard dual exhaust, and a badge on the front fenders advertised that the car had a "383 Four Barrel" engine. Front disc brakes were a mandatory option with the 383. Bucket seats and a console were part of the Formula S option.

Available transmissions included a standard 3-speed manual with all engines except the 383, with the Chrysler A833 4-speed manual with a floor-shift available as an option. The super strong and reliable 3-speed A727 TorqueFlite automatic was available as an option with all engine packages.

### Barracuda Advertising

New for 1967 was the announcement of the National Barracuda Owner's Club, an indication of the performance-oriented direction Dodge and Plymouth advertising would take beginning with the 1968 models. Barracuda enthusiast magazine advertising for 1967 pointed out that the 383 V-8 in the Formula S was equipped with chrome valvecovers, cast-iron headers, an AFB 4-barrel carburetor, and low-restriction dual exhaust, producing "a walloping" 400 ft-lbs of torque. The "Plymouth is out to win you over" campaign slogan was beginning to have real meaning, and this was only the beginning.

Advertising for the 1967 Barracuda Formula S included full-page color ads in the January 1967 issue of *Motor Trend* and the February 1967 issue of *Hot Rod*. The *Motor Trend* ad featured an overhead shot of a blue Formula S with a smartly dressed girl standing beside it. The text pointed out the 383 engine and its dual exhaust, chromed valve covers, and black crackle-finish air cleaner. The performance aspects of the cars were becoming the most important features in advertising.

The February *Hot Rod* ad also had an overhead view of a blue Barracuda but at the bottom of the page. Text above the car said that it had "383 Cubes. And a trophy room in the back." It was referring, of course, to the Barracuda's unique fastback design and large rear window glass. The ad also pointed out "Sort of makes you want to turn trophy hunter yourself, doesn't it?"

Both Dodge and Plymouth performance-oriented promotional and advertising efforts for 1967 were clearly just a warm-up for what would come in 1968 from Dodge, and later in 1970 with Plymouth. These new programs would prove to be some of the most exciting, artistic, and aggressive campaigns in automobile history.

*The lead line is "Plymouth is out to win you over," but the text of this ad tells more about the high-performance features of the 383 V-8-powered Formula S package. This same blue Barracuda was used in at least two full-page magazine ads for 1967. (Dodge, Plymouth, and the AMC design are registered trademarks of FCA US LLC)*

*A February 1967* Hot Rod *ad uses the same blue 1967 Barracuda but at the bottom of the page. The illustrations show close-up details of the 383 Formula S engine's chrome valve covers and black crackle-finish air cleaner. Notice the trophies in the backseat area. (Dodge, Plymouth, and the AMC design are registered trademarks of FCA US LLC)*

# CHAPTER 2

# 1968

## DODGE SCAT PACK PROGRAM

*" 'Welcome to Scat City.'*
*This is where Dodge performance cars are developed*
*and built."*

It did not take long for Chrysler and Dodge marketing staff to realize the direction the high-performance automobile market was taking, so by early 1967 plans were already well under way for the new aggressive advertising and publicity programs for the 1968 model year to begin development. Dodge took advantage of the skills and experience of the Ross Roy Communications ad agency to develop and plan a program designed to make the most of the momentum gained by the introduction of the new image vehicles introduced during the 1967 model year.

Although BBD&O was Dodge's primary ad agency, The Ross Roy Company had been with Dodge since its beginning in 1926 when Ross Roy, a successful Dodge dealer in Janesville, Ohio, impressed the Dodge Brothers (Horace and John) with his sales methods. When Chrysler merged with the Dodge Brothers in 1927, Roy's sales methods were extended to all Chrysler Corporation dealers. Roy continued with Chrysler into the 1930s and specialized in training and educational films and programs. By the 1960s, Ross Roy had become a full service ad agency and contributed greatly to Dodge sales and marketing ideas.

The Coronet R/T, Charger R/T, and Dart GTSport 340 (joined later in the model year by the Coronet Super Bee) would be the basis for their new performance theme that added strength to the identity already created by the attention-getting names for the cars in the lineup. Dodge had already changed its primary advertising and publicity theme from "Dodge Rebellion" used in 1967 to "Dodge Fever" for the 1968 model year, but this new push for a youthful performance image needed a new name.

From the Ross Roy group came the name "Scat Pack." It is not clear where the idea for the Scat Pack

*This magazine ad leads with the "Silken Snarl" name for the red 1968 Dodge Coronet R/T. This view shows the parking lights and black mesh grille with R/T badge. The text lists the standard equipment of the Coronet R/T. (Dodge, Plymouth, and the AMC design are registered trademarks of FCA US LLC)*

name came from but the popularity of the "Rat Pack," consisting of Frank Sinatra, Dean Martin, Joey Bishop, Peter Lawford, and Sammy Davis Jr., certainly had to have had an influence somewhere down the line. This boisterous and rowdy team of popular Las Vegas entertainers captured the attention of everyone in the country at about the same time the new cars were introduced, and their image fit the program well.

### Birth of the Scat Pack

Andy Agosta of Dodge related how the Scat Pack program came to be. "The Scat Pack came about at the request of Bob McCurry, vice president and general manager of the Dodge Division. He asked John Wilson, president of BBD&O, to develop a campaign to promote the Dodge Performance cars. He hired an ad guy from Chicago named Bill Maloney and Bill, with the help of the BBD&O creative guys, came up with the Scat Pack idea.

"Bill Maloney and a BBD&O photographer Bob Osborne came to our offices at Dodge Main, Hamtramck, Michigan. They made a presentation to George Booth, sales promotion manager, his assistant Bill Coley, Jim Howitt, production manager, and myself, as the sales promotion coordinator.

"The presentation was a series of ads promoting the Dodge performance cars tied around the Scat Pack theme with the headline 'Welcome to Scat City. This is where Dodge performance cars are developed and built.' According to Andy Agosta, Bill Maloney said, 'Scat was a spin on popular reggae singer Johnny Scat Davis and to any hot football halfback who was called a scatback. Scat City was a mythical place . . . and it was where hot cars were being made and tested.' From that point on, the Dodge performance cars were part of the Scat Pack Club."

Andy Agosta said that their team at Dodge instructed George P. Johnson Company to produce a 40-foot-wide banner, which read "DODGE Scat City" with a Bumblebee logo. That banner hung across the top of the Dodge headquarters building at Hamtramck for some time.

### Scat Pack Requirements

To make sure that the Scat Pack title had real meaning to buyers and enthusiasts, Dodge put clear requirements on becoming a member of the team. First, all of these cars had to be capable of quarter-mile ETs of 14.99 seconds or less to qualify. This level of performance would not win any NHRA Super Stock races, but it was more than enough to stir the emotions of any performance-minded driver on the street. The second requirement grew quickly into an appearance theme that caused the Scat Pak Dodges to be known as "the cars with the Bumblebee stripes" in print advertising. Although the unique standard equipment stripe treatment could be deleted if the buyer desired, it was a clear and identifiable badge of the prestige and power afforded to that car.

### Getting the Word Out

By late fall of 1967, Dodge was already placing advertising, showroom literature, and special promotional events in the hands of dealers around the country. The public could not miss the new campaign and Scat Pack became a household name among Dodge fans. Some of the promotional programs included a "Scat Pack" sweepstakes drawing at selected Dodge dealers (then known as "The Dodge Boys") offering as a prize a new Scat Pack Dodge of your choice among 250,000 prizes. An interesting piece among the Dodge "Pick of the Pack" drawing was a new Dodge 3-in-1 Road Race Set with powered scale models of Dodge racing cars. Prizes offered in this national campaign totaled $3,487,000.

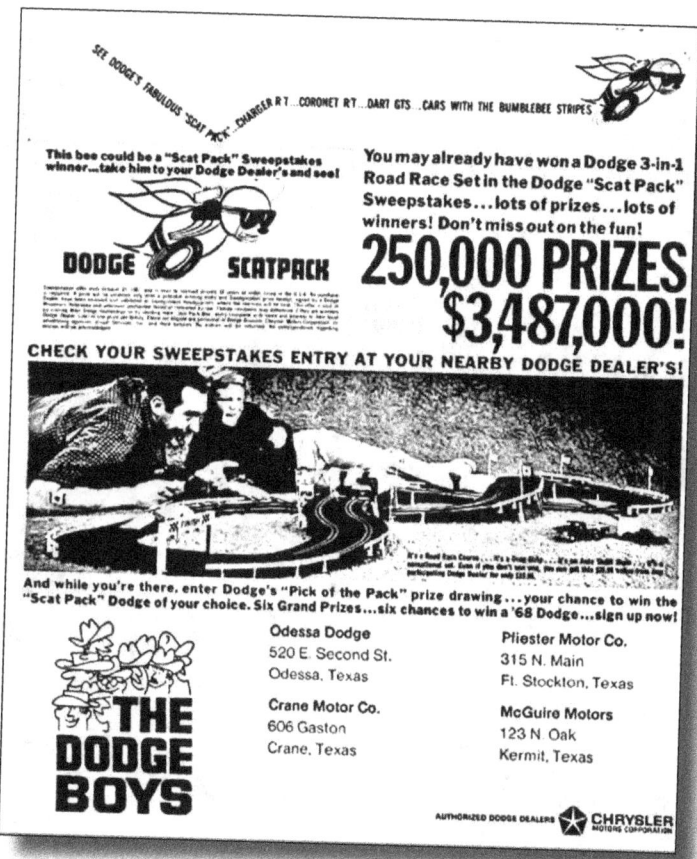

One of the promotional efforts for the new 1968 Dodge Scat pack program was this "Scat Pack Sweepstakes" that offered 250,000 prizes worth more than $3,487,000. These promotional contests brought potential buyers into their local Dodge showroom and introduced them to the Scat Pack Club and cars. (Dodge, Plymouth, and the AMC design are registered trademarks of FCA US LLC)

One of the prizes in the Scat Pack promotional program was this Dodge 3-in-1 road race set. The scale model race cars connected with the real Dodges that were winning on the drag racing and NASCAR tracks and directly related to the cars available in the showroom. (Photo Courtesy Jim Stodolka)

## Magazine Advertisements

By October 1967, full one- or two-page color ads began to appear in all of the important automobile enthusiast magazines. One of the first was featured in the October issues of both *Car Life* and *Motor Trend*. The left-side headlines on a white background stated that there were "Three Quick Ways to Catch Dodge Fever." Dodge Fever was in bright-red

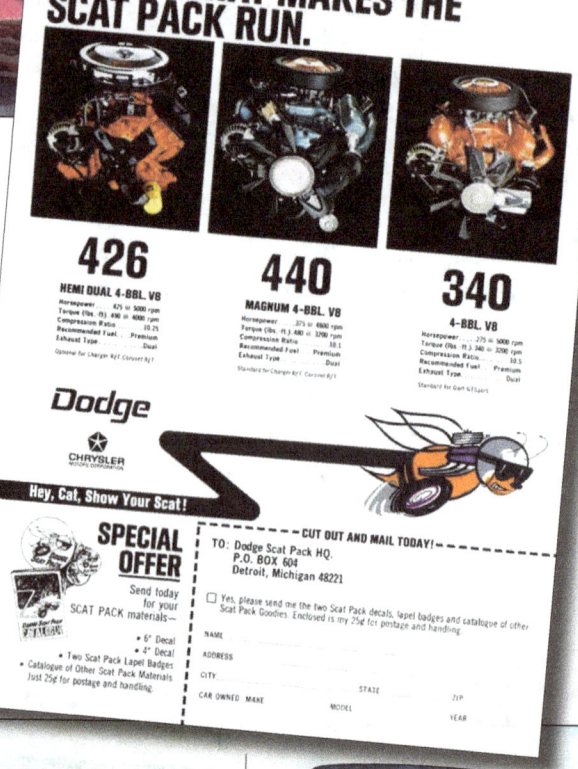

A period full-page magazine ad shows the three optional engines used in the 1968 Dodge Scat Pack performance cars. The 426 Hemi and 440 V-8 were used for the Coronet R/T, while the 340 was used in the Dart GTS. (Dodge, Plymouth, and the AMC design are registered trademarks of FCA US LLC)

A full-page magazine ad featured the same Bronze Metallic Charger R/T used in the two-page spread accompanied by smaller images of a yellow Coronet R/T and black Dart GTS. (Dodge, Plymouth, and the AMC design are registered trademarks of FCA US LLC)

A two-page 1968 Charger magazine ad featured a new Bronze Metallic Charger R/T and showed details of the trim and interior. The Scat Pack Bee and the Bumblebee stripes were a couple of the identifying features of the Scat Pack line of performance cars. (Dodge, Plymouth, and the AMC design are registered trademarks of FCA US LLC)

*This full-page magazine ad featured a red 1968 Charger R/T with black Bumblebee stripes and the same "Clean machine" slogan used in earlier ads. All used the now-familiar "Run with the Scat Pack" slogan and a form to order Scat Pack decals and badges. (Dodge, Plymouth, and the AMC design are registered trademarks of FCA US LLC)*

script letters with a full-page width image of a 1968 Dodge Charger R/T.

Two smaller images of cars were shown beneath the Charger. On the left there was a rear view of a 1968 Coronet R/T. On the right bottom was a rear top view of a black 1968 Dart GTS.

The right side of the double-page layout was a white page with square full-color images of the three high-performance engines used in the Scat Pack cars with detailed specifications beneath each one.

A black bumblebee zigzag tail swept horizontally across the middle of the page with the slogan, "Hey, Cat, Show Your

*A two-page ad for the Scat Pack that included the Charger and Coronet R/T and the Dart GTX, along with a form to order Scat Pack promotional materials. The same Bronze Metallic Charger, yellow Coronet R/T, and black Dart GTS were used in a number of magazine ads. (Dodge, Plymouth, and the AMC design are registered trademarks of FCA US LLC)*

Chapter 2: 1968    29

Scat," followed by the familiar gold bumblebee with helmet and racing goggles.

The October issue of *Hot Rod* featured a massive and colorful eight-page center-spread advertising section outlining the full Dodge Scat Pack offering for the 1968 model year. The first page was identical to the first page of the previously described ads in *Car Life* and *Motor Trend*. The second and third pages were opposing and showed a full-width picture of the Bronze Charger R/T. The lower left carried the message, "Charger R/T The Clean Machine."

The fourth and fifth pages of the spread showed a three-quarter view of the yellow Coronet R/T with the title, "Coronet R/T The Time Machine" at the lower left of page four. The lower right of the ad ended the story with, "No Wonder You've Got Scat Pack Fever."

The sixth and seventh pages of the spread showed a three-quarter view of the black 1968 Dart GTS on the left of the layout with the caption, "Dart GTS The Scat Pack Compact." The last and eighth page was the same engine specifications page shown as the second page in the *Car Life* and *Motor Trend* spread with the coupon for the Scat Pack memorabilia at the bottom.

By November 1967, additional ads began to appear with more pictures and information on Dodge's new Scat Pack program. The November issue of *Hot Rod* featured another full-color two-page spread. The first page had new and different photos of the same three 1968 Scat Pack Dodges shown in the previous month's ad, but stacked vertically and full width on the page. At the bottom of the page were just the Dodge and Chrysler Corporation logos.

The right full-page layout featured six smaller pictures of details of the Scat Pack cars.

Of course, a bumblebee and trail ran across the page reading: "Run With the Scat Pack."

### First Scat Pack Show Car: Daroo I

Even before the new 1968 Dodge Scat Pack lineup was announced to the public, Dodge Division had already begun an image program directed at new car shows around the country. Bill Brownlee of Dodge styling created the initial concept for a wild show car to be called Daroo I. Brownlee said, "We wanted to convey the feeling of a real Dart in motion, even while the car was standing still. The intent was to give a tough performance image, compatible with the style concept." His ideas were sent to famed car customizer George Barris near Hollywood, California, who crafted the Daroo I.

The Daroo I was based on a brand-new red 1967 Dart convertible, with a 383 V-8 engine. The 111-inch wheelbase was left stock but Barris added a 17-inch nose extension and cut

*This candid photo features the Dodge Daroo custom show car and one of the Dodge girls used to attract attention to the car and the rest of the Scat Pack program. This photo shows the car in its green 1969 finish. (Bill Cook Photo)*

10 inches from the rear of the body, leaving a 202-inch overall length. The convertible roof was removed, the windshield was lowered, and the beltline was restyled, giving the car a final height of 42 inches. The body was reconfigured with an overall V-design from front to rear, realizing Brownlee's pointed vision of the car. The Daroo I was finished in deep Orange Candy Apple with black accents. The nonfunctional Longhorn injectors and side exhaust pipes conveyed the power message. The car followed the show circuit in 1968, but for 1969 it was repainted in Candy Apple Green with gold accents. Although there was no direct mention of Scat Pack on the car, it did serve to draw attention to Dodge's performance line for 1968 and 1969.

Another of the Scat Pack show cars was a more stock but colorful yellow 1968 Coronet R/T with a blacked-out hood. The Scat Pack shows covered the new car show circuit not only in Detroit but also in a number of other major cities such as Chicago, New York, and Los Angeles.

### Scat Pack Trademark Battle

It was not long after Dodge's new Scat Pack program and cars were introduced in 1968 that a letter of cease and desist was received from the attorneys of Scat Enterprises, Inc., in California, a manufacturer of high-performance automotive parts such as crankshafts and connecting rods. The letter, followed by official legal court documents, advised Dodge that its use of the name Scat Pack was infringing upon the legal trademark registered by Scat Enterprises, Inc., causing great harm to its business, established in 1963. Scat Enterprise's lawyers told Dodge/Chrysler Corporation to discontinue use of that name in its products and advertising.

Chrysler's attorneys argued that the name of Scat Enterprises had no relationship to Chrysler's use of the name "Scat Pack" and called the suit meritless. Chrysler Corporation continued the use of the Scat Pack name until ceasing that program in 1971.

### Scat Pack Lineup for 1968

Of course, no matter how effective and attention-getting the advertising may be, it was the cars that were most important to prospective Dodge buyers. Although the A-Body Dart was similar to the 1967 model, the 1968 Charger and Coronet were entirely new designs. Gone were the rather straight and sharp angular themes of the 1967, replaced by a more modern, smoother, and decidedly more aerodynamic idea for the 1968 B-Body models.

### 1968 Dodge Charger R/T

Like its Dodge Coronet stable mate, the 1968 Charger changed entirely for 1968. The styling was new from top to bottom and front to rear, with a definite aerodynamic "Coke bottle" shape to the body sides. The fastback roof theme was now more integrated with the flowing bodylines, and its sail panels extended beyond the sloped rear window, much like the contemporary GTO styling. Noticeable bulges at the front and rear wheel openings accented the sharply defined upper bodylines.

A relative flat upper hood surface ended sharply at the bright-rimmed front grille opening that used a horizontal open scoop appearance. The grille still featured the distinctive hidden retractable headlights but they were now vacuum operated rather than electric. Both the Charger hood and doors featured dual nonfunctional reverse-facing scoops to add both styling cues and stiffness to hood and door surfaces.

*A rear view of the dark green 1968 Charger R/T shows the White Bumblebee stripe and Charger R/T badge on the rear deck lower panel. The round taillights are indicative of the 1968 Charger.*

The design concepts for the 1968 Charger were dramatic and were based extensively on Chrysler's racing success in NASCAR and USAC. Bill Brownlie, chief of design at Dodge, wanted the second-generation Charger to be more aerodynamic and sporty than the Coronet-based first-generation model. The path to the final appearance of the new Charger included a design contest within the Dodge studio. Brownlie wanted the car to "look like a cab sitting on top of the lower body shell." Richard Sais designed the final product, which was chosen by Brownlie and Charles Mitchell, who were responsible for the Charger program.

#### Exterior

Only one body type was offered for the 1968 Charger, which was based on the 117-inch-wheelbase steel unibody construction of the 1968 Coronet, but was 2 inches longer overall. The basic body shell was now offered in two models for 1968: the premium XP29 Charger and the performance-sports-oriented XS29 Charger R/T, both two-door hardtops. The 1968 Charger was available with V-8 power only. The 1968 Charger R/T was available in 18 acrylic enamel colors, 3 optional vinyl roof colors, and 10 all-vinyl interior trim combinations. The distinctive optional dual narrow Bumblebee stripes had no logo and the small, round side-marker lights were mounted inside the rear stripe band. The 1968 Bumblebee stripes had no R/T logo and were available in black (310), red (314), and white (317). All 1968 Chargers used a bright chrome-plated fuel filler door mounted on the driver-side rear deck.

*A driver-side view of the Dark Green Poly 1968 XP29 Charger R/T with optional white vinyl roof and Magnum 500 styled steel wheels. The white Bumblebee stripes at the rear quarter were iconic features of the Scat Pack cars.*

### Interior

The 1968 Charger was available in a variety of trim schemes with a rear bench seat for all models. The rear bucket seats of the 1966–1967 Chargers were gone. The Charger R/T standard all-vinyl interior included front bucket seats with an optional fixed center cushion and folding center armrest. The interior trim was available in blue, green, red, black, gold, and white and featured four wide, horizontal panels between smooth bolsters on both the back and seat cushions. The carpet was color coordinated except for the white interior, which was available with blue, green, gold, red, or black carpeting. A center console with gearshift was optional.

### Instrument Panel

The 1968 Charger instrument panel featured what Dodge called "sports-car-type instrumentation." A large, round 150-mile-per-hour speedometer was placed to the right of an identically sized combination tachometer and clock. To the right of the speedometer were four smaller round bezels that contained the fuel, temperature, oil pressure, and alternator gauges. The 1968 instrument cluster was mounted in a textured flat-black background panel.

### Engine Options

The standard powerplant in the 1968 Charger R/T was a 440-ci V-8 based on the RB (raised) block configuration. The single Carter AVS 4-barrel-equipped 440 Magnum produced 375 hp at 4,600 rpm and 480 ft-lbs of torque at 3,200 rpm. The 440 had a bore and stroke of 4.32 x 3.75 inches and a compression ratio of 10.1:1. All 1968 440 engines were painted turquoise.

The 426 Hemi V-8 was the only optional engine available in the 1968 Charger R/T. The Hemi had 425 hp, and its twin Carter AFB carburetors were covered with a large, round, chrome-plated air cleaner housing.

The only optional engine available with the 1968 Charger R/T was the 426 Hemi V-8 rated at 425 hp at 5,000 rpm and 490 ft-lbs of torque at 4,000 rpm. The two Carter AFB 4-barrel-equipped Hemi had a bore and stroke of 4.25 x 3.75 inches and a compression ratio of 10.3:1. The Hemi block and heads were finished in Street Hemi Orange with a black crackle-finish air cleaner. The large and unique Hemi valvecovers were black crackle finish. A total of 17,584 XS29 Charger R/Ts were built for the 1968 model year.

### Transmission Options

The 1968 Charger R/T had a standard A727 3-speed TorqueFlite automatic transmission when equipped with the 440 V-8 engine. The cast-aluminum case TorqueFlite was operated with either a column or console-mounted shift lever, depending on the interior options. An A833 4-speed manual transmission was standard with the 426 Hemi and optional with the 440. The 4-speed used a chrome-plated Chrysler Inland shifter with a black knob until early in the 1968 model year when it was replaced with a Hurst shifter that used a round walnut knob. The Hemi was available with an optional TorqueFlite automatic transmission.

### Rear Axle Options

The standard rear axle with the 1968 Charger R/T equipped with a 440 or 426 Hemi engine and TorqueFlite automatic transmission was the Chrysler 8¾-inch banjo-type, which was available in ratios from 2.94:1 to 3.91:1, with 3.23:1 standard. When a 4-speed transmission was ordered with the 440 or 426 Hemi engine, a 9¾-inch ring gear Dana 60 heavy-duty rear axle with a standard 3.54:1 gear ratio was used.

### Wheel and Tire Options

The 1968 Charger R/T had standard 14 x 5–inch stamped-steel wheels, which could be equipped with either a small hubcap or a styled wheel cover. An optional 14-inch Magnum 500 styled wheel with chrome-plated trim rings was available. For a short time, optional 15-inch cast-aluminum Kelsey Hayes road wheels were available, but they were recalled in September 1968 due to maintenance problems. All 426 Hemi–equipped Charger R/Ts were equipped with standard 15 x 6 pressed-steel wheels and no optional wheels were available.

### Advertising

Advertising for the 1968 Scat Pack Dodges was not confined to Chrysler and Dodge corporate ads. In the March 1968 issue of *Hot Rod*, a full-page ad appeared for the then-popular Cragar mag wheels. In addition to the four different styles of Cragar wheels pictured, a pretty dark-haired Dodge model in

Full-page magazine ads for 1968 featured the second-generation Dodge Charger and told potential buyers that it was a way for them to run with the Scat Pack.

This full-page magazine ad features the silver 1968 Charger R/T. The text lists all of the distinctive standard features of the 1968 Charger R/T. The lower right shows a large image of the Scat Pack bee in drag racing form. (Dodge, Plymouth, and the AMC design are registered trademarks of FCA US LLC)

A full-page ad shows a view of a 1968 Dodge Charger R/T burning its tires under hard acceleration on the dragstrip. The Bumblebee illustrations show what appears to be a drag chute behind the bee. (Dodge, Plymouth, and the AMC design are registered trademarks of FCA US LLC)

a short, white nurse's uniform exclaimed that "Dodge Fever" was "highly contagious!" when those Dodges were equipped with Cragar wheels. In the background was a new Dodge Charger R/T viewed from the passenger-side rear, plainly showing its distinctive dual Bumblebee stripes and chrome Cragar spoke wheels.

## 1968 Dodge Coronet R/T

There were four series of Dodge Coronets for the beginning of 1968, all based on a 117-inch-wheelbase platform. The sport Coronet model for 1968 was the Coronet R/T, available as a WS23 two-door hardtop and WS27 two-door convertible. A power-bulge hood and R/T nameplates identified the R/T; it had the same twin simulated side scoops as the premium model Coronet 500.

All 1968 Coronets were of steel unibody construction and were based on a shared similar platform for the hardtop, sedan convertible, and later coupe. Like the Charger, the Coronet/Chrysler unit construction concept utilized a solid floorpan with a front subframe and parallel rear longitudinal members to support the suspension and drivetrain. All cars with the 426 Hemi engine had torque boxes welded in place across the frame rails in front of the rear spring front mounting. All convertibles had the same rear reinforcements plus an additional plate welded across the front body crossmember to the body side seam. Hemi cars also had a flat reinforcement plate welded in place above the rear axle pinion snubber.

The front view of a red 1968 Dodge Coronet R/T shows the distinctive R/T badge on the driver's side of the black mesh grille. Note the round parking lights in the front bumper and the small, round side-marker on the fender.

### Exterior

A red-filled bright R/T badge mounted at the driver's side of the deep-set horizontal black front grille identified the Coronet R/T. Bright trim surrounded the entire grille assembly and quad round headlights. The R/T power bulge hood was standard but a special hood was available with a Sales Code N96 fresh-air-package that was standard with the 426 Hemi and optional with the 440 V-8. Like the 1968 Charger R/T, the Bumblebee stripes were only available in black, red, and white.

### Interior

The 1968 Coronet R/T standard interiors were all-vinyl seats with an optional center console or fixed center cushion and folding armrest. The vinyl trim was available in blue, green, red, black, gold, or white and used lateral panels with longitudinal pleats only in the center section. The carpet color choices were color-keyed except for the white interior, which was available with choices of blue, green, red, or black.

### Instrument Panel

The 1968 Coronet R/T Rallye-type instrument panel featured a wide, horizontal-design speedometer with oil pressure, coolant temperature, and ammeter gauges on either side. The steering wheel was a three-spoke design with a partial horn ring and a Dodge Tri-Star emblem in its center.

### Engine Options

The standard engine in the 1968 Coronet R/T was the 440-ci RB V-8 with a 4.32 x 3.75–inch bore and stroke and a 10.1:1 compression ratio, producing 375 hp at 4,600 rpm and 480 ft-lbs of torque at 3,200 rpm. The 440 had a single Carter AVS 4-barrel carburetor mounted on a Chrysler cast-iron intake manifold. All 1968 440 blocks and heads were painted turquoise.

Like the Charger R/T, the only 1968 Dodge Coronet R/T optional engine was the 426 Hemi V-8. The Hemi had a 4.25 x 3.75–inch bore and stroke and a 10.3:1 compression ratio. The Hemi produced 425 hp at 5,000 rpm and 490 ft-lbs or torque at 4,000 rpm. The 1968 Hemi engine used solid mechanical valve lifters operated by a camshaft with an intake lift of .484 inch and an exhaust life of .475 inch; the duration on both was 284 degrees. The Hemi had cast-iron cylinder heads and a cast-aluminum intake manifold topped with two inline-mounted Carter AFB 4-barrel carburetors. The 1968 Hemi was finished in Street Hemi Orange with black crackle-finish valvecovers. A total of 10,280 Coronet R/T two-door hardtops and 569 Coronet R/T convertibles were built for the 1968 model year.

## Transmission Options

The 1968 Dodge Coronet R/T had a standard aluminum case A727 3-speed TorqueFlite automatic transmission when equipped with the 440 V-8 engine. The TorqueFlite was operated with either a column- or console-mounted shift lever depending on the interior options. An A833 4-speed manual transmission was standard with the 426 Hemi and optional with the 440. The 4-speed used a Chrysler Inland shifter until early in the 1968 model year when it was replaced with a Hurst shifter that used a round walnut knob. The Hemi was available with an optional TorqueFlite automatic transmission.

## Rear Axle Options

The standard rear axle with the 1968 Coronet R/T with a 440 or 426 Hemi engine and TorqueFlite automatic transmission was the Chrysler 8-3/4-inch banjo-type, which was available in ratios from 2.94:1 to 3.91:1, with 3.23:1 being standard. A special Performance Axle Group option (Sales Code 358) was available that provided a 3.55:1 rear axle gear ratio, special slip-drive fan, and an extra-wide high-performance radiator fan shroud. When a 4-speed transmission was ordered with the 440 or 426 Hemi engine, a 9-3/4-inch ring gear Dana 60 heavy-duty rear axle with a 3.54:1 gear ratio was used.

## Wheel and Tire Options

The 1968 Coronet R/T was equipped with standard 14 x 5-inch stamped-steel wheels, which could be equipped with either a small hubcap or a styled wheel cover. An optional 14-inch Magnum 500 styled wheel with chrome trim rings was available. For a short time, optional 15-inch cast-aluminum Kelsey Hayes road wheels were available, but they were recalled in September 1968 due to maintenance problems. All 426 Hemi–equipped Coronet R/Ts were equipped with standard 15 x 6 pressed-steel wheels and no optional wheels were available.

## Advertising

Some of the earliest advertising for the 1968 Coronet R/T was published in the October 1967 issue of *Hot Rod*. A two-page set included a great front view of a yellow 1968 Coronet R/T with a black vinyl roof and red-stripe tires posed on a hilly country road. The rear view of the Coronet prominently featured the black Bumblebee stripes. The Coronet was one of three shots that included a red Charger R/T at the top and a black Dart GTS on the bottom.

The second page included six smaller photos of the three cars with text pointing out the details of all of them. The text for the Coronet was beneath a large Bumblebee logo and "Run with the Scat Pack" lettering and began with, "Coronet R/T. The Time Machine: A great example of how to put more in a new car than just good looks." The rest of the text highlighted the special performance catalog available at the Dodge dealer containing all of the specifications, options, and parts for Dodge performance cars. The bottom of the page featured an order form for Scat Pack decals, lapel pins, badges, and a catalog of goodies.

Another full-color vertical ad appeared in the May 1968 issue of *Car Life* with an angled front view of a red 1968 Coronet R/T on a racetrack. The black section below began with large red text that read, "The Silken Snarl." A large Scat Pack Bee was placed at the bottom of the page with smaller text on the left side listing the standard and optional equipment of the R/T. Of course, the bottom of the page held the slogan that read "Dodge Scat Pack. The cars with the Bumblebee stripes."

This magazine ad leads with the "Silken Snarl" name for the red 1968 Dodge Coronet R/T. This view shows the parking lights and black mesh grille with R/T badge. The text lists the standard equipment of the Coronet R/T. (Dodge, Plymouth, and the AMC design are registered trademarks of FCA US LLC)

The Coronet R/T was also featured as one of the three Scat Pack cars on the cover and in an article inside the April 1968 issue of *Car Life* with one of the first tests of all three cars. The program was off to a powerful start.

### 1968 Dodge Dart GTSport

The third original member of the 1968 Dodge Scat Pack team was the A-Body Dart GTSport. The 1968 Dart was very much like the 1967 model except for the addition of round

GTS 1968 Darts received this badging on the front fenders. (Photo Courtesy Hanksters Hot Rods & Muscle Cars)

*Before crazy names such as Lemon Twist and Citron Yella, there was just Yellow. That's the color adorning this 1968 Dart GTS wearing black interior, vinyl roof, and Bumblebee stripe. (Photo Courtesy Hanksters Hot Rods & Muscle Cars)*

*A detailed view of the grille and hood shows its non-functional scoops on a 1968 Dodge Dart GTS two-door hardtop. This Dart is equipped with the 340 V-8 engine, standard on the GTS.*

The bright nonfunctional scoops on the 1968 Dart GTS gives a distinctive performance-oriented appearance to the otherwise economy-equipped Dart. The GTS had a standard 340 V-8 engine and other equipment to put it squarely in the Scat Pack.

side-marker lights and a redesigned grille with round parking lights moved slightly inboard on either side and a mesh pattern with a vertical cross in the center. Like the 1967 model, the 1968 Dart was based on a 111-inch-wheelbase unibody chassis. The Dart GTS hood had two longitudinal fake scoops with bright trim that set it apart from the standard Dart models. A GTS badge on the upper rear of the front fenders identified the sport model Dart to the public. The 1968 Dart GTS was available in 21 body colors and 9 interior trim schemes. The 1968 Dart GTS had standard Bumblebee stripes on the rear quarters available in red, white, and black only. The stripes could be deleted, if desired.

### Interior

The Dart GTS interior had standard all vinyl trim and carpeting with standard bucket seats and color-coordinated carpeting. A center console was optional and could be equipped with a chrome handle shifter for either a Torque-Flite or 4-speed manual transmission. Without the console, the automatic shift was mounted on the steering column. The instrument panel had a wide, horizontal design with rectangular gauges and speedometer. The steering wheel had a bright partial horn ring with three spokes and a Dodge Tri-Star badge in its center.

### Engine Options

The standard powerplant of the 1968 Dart GTS was the 340-ci LA-Series small-block V-8. The 340 developed 275 hp at 5,000 rpm and 340 ft-lbs of torque at 3,200 rpm with a single Carter Thermo-Quad 4-barrel carburetor. The 340 had a bore and stroke of 4.04x3.31 inches and a compression ratio of 10.5:1, as well as dual exhaust with a 2.25-inch-diameter. The LA-series engines are easily identified by their ignition distributor mounted at the rear of the block.

Two different camshafts were used in the high-performance 340 GTS engine, depending upon whether a manual or automatic transmission was ordered. A smoother, low-speed idle was desirable with the TorqueFlite, so the camshaft had an intake valve lift of .430 inch and a duration of 268 degrees. The exhaust valves had a lift of .445 and a duration of 276 degrees. Darts with a 4-speed manual transmission had a camshaft with .445-inch lift on both intake and exhaust, and duration of 276 degrees on the intake and 286 degrees for the exhaust.

The only optional engine for the Dart GTS was the 383-ci V-8 that was standard in 1967. Like its 1967 counterpart, the single 4-barrel 383 had a bore and stroke of 4.25x3.38 inches and a compression ratio of 10.1:1. The 383 developed 300

The office of this GTS features an auto on the console and a pair of cushy bucket seats. GTS emblems flank both doors between the window crank and armrest. (Photo Courtesy Hanksters Hot Rods & Muscle Cars)

The engine compartment of a red 1968 Dodge Dart GTS shows the LA-based 340-ci V-8 engine that provided enough power to put the GTS in the Dodge Scat Pack for 1968. The Dart GTS had an immediate high-performance image for the buying public.

hp at 5,200 rpm and 400 ft-lbs of torque at 2,400 rpm. The B-block–based 383 was easily identified by its passenger side front-mounted ignition distributor.

### Transmission Options

The standard transmission on the 1968 Dart GTS was the cast-iron case Chrysler New Process A833 4-speed manual with a 2.66:1 low-gear ratio. A Chrysler Inland design floor shift with a black plastic knob was used with the 4-speed at the beginning of the model year, but it was replaced later with a chrome-handled Hurst shifter with a walnut shift knob. The super strong aluminum case A727 TorqueFlite 3-speed automatic was optional and was equipped with a 2.45:1 low gear. Both transmissions were extra cost.

### Rear Axle Options

The standard rear axle with the TorqueFlite or 4-speed manual transmission was the Chrysler 8¾-inch banjo-type unit with a standard 3.23:1 gear ratio. Sure Grip limited-slip was optional with the 3.23:1 gears. The rear axle was supported by Chrysler-designed heavy-duty longitudinal parallel leaf springs.

### Wheels, Tires, and Brakes

The 1968 Dart GTS brakes were up to the performance levels of the car. It had 10-inch rear drums and 10.79-inch front power disc brakes. Tires were E7014 redline mounted on 5.5-inch steel wheels. Quarter-mile times of around 14.38 seconds at 97 mph were possible with stock gearing. A total of 8,745 Dart GTS hardtops were produced for the 1968 model year. The majority (4,232) had a TorqueFlite automatic transmission.

### Advertising

The 1968 Dart GTS was featured in only a few full color magazine ads published in late 1967, all but one alongside a Charger R/T and a Coronet R/T. The same black Dart GTS with a white Bumblebee stripe was shown in all of those ads. A single two-page ad was published featuring only the black Dart GTS.

The 1968 Dart GTS was featured in at least two other ads with a Coronet and Charger, but only one magazine ad was published showing only the Dart GTS. The two-page spread described the GTS as the "Scat Pack Compact." (Dodge, Plymouth, and the AMC design are registered trademarks of FCA US LLC)

# Maximum Performance 1968 Dart

In addition to the standard line of Darts, the 1968 model year lineup included the limited-production 1968 Dart Hemi Super Stock package cars. The Hemi Dart was a specially built car, created for the NHRA Super Stock drag racing program. It was not sold or intended for street use and was issued a unique VIN and Special Order Code that identified it for that purpose. Every Hemi Dart had yellow warranty avoidance decals posted at multiple locations on the body, warning owners that it was intended only for supervised acceleration trials and the regular warranty did not apply.

Although marketed as a Dart GTS, the Hemi-powered Dart was actually built from a standard Dart with Dart 270 body and interior trim. They were built to a partially finished level on the assembly line but coded as a 383 V-8 car. The body was not finish painted and was taken from the line with only light gray primer and gloss-black paint on the interior of the engine compartment, trunk interior, and door jambs.

The unfinished Darts, without engine, transmission, driveshaft, doors, and quarter glass or interior trim were hauled to the Hurst Performance Research Corporation's rented warehouse near the Hazel Park, Michigan, facility. David Landrith directed the completion of the cars at this building.

While at Hurst, the Darts had the 426 Hemi engine with crossram intake manifold and dual Holley 4-barrel carburetors installed. The interior was equipped with two lightweight Bostrum bucket seats, a rear seat delete panel, and lightweight carpet. The rear suspension was removed and special Super Stock leaf springs installed along with either an 8¾ Chrysler or Dana 60 rear axle, depending on whether an automatic or manual transmission was used. The front fenders and hood were replaced with fiberglass components and the doors were replaced with lightweight steel versions. The hood included a large, wide air scoop to accommodate the dual carburetors.

The finished cars were then shipped back across town to the U-drive pickup area or to dealers. A total of 80 1968 Hemi Darts were built and delivered in early 1968. Although not directly Scat Pack Darts, the image of these cars contributed to 1968 sales and carries on today to the current Hemi Shoot Out, where these 1968 Darts and their stablemate, Hemi Barracudas, are the quickest and fastest Super Stock cars ever, running in their own SS/AH class at NHRA events.

*Northern Illinois driver and owner Larry Griffith won three consecutive NUDRA Super Stock Championships with this 1968 Hemi Dart. The car is posed here at Cordova Dragway after an extensive full restoration in 2007.*

*The 1968 Hemi Darts, along with its 1968 Barracuda stablemates, are still considered the fastest and quickest factory-built Super Stock cars. NHRA allows them to compete in their own special Super Stock/AH class because no other manufacturer's offerings are capable of their speeds and ETs.*

### First Marketing Appearance of the Scat Pack

One of the first magazines to feature the new Dodge Scat Pack lineup was *Car Life*, and its April 1968 issue screamed that point. The cover image was an impressive overhead view of the Dart GTS, Cornet R/T convertible, and Charger R/T with "How Much Scat In the Scat Pack?" at the top of the photo. There was no missing the impact of these three hot machines from Dodge racing down a track side by side.

The eight-page, fully detailed article and road test review inside left no stone unturned in revealing the performance and image-grabbing power of the Scat Pack program and its cars. The lead page width was filled with large red letters stating, "The Dodge Scat Pack." Inside the article the writers at *Car Life* gave all three Dodges a good thrashing. A page of specifications for each car and 13 photos

A black-and-white photo of the 1968 Charger R/T, Coronet R/T, and Dart GTS appeared with the article and tests in the April 1968 issue of *Car Life*.

left readers with a desire to find a local dealer and try them out for themselves. Detail shots of the engines, interior, trunk, and body brought them to life.

The favorite car of the three for *Car Life* writers was clearly the Dart GTS, but all three had defects that took something away from the experience. Both the Dart GTS and the Coronet convertible posted quarter-mile times of 14.68 and 14.69 seconds, but the 426 Hemi Charger R/T left them disappointed because they could not seem to get the Hemi up to its proper level of tune, turning a 15.35 at 94.6 mph. That was not unusual at that time, as few dealer service departments knew how to tune the Hemi well. At around the same time, *Car and Driver* tested a similar 1968 Hemi Charger, also with 3.23:1 gears, and were able to get times closer to what they should be with an ET of 13.5 seconds and a quarter-mile trap speed of 105 mph. Obviously, this Charger was tuned and driven properly.

### 1968 Dodge Coronet Super Bee

The March 1968 issue of *Hot Rod* posted some of the first ads for the new member of the Scat Pack Dodge team. The full-page color ad on the inside front cover showed the first view of a new light-yellow 1968 Dodge Coronet Super Bee with black Bumblebee stripe at the top of the page. Just below were four smaller images of the 383 Magnum engine, Rallye instrument panel, redline tires, and a close-up view of the black rear Bumblebee stripe and Super Bee decal.

Below the pictures the message stated: "Announcing: Coronet Super Bee. Scat Pack performance at a new low price." The text beneath the headline read: "Beware the Hot-Cammed, 4-barrel 383 Mill in the Light Coupe Body." The remainder of

The cover of the April 1968 issue of *Car Life* made it clear that the big news for the 1968 season was the triple play of Dodge's three Scat Pack offerings. The article inside tested all three cars and provided details of the equipment and trim available.

This original unrestored WM21 1968 Dodge Coronet Super Bee coupe is finished in QQ-1 Bright Blue Poly with a white Bumblebee stripe at the rear. It also has Magnum 500 styled steel wheels and red streak tires.

the detailed text related all of the important specifications of the new high-performance Dodge. A horizontal orange zigzag stripe across the middle of the page led to an image of the orange and black bee. The text inside the stripe read, "Run With the Dodge Scat Pack."

Because of the sales success of the 1968 Plymouth RM21 Road Runner, announced at the start of the model year and based on the low-line RL21 Belvedere coupe, Dodge decided that they had to offer a comparable model. Dodge Division General Manager Robert McCurry was behind the idea for the Super Bee, but Dodge Styling office senior designer Harvey J. Winn won a contest within the styling section with the name "Super Bee" and a new logo based on the Dodge "Scat Pack" Bee medallion.

In February 1968, Dodge introduced the WM21 Coronet Super Bee, similarly based on

The H4W white vinyl interior trim of a Medium Dark Turquoise 1968 Coronet Super Bee coupe. The trim combination includes a bench seat and black loop-pile carpeting.

The passenger-side taillight and rear deck lower panel on a QQ-1 Bright Blue Poly 1968 Coronet Super Bee coupe. Note the Scat Pack Bumblebee on the passenger's side of the rear deck panel.

Shown here is the passenger-side door panel of a 1968 Coronet Super Bee coupe with H4W white vinyl interior and black painted upper and lower doorframe. This car has standard window regulators.

the low-line Coronet coupe. The coupe version had foldout rear quarter windows that replaced the two-door hardtop's roll-down windows and had a solid post installed at the front of the glass. The marketing point of both the Road Runner and the Super Bee was to offer high performance based on a less expensive model with fewer luxury options available to give the entry-level buyer a more affordable but still attention-grabbing choice. The Dodge Super Bee was sure to become a member of the Scat Pack lineup. The Super Bee name and badging were, of course, related to the midsized Dodge B-Body line.

The basic Super Bee was similar to the low-line WL21 Coronet Deluxe Coupe but differed in the addition of a small die-cast Super Bee badge featuring the Scat Pack Bee on the passenger-side rear tail panel and the standard Bumblebee stripe on the rear quarters. A change and improvement to the interior was the optional Charger R/T Rallye-type instrument panel with its large, round gauges and tachometer, which replaced the wide, horizontal-design standard Coronet panel. A total of 7,844 1969 Coronet Super Bee two-door hardtops were built.

### Engine Options

The standard engine for the 1968 Dodge Coronet Super Bee was a special high-performance version of the B-block–based 383-ci V-8. Dodge called the performance version of the single 4-barrel 383 was called a 383 Magnum. It had a bore and stroke of 4.25 x 3.38 inches and a compression ratio of 10:1, producing 335 hp at 5,200 rpm, 5 more than the standard single 4-barrel 383. The 383 Magnum was equipped with an unsilenced air cleaner and dual exhaust, making 425 ft-lbs of torque at 3,400 rpm. Most significant was the special high-performance camshaft used only in the Magnum V-8 and its Plymouth Road Runner counterpart. This camshaft had a lift of .450 inch on the intake and .465 inch on the exhaust valve. Intake and exhaust duration was 268 degrees for the intake and 284 degrees for the exhaust, with 46 degrees of overlap. The 383 Magnum was also equipped with a standard windage tray and dual exhaust.

The only optional engine offered with the Dodge Super Bee was the impressive 426 Hemi V-8, producing 425 hp at 5,000 rpm and 490 ft-lbs of torque at 4,000 rpm. The 426 Hemi had a camshaft with mechanical valve lifters and a lift of .490 inch on the intake valve and .480 inch on the exhaust with 284 degrees of duration on both. The Hemi had a cast-aluminum intake manifold that mounted two Carter AFB 4-barrel carburetors. Low-restriction cast-iron headers and dual pipes handled the exhaust. Of course, like all Street Hemi engines, this one was equipped with distinctive black crackle-finish valve covers and was painted Street Hemi Orange.

### Transmission Options

The standard equipment transmission on the 1968 Dodge Super Bee was the super strong cast-iron case Chrysler New Process A833 4-speed manual transmission with a chrome-handled Chrysler Inland floor-mounted shifter with a black plastic knob. The Inland shifter was replaced later in the 1968 model year by a Hurst shifter with a round walnut knob. The cast-iron case A833 had a standard 2.66:1 low-gear ratio to help with hard launches and quick

*This engine compartment is in a 1968 Coronet Super Bee with a 383 Magnum engine. Note the optional air conditioner and correct Chrysler Blue engine color and crackle-finish air cleaner with identification plate.*

*This black vinyl bench seat interior is in a Bright Blue Poly 1968 Coronet Super Bee coupe. This car is equipped with a 4-speed transmission and chrome-plated Inland shifter handle with a black plastic knob.*

acceleration. The optional transmission was the aluminum case A727 Chrysler TorqueFlite 3-speed automatic with a 2.45:1 low gear. A special small-diameter (11-inch) and high-stall-speed torque converter was standard equipment with the Super Bee.

### Rear Axle Options

The standard rear axle with the TorqueFlite or 383 with the 4-speed manual transmission was the Chrysler 8¾-inch banjo-type unit with a standard 3.23:1 gear ratio. When the 426 Hemi and a 4-speed transmission were ordered, a stronger Dana 60 9¾-inch ring gear axle with a 3.54:1 ratio was installed with its standard Sure Grip. Both axles were supported with the standard and very effective Chrysler-designed heavy-duty longitudinal leaf springs.

### Wheel and Tire Options

Standard tires on the 383 Coronet Super Bee were F70x14–inch red streak that were only available with the heavy-duty suspension and power disc brakes that came with the Super Bee. When equipped with the optional 426 Hemi engine, standard tires were F70x15–inch red stripes mounted on pressed-steel painted wheels. No optional tires and wheels were available with the Hemi.

*This ad likens the Super Bee to "discovering that Piper-Heidsieck is selling at beer prices." The Super Bee borrowed many components from its model stablemate, the Coronet R/T, hence the analogy. (Dodge, Plymouth, and the AMC design are registered trademarks of FCA US LLC)*

*These optional Magnum 500 styled steel wheels with chrome rims were used on the 1968 models. They were not available with a trim ring. These wheels were ordered with Sales Code 580 in 1968 and cost $97.30.*

### Advertising

With Super Bee's addition to the Scat Pack lineup it was clear that the Plymouth Road Runner would now have a direct competitor across the way at Chrysler. One way to do this was to showcase the Super Bee with its in-house companions through Scat Pack advertisement. While the Road Runner would continue to outsell the Super Bee, there's little doubt that the Super Bee ate away at sales. While 1968 Road Runner ads consisted of static cars with generic backgrounds, the Super Bee ads featured advertisements containing the lively Scat Back zipping or charging at you through them. The "Bee" would continue to be a stinging thorn in the side of Road Runner until it's dismissal in 1971.

### Scat Pack Dealership Advertising

Although the Dodge Scat Pack Program was directed by Chrysler and Dodge Division, dealers were expected to contribute not only money to accomplish the goals of the program, but they were also required to participate by presenting Scat Pack Club activities, advertising, and promotional efforts. As instructions from Dodge stated, "Nationally, the club was designed to function without dealer involvement, but its number one objective, of course, is to send members to Dodge dealerships."

This full-page ad shows a white 1968 Coronet Super Bee with a black Bumblebee stripe. The text describes the standard equipment and features of the Super Bee. (Dodge, Plymouth, and the AMC design are registered trademarks of FCA US LLC)

This color ad appeared in the March 1968 issue of Hot Rod. It shows the yellow Dodge Coronet R/T that was shown in earlier ads but announces a new lower price to stir up sales. (Dodge, Plymouth, and the AMC design are registered trademarks of FCA US LLC)

A detailed 31-page brochure titled "Club Operator's Manual" laid out the instructions for dealers about how to promote the club and the cars to customers and potential customers. The manual reinforced the value of the program by pointing out that "nearly one in every five Dodges sold is a Scat Pack." Dealers were told, "The objective of your local club operation is to promote your dealership as a Scat Pack Performance Headquarters."

In addition to detailed instructions on how to start and run their local Scat Pack Club, dealers were given examples of the text for radio and newspaper spots so that dealers across the country would have standardized material to keep everyone heading in the right direction and on the same page for the most successful results. Radio spots were provided in 10-, 20-, and 30-second blocks so that dealers would not have to create their own messages. Additional examples were provided for direct mail and telephone efforts.

The manual also included detailed instructions on how to start and conduct meets for the local Scat Pack Club and provided examples of events and programs that could be presented by the dealer staff for the local club. The manual also provided a list of films and printed materials that were available from Dodge that could be used to enhance the interest in local club meetings and events. Suggested events were explained that included Drag Racing, Gymkhanas, Rallys, and car shows.

A more aggressive program available to dealers who had the resources was a list radio and TV show material. The Dodge manual provided the dealer with choices of TV spots including films, commercials, and everything else they might need to produce a successful and entertaining program. The manual finished up with copies of print advertising that the dealer could use for his own local promotional programs.

# CHAPTER 3

# 1969

## DODGE SCAT PACK PROGRAM

*"Dodge Scat Pack: The Cars with the Bumblebee Stripes."*

By September 1968, the new 1969 Dodge Scat Pack lineup had already been announced to the public and was appearing in many popular enthusiast magazines in addition to the regular dealer posters, ads, and brochures. The lineup and availability of high-performance options was increased for the 1969 model year, giving buyers even more opportunities to choose their weapons. In addition to the stalwarts of the 1968 model year, 1969 offered some new fare for the road.

### Scat Pack Lineup for 1969

The Dodge Charger stable for 1969 was expanded by the addition of the Charger 500 and later in the year, the Charger Daytona, along with the already well-qualified Charger R/T. Both the Charger 500 and the Daytona were expressly created to satisfy NASCAR aerodynamic needs, but they had to be made available to the public to fill homologation sales requirements.

The Coronet R/T hardtop and convertible were still around, along with the Coronet Super Bee, offering power and performance at a lower price. Engine performance was improved in both cars by the use of an optional functional fresh air system. In February 1969, a new option became available for the Coronet Super Bee in the form of the A12 Six-Pack option. Called a 1969-1/2 model, the A12 was so distinctive that it almost represents a separate model. These cars, along with their Plymouth Road Runner brothers, came to be recognized as the ultimate street-performance B-Body Mopars.

Dart GTS was back for its sophomore campaign. In addition to the standard 340 and optional 383 engines, the relatively

*A passenger-side front quarter view of a 1969 XX29 Charger 500 finished in T5 Copper poly with a white Bumblebee stripe and 500 logo. The Charger 500 used a modified Coronet grille and a flush backlight.*

tight Dart engine compartment for 1969 would be filled with the exceptionally formable 375-hp 440-ci Magnum V-8. The idea was first proposed by dealer extraordinaire "Mr. Norm" Kraus in Chicago, whose staff stuffed a 440 V-8 into a Dart chassis and demonstrated to Dodge engineers in Detroit that it could be done successfully, if not easily.

Overall, the styling changes for 1969 were subtle, but noticeable. The grille and front bumper of the Dart GTS were changed to set them apart from the 1968 models. The grille

This ad shows the full Scat Pack lineup for the 1969 model year. The country road caravan here is led by a red 1969 Dart GTS, followed by a green Coronet Super Bee, Coronet R/T, Dart Swinger, and a Charger R/T. (Dodge, Plymouth, and the AMC design are registered trademarks of FCA US LLC)

A 1969 Dodge showroom brochure shows all of the Scat Pack cars and lists the details of their equipment and standard features. (Dodge, Plymouth, and the AMC design are registered trademarks of FCA US LLC)

on the Coronet was given more sculptured lines at both ends around the quad headlights and a new two-door hardtop model was added to the Coronet Super Bee body type choices. The Charger grille was given a new vertical center bar to separate it easily from the 1968 front end styling on the street. Side markers changed from round to rectangle as well.

### 1969 Dodge Charger R/T

The 1969 Charger styling was much like that of the 1968 model, and there were few, if any, dramatic changes. The popular flowing "Coke bottle" lines continued from 1968, causing magazine writers to compare the lines of the Charger to

*This dark green 1969 Charger R/T has a red Bumblebee stripe and has Magnum 500 styled steel wheels. This Charger also has an optional black vinyl roof.*

those of the Chevrolet Corvette in their general feeling. The most obvious update to the body was the deep-set grille, which added a bright vertical trim to its center. The Charger's quad headlights were still hidden and mechanically operated by vacuum solenoids. The taillights were changed from the four small, round, bright-trimmed units used in 1968 to bright-trimmed dual wide sculptured lights in 1969. All side-marker lights were now rectangular.

**Exterior**

Like the 1968 model, the 1969 Charger was offered in only one body type: a two-door hardtop based on the same 117-inch-wheelbase chassis and all-steel unibody. There were three models available at the beginning of the 1969 year: XP29 Charger two-door hardtop, XS29 Charger R/T two-door hardtop, and XX29 Charger 500. Only the Charger R/T and Charger 500 were considered to be sports-performance models and part of the Scat Pack program. The 1969 Charger was available in 19 acrylic enamel body colors and four optional vinyl roof colors. The 1969 Bumblebee stripe at the rear quarters was now a singlewide stripe with thin stripe lines on both sides. An R/T logo was cut into the stripe at the rear quarters.

The Bumblebee stripe was available in black (V-8X), red (V-8R), and white (V-9W). A similar stripe was used on the 1969 Charger 500 that replaced the "R/T" cutout with a "500" cutout. The 1969 Charger Daytona used a wider, one-piece stripe with a "Daytona" cutout that lined up with and matched the color of the rear wing vertical stabilizers.

*A passenger-side rear view of a dark green 1969 Charger R/T clearly shows the unique Charger rear window design, black vinyl roof, and red Bumblebee stripe with prominent R/T logo.*

*The red Bumblebee stripe with R/T logo and the distinctive Charger bright racing-type fuel filler cap were features unique to the Scat Pack line. The rectangular side-marker identifies a 1969 model.*

### Interior

The 1969 Charger was available in 12 all-vinyl interior trim combinations with front bucket seats and a rear bench seat for all models. The Charger R/T standard interior included front bucket seats with an optional fixed center cushion and folding center armrest. The interior trim was available in dark blue, dark green, red, tan, black, and white. The pattern consisted of six sections with buttons at the apex on both the seat cushion and back. The pile carpet was color coordinated except for the white interior, which was available with blue, green, gold, red, or black carpeting. A center console with gearshift was optional.

The 1969 Charger R/T was available in a Special Edition Décor Group, Sales Code A47, which added leather and vinyl front bucket seats, wood-grain steering wheel with stainless-steel spider and vinyl-covered padded horn button, wood-grain inserts in the instrument panel, hood-mounted turn signals, pedal dress-up, deep-dish wheel covers, light package, and Special Edition nameplate.

*The interior of this F8 Dark Green Poly 1969 Charger R/T is C6G Dark Green vinyl with bucket seats and a center console with automatic transmission shifter. The 1969 seats differ from the 1968 versions by the addition of adjustable head restraints.*

### Instrument Panel

The 1969 Charger instrument panel was nearly identical to the 1968 model and featured what Dodge called "sports-car-type instrumentation." A large, round 150-mile-per-hour speedometer was placed to the right of an identically sized combination tachometer and clock. To the right of the speedometer were four smaller, round bezels that contained the fuel, temperature, oil pressure, and alternator gauges. The instrument cluster was mounted in a textured flat-black background panel.

A total of 18,974 1969 Charger R/Ts were built.

## 1969 Dodge Charger 500

The XX29 Charger 500 two-door sports hardtop was a new model for 1969, designed and intended to satisfy the needs of racing and winning on the long NASCAR tracks. All of its special features were designed to increase aerodynamic efficiency at high speed. Most noticeable at the front was the specially designed flush-mounted grille made from a standard quad nonretractable headlight 1968 Coronet grille and mounted in the Charger front fascia. A unique script Charger and red "500" nameplate was mounted at the passenger's side of the grille. A similar badge was also mounted on the deck faceplate.

The only modification to the 1968 Coronet grille was the addition of brackets to mount it to the Charger body opening. Because the headlights were no longer retractable, backing plates were used, along with standard 1968 Coronet bezels. The original vacuum hoses for the standard Charger lights were cut off, and the remainder hung behind the grille.

At the rear of the Charger 500, the normally deep-set Charger rear window and roofline C-pillars were modified and moved back to be made flush with the rear of the roofline to create smooth aerodynamic flow without the previous design's tunnel-roof effect. Special chrome-clad covers were added to the A-pillar posts to improve airflow around the windshield. Because of the redesigned rear window and roofline, the 1969 Charger 500 used a shorter deck lid and special deck lid hinges to work with the deck lid.

*Shown here is a passenger-side front quarter view of a red 1969 Charger 500 equipped with a 426 Hemi engine. Note the wider front windshield post moldings added to increase aerodynamic efficiency.*

## 1969 Charger Daytona

In April 1969, Dodge introduced the new XX29 1969 Charger Daytona two-door sports hardtop to replace the Charger 500 as the lead in their efforts to win at NASCAR long tracks because the former did not accomplish the goals set for it at the races. The Daytona, and its later corporate brother, the 1970 Plymouth Roadrunner Superbird, represented the ultimate in extreme factory track performance. Its outstanding aerodynamic attributes clearly set it apart from anything done before or since.

The 1969 Dodge Charger Daytona was based on a standard Charger unibody construction two-door sports hardtop

*The hood, grille, and bumper of a red XX29 1969 Charger 500. The grille is a modified Coronet unit. The front was customized to increase aerodynamics for NASCAR racing. This design became obsolete when the Daytona was introduced.*

*This 1969 Dodge XX29 Daytona is finished in Y2 Yellow with a white stripe and wing. Optioned on the Daytona are the Magnum 500 styled steel wheels and red streak tires. Note the correct lower front spoiler and mesh grille opening above.*

*The 1969 Charger 500s all wore Bumblebee striping in Red, White, or Black. The special rear window was used on the 1969 Charger 500 and Daytona only.*

Standard equipment on the Charger 500 included a standard 440-ci single 4-barrel V-8, 4-speed manual transmission with Hurst linkage, heavy-duty suspension and brakes, and F70x15 red streak fiberglass tires. A 426 Hemi engine and 3-speed TorqueFlite automatic transmission were optional. Bumblebee stripes with "500" stripes were standard across the rear deck and fenders.

A total of 580 1969 Charger 500s were produced.

*Left rear quarter of a 1969 Charger Daytona finished in Y2 Yellow with a white stripe. The Daytona spoiler is different from the one used later on the 1970 Plymouth Superbird.*

body shell that included the already major design modifications of the previous Charger 500 model. Both the Charger 500 and Daytona packages were ordered under Sales Code A11. The most obvious changes to the original Charger 500 were the addition to the front of the body of an 18-inch-long steel nose and a large aerodynamic wing to the rear deck. Creative Industries of Detroit, an outside vendor, performed these modifications. These machines, which came to be known as "Winged Warriors," dominated the long tracks of NASCAR and easily brought speeds up to the 200-mph mark.

### Exterior

The 1969 Charger Daytona front-end treatment consisted of a steel nose cone assembly that included retractable rectangular headlight doors on its top surface. The underside of the nose cone used a full valance that attached to the lower edge of the front fenders. The small, rectangular screened grille panel was mounted into the center of the nose cone. A wide spoiler was mounted under the grille opening.

The Daytona used front standard Charger fenders but without marker light openings. The rectangular side markers on a Daytona were mounted in a separate lower transverse panel below the front fascia. Reverse air scoops were mounted in the top center of each Daytona front fender. On the actual Daytona race cars, this scoop was designed to allow clearance for the larger front tires and lower front suspension, but they were nonfunctional on the cars available to the public. The 1969 Charger Daytona used the same hood as a standard Charger except for the Daytona's chrome hood pins and plates. The Daytona did not use a hood latch, but it did have a safety catch.

The most significant addition to the 1969 Charger rear quarter was the massive wing that was standard on the Daytona. The Daytona wing assembly consisted of three parts: the two vertical stabilizers and the adjustable horizontal wing. The vertical stabilizers were attached to the rear body with reinforcements. A black rubber gasket was used between the body and the vertical stabilizers. The wing and stabilizers were painted the same semi-gloss color as the stripe. The wing assembly served two purposes on the track. The vertical stabilizers did just that: stabilize the side-to-side or lateral forces. The horizontal wing provided considerable downforce to keep the rear tires on the ground at speed. The 1969 Charger Daytona was available with the same interior trim schemes, body colors, and engine and transmission choices as the Charger R/T and 500. A total of 503 1969 Charger Daytonas were produced, although dealer sales to the public of this outlandishly styled machine were decidedly slow.

### Road Test

The Charger Daytona was so rare and specialized that few magazine ads or articles appeared announcing the cars. One was a *Road Test* article from December 1969 describing the details of the Daytona's development and production. The article mentioned that the Daytonas had been shut out for the season from the superspeedways such as Daytona, Darlington, and Rockingham, although Richard Brickhouse's Daytona won Talladega later in the year. The damage to Dodge advertising was serious because these long tracks held the greatest potential impact.

The Daytona used in this test was a 375-hp 440 4-barrel and was connected to the rear wheels by a 3-speed Torque-Flite automatic and a 3.23:1 ratio rear axle with Sure Grip. The 3,875-pound Daytona with Rallye suspension was tested for its handling and performance on the Chrysler Proving Grounds by veteran NASCAR driver Charlie Glotzbach, who said, "There is no comparison to what the other cars handle like. This one is a lot more stable. You go right down into the corner and then with one hand you go right through." The car also achieved an ET of 14.48 seconds at 96.15 mph on the quarter-mile dragstrip during this test session.

### Engine Options

The standard engine in the 1969 Charger R/T, Charger 500, and Charger Daytona was the 440-ci RB V-8. The 1969 Charger R/T, Charger 500, and Charger Daytona engine options were

*The 1969 Dodge Charger R/T was equipped with a standard 440 Magnum V-8. This dark green Charger has an optional air conditioner, which was rare in that era.*

the same as those in the previous 1968 model. The standard powerplant was a 440-ci V-8 based on the RB (raised-block) configuration. The single Carter AVS 4-barrel-equipped 440 Magnum produced 375 hp at 4,600 rpm and 480 ft-lbs of torque at 3,200 rpm. The 440 had a bore and stroke of 4.32 x 3.75 inches and a compression ratio of 10.1:1. All 1969 440 engines were 440 Engine Orange to more closely relate to the performance image of the optional 426 Hemi. The 440 Magnum engine used a black crackle-finish unsilenced air cleaner.

The only optional engine available with the 1969 Charger R/T, Charger 500, and Charger Daytona was the 426 Hemi V-8 rated at 425 hp at 5,000 rpm and 490 ft-lbs of torque at 4,000 rpm. The two Carter AFB 4-barrel-equipped Hemis had a bore and stroke of 4.25 x 3.75 inches and a compression ratio of 10.3:1. The Hemi block and heads were finished in Street Hemi Orange with a black crackle-finish air cleaner. The large, wide Hemi valvecovers were black crackle finish.

### Transmission Options

The 1969 Dodge Charger R/T, Charger 500, and Charger Daytona had a standard cast-aluminum case A727 3-speed TorqueFlite automatic transmission when equipped with the 440 V-8 engine. The TorqueFlite was operated with either a column- or console-mounted chrome shift lever, depending on the interior options. An A833 4-speed manual transmission was standard with the 426 Hemi and optional with the 440. The 4-speed used a Hurst shifter with a round chrome-plated steel handle and a round, white plastic knob. The Hemi was also available with an optional TorqueFlite automatic transmission.

### Rear Axle Options

The standard rear axle with the 1969 Charger R/T, Charger 500, and Charger Daytona with a 440 or 426 Hemi engine and TorqueFlite automatic transmission was the Chrysler 8¾-inch banjo-type, which was available in ratios from 2.94:1 to 3.91:1 with 3.23:1 being standard. A special Performance Axle Group option (Sales Code 358) was available that provided a 3.55:1 rear axle gear ratio, special slip-drive fan, and an extra-wide high-performance radiator fan shroud. When a 4-speed transmission was ordered with the 440 or 426 Hemi engine, a 9¾-inch ring gear Dana 60 heavy-duty rear axle with a 3.54:1 gear ratio was used.

### Wheel and Tire Options

The 1969 Charger R/T and Charger 500 were equipped with standard 14 x 5–inch stamped-steel wheels, which could be equipped with either a small hubcap or a styled wheel cover. Optional 14-inch Magnum 500 styled wheels with chrome trim rings was available. For a short time, optional 15-inch cast-aluminum Kelsey Hayes road wheels were available, but they were recalled in September 1968 due to maintenance problems. All 426 Hemi-equipped 1969 Charger R/Ts and Charger 500s were equipped with standard 15 x 6 pressed steel wheels, and no optional wheels were available.

### Production Numbers

A total of 18,974 Charger R/Ts, 580 Charger 500s, and 503 Charger Daytonas were built for the 1969 model year.

### 1969 Charger R/T, Charger 500, and Charger Daytona Advertising

Some of the earliest advertising pieces for the 1969 Charger models appeared in the October 1968 issue of *Motor Trend*. The full-page color Charger ad was among three used in a group to promote Dodge's new models for 1969. The Charger ad was dramatic with a full front view of a red 1969 Charger R/T with a black vinyl roof placed strategically at a diagonal on the page to get the reader's immediate attention. Behind the car

*This magazine ad displays a red 1969 Charger 500 and lists all of the standard equipment and features. As always in 1969, the Scat Pack bee is a prominent part of the advertising. Note the Charger 500 badge on the grille.*

*This 1969 Charger R/T ad appeared in the October 1968 issue of* Motor Trend. *Like all in this series, it lists the standard equipment and features of the 1969 Charger R/T and prominently includes the Scat Pack bee. (Dodge, Plymouth, and the AMC design are registered trademarks of FCA US LLC)*

*A 1969 Charger ad shows a young couple and explains how owning their new Charger R/T brought them closer together. The automobile was a significant part of the lives of young people in the 1960s. (Dodge, Plymouth, and the AMC design are registered trademarks of FCA US LLC)*

was a hazy blue sky with a partially cloud-blocked dark-red sun. Beneath the image the headline in red block letters read, "We've Got You Cornered: Charger R/T."

Directly below was a large image of the Scat Pack Bee. The bee was accelerating on wide black tires in a trail of billowing white and blue tire smoke. The lower right of the page listed the standard equip-

*The power and authority of a Dodge Scat Pack member is brought to the attention of every reader in this 1969 Charger R/T magazine ad. Charger identification is clear due to the divider in the grille and the R/T model by the badge on the driver's side. (Dodge, Plymouth, and the AMC design are registered trademarks of FCA US LLC)*

ment of the Charger R/T and text that described some of the features and attributes of the car. Of course, the optional 426 Hemi engine was mentioned at the bottom of the list. The bottom of the page finished with the slogan, "Dodge Scat Pack: the cars with the Bumblebee stripes."

A later full-page magazine ad for the new Charger R/T was a bit more subtle and showed a nice-looking sexy young couple posing on the edge of a serene lakeside scene in front of their white 1969 Charger R/T. The young woman was wearing a stylish short white dress with the man's blue sport coat draped around her shoulders. Large black letters read, "The Eternal Triangle" and the text told about the woman's concerns about her man's new love and how she learned to live with it. There was no mention of the Scat Pack this time and only: "Dodge Fever: The Catch of The Year" text appeared at the bottom of the page.

Another full-page 1969 Charger R/T ad appeared a little later in the season. A red 1969 Charger R/T filled the top third of the page with the word "Wailer" below in large block red letters. To the lower left, a color image of the yellow-helmeted Scat Pack bee was shown with white smoke billowing from its tires and a colorful yellow-and-green striped tail behind it. To the right of the bee was smaller bold red text that simply said, "Charger R/T" and beneath it was related marketing text and a list of Charger R/T standard features. "Dodge Scat Pack: the cars with the Bumblebee stripes" filled the lower edge of the page.

### 1969 Dodge Coronet R/T

There were five series of Dodge Coronets for 1969, all based on a 117-inch-wheelbase platform. The sport Coronet model for 1969 was the Coronet R/T, available as a WS23 two-door hardtop and WS27 two-door convertible. The standard R/T engine was the 440-ci single 4-barrel V-8 with the 426 Hemi as the only option. The R/T was identified by a power bulge hood and R/T nameplates like the 1968 model, and was equipped with the same twin simulated side scoop panels as the premium model Coronet 500. New for 1969 were optional simulated separate air scoops mounted on the sides of the rear quarters.

All 1969 Coronets were of steel unibody construction and were based on a shared similar 117-inch-wheelbase platform for the hardtop, sedan convertible, and later coupe. Like the Charger, the Coronet/Chrysler unit construction concept utilized a solid floorpan with a front subframe and parallel rear longitudinal members to support the suspension and drivetrain. All cars with the 426 Hemi engine had torque boxes welded in place across the frame rails in front of the rear spring front mounting. All convertibles had the same rear reinforcements plus an additional plate welded across the front body crossmember to the body side seam. Hemi cars also had a flat reinforcement welded in place above the rear axle pinion snubber.

### Exterior

The styling changes to the 1969 Coronet R/T from the previous model year were subtle, but available options were added to allow owners to personalize their cars from others and from the 1968 models, if desired. In the front, the grille was narrowed in its center, with the quad headlight pods becoming more pronounced. The body lines remained much the same and the dual scoop-like insets were still stamped into the rear quarters just to the rear of the door openings. The taillights and rear fascia were redesigned to change the wedge-shaped 1968

*A number of similar ads for 1969 Dodge Scat Pack cars were featured in enthusiast magazines, including* Car Life *and* Motor Trend. *The ads always gave a performance-oriented name to each of the cars along with an attention-grabbing picture and detailed technical information.*

lights to two wide rectangular bezels with three smaller lights in each side. Bumblebee stripes with a Scat Pack logo cutout on each side of the rear quarters were standard and available in red, white, and black.

The R/T was again available as a WS23 two-door hardtop and a WS27 two-door convertible, both on Dodge's proven unibody construction. Rectangular markers replaced the small, round side-marker lights of 1968 for 1969.

A red-filled bright R/T badge mounted at the passenger's side of the deep-set horizontal black front grille identified the Coronet R/T. Bright trim surrounded the entire grille assembly and quad round headlights. The R/T hood had a power bulge standard, but a special hood was available with a Sales Code N96 fresh-air package that was standard with the 426 Hemi and optional with the 440 V-8.

### Interior

The 1969 Coronet R/T standard interiors were all-vinyl seats with an optional center console or fixed center cushion and folding armrest. The vinyl trim was available in blue, green, red, black, gold, or white and used lateral panels with longitudinal pleats only in the center section. The carpet color choices were color-keyed except for the white interior, which was available with choices of blue, green, red, or black.

### Instrument Panel

The 1969 Coronet R/T Rallye-type instrument panel featured a wide horizontal-design speedometer with oil pressure, coolant temperature, and ammeter gauges on either side. The steering wheel was a three-spoke design with a partial horn ring and a Dodge Tri-Star emblem in its center.

### Engine Options

The standard engine in the 1969 Coronet R/T was the 440-ci RB V-8 with a 4.32 x 3.75–inch bore and stroke and a 10.1:1 compression ratio, producing 375 hp at 4,600 rpm and 480 ft-lbs of torque at 3,200 rpm. The 440 had a single Carter AVS 4-barrel carburetor mounted on a Chrysler cast-iron intake manifold. All 1969 440 blocks, heads, and valve covers were painted 440 Engine Orange.

Like the Charger R/T, the only 1969 Dodge Coronet R/T optional engine was the 426 Hemi V-8. The Hemi had a 4.25 x 3.75–inch bore and stroke and a 10.3:1 compression ratio. The Hemi produced 425 hp at 5,000 rpm and 490 ft-lbs of torque at 4,000 rpm. The 1969 Hemi engine used solid mechanical valve lifters operated by a camshaft with an intake lift of .484 inch and an exhaust lift of .475 inch with a duration on both of 284 degrees. The Hemi had cast-iron cylinder heads and a cast-aluminum intake manifold topped with two inline-mounted Carter AFB 4-barrel carburetors. The 1968 Hemi was finished in Street Hemi Orange with black crackle-finish valvecovers.

### Transmission Options

The 1969 Dodge Coronet R/T had a standard cast-aluminum case A727 3-speed TorqueFlite automatic transmission when equipped with the 440 V-8 engine. The TorqueFlite was operated with either a column- or console-mounted chrome shift lever, depending on the interior options. An A833 4-speed manual transmission was standard with the 426 Hemi and optional with the 440. The 4-speed used a chrome-handled Hurst shifter with a white plastic knob. The Hemi was also available with an optional TorqueFlite automatic transmission.

**The 1969 Coronet R/T was equipped with a Hurst shifter with a round chrome-plated handle and small walnut ball-knob shifter. The shifter on a console-equipped Charger had a sharp bend to the left and up to clear the console housing.**

### Rear Axle Options

The standard rear axle with the 1969 Coronet R/T with a 440 or 426 Hemi engine and TorqueFlite automatic transmission was the Chrysler 8¾-inch banjo-type, which was available in ratios from 2.94:1 to 3.91:1, with 3.23:1 being standard. A special Performance Axle Group option (Sales Code 358) was available that provided a 3.55:1 rear axle gear ratio, special slip-drive fan, and an extra-wide high-performance radiator fan shroud. When a 4-speed transmission was ordered with the 440 or 426 Hemi engine, a 9¾-inch ring gear Dana 60 heavy-duty rear axle with a 3.54:1 gear ratio was used.

### Wheel and Tire Options

The 1969 Coronet R/T was equipped with standard 14 x 5–inch stamped-steel wheels, which could be equipped with either a small hubcap or a styled wheel cover. Optional 14-inch Magnum 500 styled wheels with chrome trim rings were available. For a short time, optional 15-inch cast-aluminum Kelsey Hayes road wheels were available, but they were recalled in September 1968 due to maintenance problems. All 426 Hemi-equipped Coronet R/Ts were equipped with standard 15 x 6 pressed-steel wheels, and no optional wheels were available.

## 1969 Dodge Coronet Super Bee

The Coronet Super Bee, based on the low-line Coronet coupe, was continued much unchanged for 1969. The WM21 coupe version had foldout rear quarter windows that replaced the two-door hardtop's roll-down windows and had a solid post installed at the front of the glass. For 1969, a WM23 two-door hardtop version was also offered. The marketing point of the Super Bee was to offer a high-performance model based on a less expensive model with fewer luxury options available to give the entry-level buyer a more affordable but still attention-grabbing choice.

The basic Super Bee was similar to the Coronet low-line WL21 Coronet Deluxe and WH23 Coronet 440 but differed in the addition of a small die-cast Super Bee badge featuring the Scat Pack Bee on the passenger-side rear tail panel and the standard Bumblebee stripe on the rear quarters. A change and improvement to the interior was the optional Charger R/T Rallye-type instrument panel with its large, round gauges and tachometer, which replaced the standard wide, horizontal-design Coronet panel. Super Bee Bumblebee stripes were available in red, black, and white.

### Engine Options

The standard engine for the 1969 Dodge Coronet Super Bee was a special high-performance version of the B-block–based 383-ci V-8. Dodge called the performance version of the single 4-barrel 383 a 383 Magnum. It had a bore and stroke of 4.25 x 3.38 inches and a compression ratio of 10:1, producing 335 hp at 5,200 rpm, five more than the standard single 4-barrel 383. The 383 Magnum was equipped with an unsilenced air cleaner and dual exhaust, making 425 ft-lbs of torque at 3,400 rpm. Most significant was the special high-performance camshaft used only in the Magnum V-8 and its Plymouth Road Runner counterpart. This camshaft had a lift of .450 inch on the intake and .465 inch on the exhaust valve. Intake and exhaust duration was 268 degrees for the intake and 284 degrees for the exhaust, with 46 degrees of overlap. The 383 Magnum was also equipped with a standard windage tray and dual exhaust and was painted turquoise.

The only optional engine offered at the beginning of the year for the Dodge Super Bee was the impressive 426 Hemi V-8, producing 425 hp at 5,000 rpm and 490 ft-lbs of torque at 4,000 rpm. The 426 Hemi had a camshaft with mechanical valve lifters and a lift of .490 inch on the intake valve and .480 inch on the exhaust, with 284 degrees of duration on both. The Hemi had a cast-aluminum intake manifold that mounted two Carter AFB 4-barrel carburetors. Low-restriction cast-iron headers and dual pipes handled exhaust. Of course, like all Street Hemi engines, this one was equipped with distinctive black crackle-finish valvecovers and was painted Street Hemi Orange.

*An original unrestored 1969 Coronet Super Bee finished in B5 Bright Blue Poly with a black Bumblebee stripe. A 425-hp 426 Hemi engine powers this Super Bee. The 15-inch body color steel wheels and small hubcaps were standard with the Hemi engine.*

*A detail view of a Bright Blue Poly 1969 Coronet R/T 426 Hemi engine and Ramcharger fresh air intake system. Notice the rubber boot that fits over the brake master cylinder.*

### Transmission Options

The standard equipment transmission on the 1969 Dodge Super Bee was the super strong cast-iron case Chrysler New Process A833 4-speed manual with a chrome-handled Hurst floor-mounted shifter. The cast-iron case A833 had a standard 2.66:1 low-gear ratio to help with hard launches and quick acceleration. The optional transmission was the aluminum case A727 Chrysler TorqueFlite 3-speed automatic with a 2.45:1 low gear. A special small-diameter (11-inch) and high-stall-speed torque converter was standard equipment with the Super Bee.

### Rear Axle Options

The standard rear axle with the TorqueFlite or 383 with the 4-speed manual transmission was the Chrysler 8¾-inch banjo-type unit with a standard 3.23:1 gear ratio. When the 426 Hemi and a 4-speed transmission were ordered, a stronger 9¾-inch ring gear Dana 60 axle with a 3.54:1 ratio was installed with its standard Sure Grip. Both axles were supported with the standard and very effective Chrysler-designed heavy-duty longitudinal leaf springs.

### Wheel and Tire Options

Standard tires on the 383 Coronet Super Bee were F70x14–inch red streak that were only available with the heavy-duty suspension and power disc brakes that came with the Super Bee. When equipped with the optional 426 Hemi engine, standard tires were F70x15–inch red stripes mounted on pressed-steel painted wheels. No optional tires and wheels were available with the Hemi.

### 1969 Coronet R/T and Super Bee Advertising

One of the first print ads to appear for the 1969 Coronet Super Bee was an announcement that the Manufacturer's Suggested Retail Price had been reduced from the 1968 Coronet R/T. The full color ad featured a full-width image of the front of a yellow 1969 Super Bee with the optional twin hood scoops posed on a dragstrip. The text at the lower left stated, "Super Bee can lower your ET and your payments at the same time."

Three more columns of informative text explained that the list price of the Dodge Coronet Super Bee was $219 lower than the 1968 R/T. The remainder of the text listed and explained the standard features and options with prices and also provided details of how drag racing king Dick Landy had tested both cars for comparison. Nowhere on the ad was Scat Pack

*Tongue-in-cheek is the best way to describe this 1969 Yellow Super Bee magazine ad explaining that you can lower your E.T. and your payments at the same time due to the lower price compared to the same model in 1968. (Dodge, Plymouth, and the AMC design are registered trademarks of FCA US LLC)*

*"Cool It" was the title of this full-color ad, which was published in the October 1968 issue of* Motor Trend. *It shows a 1969 Coronet Super Bee, which is presumed to be equipped with the Ramcharger fresh air intake system. (Dodge, Plymouth, and the AMC design are registered trademarks of FCA US LLC)*

mentioned, but a small image of the Scat Pack Bee was placed at the lower left edge.

The October 1968 issue of *Motor Trend* featured a full-page color ad for the new 1969 Coronet Super Bee. The ad showed an action front view of a dark-red Super Bee with the optional functional dual hood scoops. The large headline read, "Cool It" in bright-red block letters. The text beneath the headline began with another smaller red headline that read, "Coronet Super Bee" that was followed with a short story. "You're sitting watching the Christmas tree, when this thing with scoops on the hood throbs up. There're crazy stripes on the rear and some kind of bee. Goodbye. It's Super Bee. The scoops scoop." The rest of the text describes the Ramcharger functional air scoops plus the standard and optional features and equipment of the 1969 Super Bee. The bottom of the page ends with the red Dodge Scat Pack logo and "The cars with the Bumblebee stripes."

### 1969 Super Bee Dealer Promotion

On March 28, 1969, a letter was sent to all Dodge dealers from Dodge General Sales Manager A. G. Kirchner Jr. describing what was called "A Springboard to Spring Selling Action." The letter told dealers of the Super Bee "Scat Pack" Special promoting both the Super Bee and the Scat Pack programs at the same time. The letter began, "This is the time of year when more and more young guys with a gleam in their eye will start drifting in for a look-see at Super Bee." Mr. Kirchner offered a bargain package of Appearance-Performance options to attract these new young buyers.

The package included a functional Ramcharger hood scoop to boost engine performance, chrome hood hold-down pins, 3-speed wipers, F70x14 fiberglass-belted Wide Oval tires, and an optional vinyl roof. This package represented a savings to the dealers' wholesale price of $41 to $66, depending upon whether or not the vinyl roof was ordered. Of course, this special Scat Pack deal was not available with the 426 Hemi engine, air conditioning, speed control, or the new 440 Six-Pack engine.

### 1969½ Super Bee A12

Around the mid-1969 model year, a new and exciting model option was announced for the Coronet Super Bee. After February 1969, Dodge offered the Sales Code A12 1969½ Six-Pack engine conversion package to the Super Bee (and on its Plymouth Road Runner cousin). The package was priced at $462.80 more than the cost of a standard Super Bee 117-inch-wheelbase WM21 coupe and WM23 two-door hardtop. Although its primary position was the replacement of the standard 383 Magnum V-8 4-barrel V-8, the package included a substantial list of unique components. The catchy Six-Pack name was the creation of Bob Osborn at BBD&O, Dodge's advertising agency.

The standard engine in the 1969 Super Bee was the 383 4-barrel with the 426 Hemi as the only option. The 440 4-barrel V-8 was normally only available as the standard powerplant in the Coronet R/T, so the VIN on the A12 package will always show an "M" code, indicating a

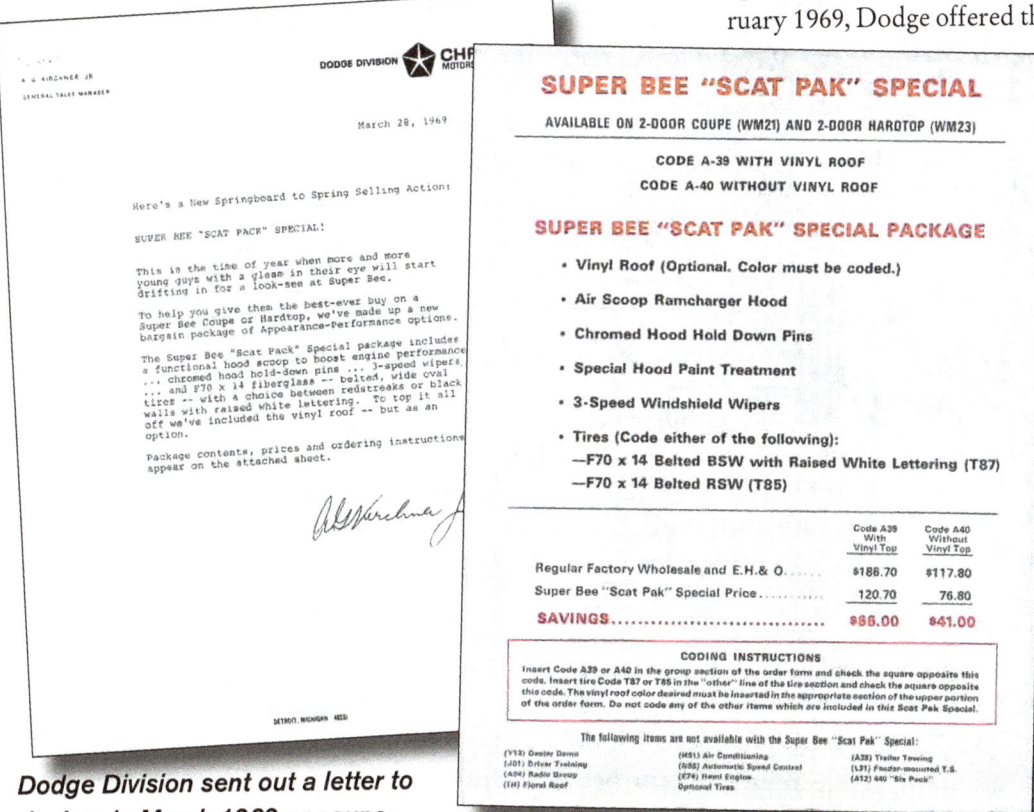

**Dodge Division sent out a letter to dealers in March 1969 announcing a new Scat Pack Spring Selling action to encourage them to promote the Scat Pack program to customers in their area. (Dodge, Plymouth, and the AMC design are registered trademarks of FCA US LLC)**

**A special notice from Dodge Division in March 1969 announced a new Scat Pack Special Super Bee package at a great discount to potential customers. (Dodge, Plymouth, and the AMC design are registered trademarks of FCA US LLC)**

*This is a 1969-1/2 A12 Six-Pack WM23 Super Bee equipped with a 440-ci V-8 engine and three Holley 2-barrel carburetors. This Six-Pack Super Bee is finished in F6 Forest Green and has a flat-black fiberglass hood. The gloss-black steel wheels without hubcaps were standard with the A12 package.*

*The functional large hood scoop and lift-off fiberglass hood that was part of the 1969-1/2 Super Bee A12 Six-Pack package. The flat-black hood was held in place by four chrome-plated hood pins.*

special-order V-8. The body code plate will always show the E63 engine code for a 383 4-barrel V-8 at the bottom line and a 999 on the top line to indicate a special order V-8. The special package is indicated by the A12 code on the third line of the plate.

The 390-horsepower 440-ci engine was essentially the same as the 4-barrel version, except for a number of performance and durability improvements. The intake manifold was a special Edelbrock-built aluminum piece with three 2300-series Holley 2-barrel carburetors with special linkage. The camshaft and lifters were specially selected and fitted, the rocker arms were heavier and the valvestems were chromed. The complete engine was painted Street Hemi Orange. All fuel lines were 5/16-inch and the vapor return lines 1/4-inch, as in a standard 440 4-barrel engine installation.

In addition to the significant performance equipment, such as heavy-duty suspension, heavy-duty 11-inch drum brakes, 4.10:1 Dana 60 rear axle, and Hemi 4-speed or TorqueFlite transmission configuration, the A12 package included a number of distinctive appearance features. The standard body color steel hood was replaced with a flat-black lift-off fiberglass hood with a large, efficient integral air scoop. The hood was held in place with four special chrome hood pins and lanyards, and each side of the scoop was decorated with a large red Six-Pack decal. The hood pins and mountings were unique and different from those used on the 1969 Charger Daytona. There should always be a circular orange Lynch Road paint inspection stamp near the passenger-side pin mounting plate on an original car.

Unlike the 1969 440 Darts and Barracudas, the 1969-1/2 A12 Six-Pack cars were never intended as pure drag racing contenders. Rather, the attractive and unique all-around performance street package was designed at a reasonable price for the youthful enthusiast market. Apparently, this idea was not clear to NHRA officials, who contacted Chrysler's Product Planning staff in early 1969 to demand a list of the first 50 owners of this new race car. For a car to be legal in Super Stock, there had to be proof that at least 50 had been delivered to owners. Five hundred copies were required for stock classes. Strangely, the NHRA did not seem to require the same standards for the 427 COPO Camaros and Chevelles that were already accepted as legal competitors.

Chrysler's answer to the NHRA was simply that these were not race cars and were never marketed as such. They had no list of owners because the cars were available to anyone. Product Planning dutifully provided verification that 137 Super Bee A12 cars had been delivered as of April 15, 1969. Tom Hoover later sent a note to Bill "Farmer" Dismuke at the NHRA verifying that by May 13, 1969, 534 Super Bees had been shipped to dealers, satisfying the minimum requirements for stock classes. The NHRA factored the A12 cars at 410 hp, placing them squarely in C/Stock class.

The street performance of the A12 cars was impressive, but with the torque of the massive 440 engine, traction was the limiting factor. They still easily qualified for Dodge's Scat Pack requirements. Magazine tests from 1969 were able to produce admirable quarter-mile times of 13.69 seconds at 106.50 mph with the standard G70x15 Polyglas tires and a 4-speed transmission. The addition of Goodyear 9.50x15 slicks with some work on air pressure reduction improved those times to about 13.18 seconds at 107 mph.

### Engine Options

The only engine available with the 1969 Super Bee A12 package was a 440-ci raised-block V-8. The special engine was rated at 390 hp at 4,700 rpm and 490 ft-lbs of torque at 3,200 rpm. The bore and stroke was 4.32 x 3.75 inches, respectively, and the compression ratio was 10.5:1. The pistons were forged aluminum with moly-filled top ring and weighed 864 grams. Piston clearance at the top of the skirt was .0015 to .003 inch. The pistons were attached to forged 8640 heavy-duty steel I-beam 6.768 inches long connecting rods with pressed-fit 1.0310- to 1.0312-inch-diameter pins.

The crankshaft was forged steel with shot-peened fillets and flame-hardened journals measuring 2.7495 to 2.7505 inches for the main bearing journals and 2.374 to 2.375 inches for the rod bearing journals. Cylinder heads were cast iron with wedge combustion chambers with 2.08-inch intake valves and 1.74-inch-diameter exhaust valves. The rocker arms were heavy-duty stamped steel and different from those used in the 440 4-barrel engines. Pushrods had 3/8-inch diameters.

The special camshaft used hydraulic lifters and had a lift of .450 inch for both the intake and exhaust valves. The duration was 268 degrees on the intake and 284 degrees for the exhaust with 46 degrees of overlap. The cast-aluminum intake manifold was made by Edelbrock and mounted three Holley 2300 series 2-barrel carburetors with a total of 1,350 cfm. The 440 engine included the N51 maximum cooling package with a 26-inch radiator. The entire 440 Six-Pack engine was painted 440 Engine orange.

### Transmission Options

The standard equipment transmission on the 1969 Dodge Super Bee A12 Six-Pack was the super strong cast-iron case Chrysler New Process A833 4-speed manual with a chrome-handled Hurst floor-mounted shifter. The cast-iron case A833 had a standard 2.66:1 low-gear ratio to help with hard launches and quick acceleration. The optional transmission was the aluminum case A727 Chrysler TorqueFlite 3-speed automatic with a 2.45:1 low gear. A special small-diameter (11-inch) and high-stall-speed torque converter was standard.

### Rear Axle Options

The standard rear axle assembly was replaced with a stronger 9-3/4-inch ring gear Dana 60 axle with a 4.10:1 ratio, installed with its standard Sure Grip limited-slip differential. The axle was supported with the standard and very effective Chrysler-designed heavy-duty longitudinal parallel leaf springs, but they were part of the S15 police handling package with a higher spring rate than normal. The front suspension modifications included a .224-inch spacer under each lower control arm bumper for tire clearance.

### Wheel and Tire Options

The standard 14-inch steel wheels were replaced with 15 x 6-inch gloss-black painted steel wheels with hubcaps and wheel covers deleted. The wheel lug nuts were chrome plated. The tires were Goodyear redline G70 x 15–inch Custom Wide-Tread Polyglas tubeless. No optional wheels or tires were available. The A12 package cars were not available with air-conditioning, speed-control, disc brakes, or trailer-towing package.

*The standard wheels on a 1969½ Six-Pack Super Bee were special gloss-black 15-inch steel wheels. The hubcaps were deleted and the standard lug nuts replaced with these chrome-plated examples. The standard tires were red streak.*

### Advertising

The only known full-width color print ad for a Six-Pack Super Bee featured an overhead front view of a red 1969-1/2 Six-Pack Super Bee posed on a dragstrip, showing the flat-black hood and large hood scoop. The headline simply stated, "Six-Pack to Go" in large white letters. Text below the headline told readers, "This is the new 440 Magnum V-8 powered Dodge Super Bee Six-Pack." The rest of the text described the power and features of the Six-Pack Super Bee and said that you should "Get With It. At Your Nearby Dodge Dealer's." The bottom of the page held the red "Dodge Scat Pack" logo followed by an image of the white-helmeted Scat Pack Bee blasting ahead in a cloud of white and blue tire smoke.

Possibly the only published magazine ad for a 1969-1/2 Coronet Super Bee A12 Six-Pack was this one published in the July 1969 issue of *Hot Rod*. It shows a red Six-Pack Super Bee on a blacktop road or dragstrip. (Dodge, Plymouth, and the AMC design are registered trademarks of FCA US LLC)

**1969 Dart GTS**

The last and smallest member of the 1969 Dodge Scat Pack team was the LS23 Dart GTSport two-door hardtop and LS27 two-door convertible. The 1969 Dart compact was still based on the 111-inch-wheelbase platform that had been used since the 1967 model year with only minor styling changes. Most obvious was the front end treatment. The 1968 grille design with its round parking lights and distinctive cross pattern of vertical and horizontal chrome bars in the center became a cleaner but similar design with a subtle rectangular mesh grille pattern and smaller, rectangular parking lights on both sides of the grille opening. The square bright-trimmed taillights were much the same as the 1968 versions.

**Exterior**

The GTS set itself apart from the run-of-the-mill Darts by a black rear deck lower panel with a GTS logo on its passenger's side. Of course, the GTS hood had the distinctive twin die-cast nonfunctional longitudinal Power Bulge scoops on either side with engine identification decals inside. A total of three high-performance engine packages were available for the 1969 Dart GTS: the 340 4-barrel LA V-8, the 383 4-barrel B-block V-8, and the later issue, limited availability 440 4-barrel RB V-8. The 3-speed TorqueFlite automatic transmission was standard, along with Rallye Suspension, Firm-Ride shock absorbers, and 14x5.5j steel wheels, with E70x14 redline wide-tread tires.

Of course, the Dart GTS offered a standard but optional contrasting rear Bumblebee stripe like all Scat Pack cars. The stripe was split horizontally at the rear quarter sides with a "GT" logo cut-out on top and a "Sport" logo on the bottom half. The Bumblebee stripes were available in white, black, and red. Bright dual exhaust tips completed the rear view trim. The Dart GTS hardtop had standard all-vinyl front bucket seats that were available in nine color combinations. The Dart GTS convertible had standard all-vinyl bench seat with front bucket seats optional.

**1969 Dart Swinger 340**

New for 1969 was the Dart Swinger, also based on the 111-inch-wheelbase compact platform. The Swinger was advertised as the lowest priced Dodge hardtop with differences that included a plainer vinyl standard interior trim with rubber mats and standard full-width front bench seat. Carpeting (standard with the TorqueFlite only), dual horns, partial horn ring, and cigarette lighter were deleted from the Swinger package. The base Dart Swinger was comparable to the low-priced Dart sedan, but a special high-performance model was offered as the LM23 Dart Swinger 340 two-door hardtop, equipped only with the 275 hp 340 V-8 engine and standard 4-speed manual transmission and optional TorqueFlite automatic. No convertible model was available.

The Dart Swinger 340 had standard D70x14 tires, compared to the Dart GTS that had E70x14 redline tires that were optional when air conditioning was ordered on the Swinger. The Dart Swinger 340 had a standard but optional Bumblebee stripe on the rear quarters, making it a full member of the Scat Pack team, but it did not have a badge on the front fenders like the GTS. The Bumblebee stripes were available in white, black, and red.

The price was the primary difference, with a base price of $2,836 for the Dart Swinger 340 two-door hardtop and $3,226 for the Dart GTS two-door hardtop. The GTS convertible was $3,419. A total of 20,000 Dart Swinger 340s were built for the 1969 model year.

The 1969 Dart Swinger received the Scat Pack Bumblebee stripe. If the tail stripe was deleted, the words "Dart" and "Swinger" were moved to the front fenders. (Kenny Flanagan Photo)

The Dodge Dart Swinger was new for 1969 and offered a 340-ci V-8 equipped with a single 4-barrel carburetor with a black crackle-finish air cleaner housing. This original unrestored 340 engine is painted Chrysler Engine Blue.

### 1969 Dart GTS and Dart Swinger 340 Engine Options

The standard engine available with the 1969 Dart GTS and the only engine available with the Dart Swinger 340 was the LA-series-based 340-ci V-8. The 340 was rated at 275 hp at 5,000 rpm and 340 ft-lbs of torque at 3,200 rpm. The 340 V-8 had a bore of 4.04 inches and stroke of 3.31 inches and was equipped with a single Carter Thermo-Quad 4-barrel carburetor. The 340 had a 10.5:1 compression ratio, so premium fuel was required. All 340 V-8 engines had hydraulic valve lifters and dual exhausts with chrome tips.

An optional engine for the 1969 Dart GTS was the 383-ci V-8. Like its 1968 counterpart, the single 4-barrel 383 had a bore and stroke of 4.25 x 3.38 inches and a compression ratio of 10.1:1. The 383 developed 300 hp at 5,200 rpm and 400 ft-lbs of torque at 2,400 rpm. The B-block–based 383 had hydraulic valve lifters and was easily identified by its passenger-side-front-mounted ignition distributor. The 383 block and heads were painted Chrysler Turquoise, but the valve covers were chrome plated on the Dart GTS 383.

### Transmission Options

The standard transmission on the 1969 Dart GTS was the super strong aluminum-case A727 TorqueFlite 3-speed automatic; a 2.45:1 low gear was optional. A column shift was standard but a floor shifter was included when the optional console was ordered. The optional transmission was the cast-iron case Chrysler New Process A833 4-speed manual with a 2.66: low-gear ratio. The 4-speed equipped 1969 Dart GTS had a chrome-handled Hurst shifter with a white plastic shift knob.

### Rear Axle Options

The standard rear axle with the TorqueFlite or 4-speed manual transmission was the Chrysler 8¾-inch banjo-type unit with a standard 3.23:1 gear ratio. Sure Grip limited-slip was optional with the 3.23:1 gears. The rear axle was supported by Chrysler-designed heavy-duty longitudinal parallel leaf springs.

### Wheel and Tire Options

The 1969 Dart GTS brakes were up to the performance levels of the car. It was equipped with 10-inch front and rear drums and available with optional 10.79-inch front power disc brakes. Standard tires were D70x14 redline mounted on 5.5-inch steel wheels. Small hubcaps were standard equipment. Quarter-mile times of around 14.38 seconds at 97 mph were possible with stock gearing.

# The 1969 Dart GTS 440

The year 1969 was not the first time the big raised-block–based 440-ci V-8 was available in a Dodge Dart. In early 1968, "Mr. Norm" Kraus of Grand Spaulding Dodge in Chicago talked with Chrysler engineers about the possibility of offering the 440 V-8 in the Dart. Mr. Norm's dealership was the largest high-performance dealer in the country so a new product to match the big engine offerings from Ford and General Motors was a priority. The engineers at Chrysler told him the engine could not fit into the Dart engine compartment and there would be problems with heat near the brake proportioning valve. Apparently, Norm had his mechanics work out those problems and took the car back to Chrysler to show them it could be done. His crew, including race car driver Gary Dyer, had solved the heat problem with a special heat shield.

These distinctive hood scoop decals were used on the 1969 Dart GTS 440 and were the only evidence of the powerful engine under the hood. This decal was actually installed over the existing 383 decal as that is what the car was built with on the assembly line.

This 1969 Dart GTS 440 is finished in R6 Red with a black vinyl interior and has the standard 14-inch painted steel wheels and F70x14 tires. This Dart has the standard black Bumblebee stripe and GTS logo. (Angelo van Bogart Photo)

This rear view of a 1969 Dart GTS 440 shows the standard black Bumblebee stripe with GTSport logo and standard 14-inch wheels, F70x14 tires, and small hubcaps. (Angelo van Bogart Photo)

This is a driver-side front quarter view of a black 1969 Dart GTS 440 two-door hardtop. A number of special modifications were required to install the 440 V-8 into the A-Body Dart chassis. The small hubcaps were standard equipment.

## Conversions

Norm convinced Chrysler to build 48 to 50 new 1968 Darts as a 383 GTS but without the engine and drivetrain. These Darts were sent to Hurst-Campbell for modifications so they would receive the 440 engine. Because of the increased power and mechanical linkage problems, the cars would only be available with an A727 TorqueFlite automatic transmission and not the A833 4-speed. The battery was moved to the trunk to gain engine compartment space and to improve weight transfer to the rear to compensate for the heavy engine. Grand Spaulding Dodge had the cars re-badged as a GSS, for Grand Spaulding Special, and were available only through that dealership. The Dart GSS could be seen in many of the magazine ads for Grand Spaulding Dodge in 1968. The Success of the GSS caused Dodge to decide to offer a 1969 Dart GTS 440 from the factory.

*Like many 1969 Dart 440 GTS hardtops, this one, driven by me from 1969 to 1972 was used for competition on the dragstrip. The red Dart was raced in the St. Louis area and sponsored by King Dodge.*

The Dart GT Sport was available with the 383 at the beginning of the 1969 model year, but the RB added a few additional problems to the already tight installation. Because the 440 block had .75 inch more deck height than the 383, the overall width of the assembled engine was increased by about 2.5 inches with the stock exhaust manifolds. This increase necessitated that a completely new driver-side exhaust manifold be designed and manufactured. This restriction effectively reduced the horsepower and torque output.

That and other problems involved with the 440 engine installation were more than the factory assembly line could handle, so Chrysler decided to have the installation done at the nearby Hurst Performance facility. The Darts (and Barracudas) were completely built and coded as 383s, but without the engine and drivetrain, then sent across town for the conversion. This Chrysler Hurst business relationship had already been worked out when the 150 Hemi Darts and Barracudas were built in 1968.

## Call-Outs

One of the smaller changes required was the addition of the identifying badges and decals. The Dart GTS had simulated long scoops, or power bulges, on the hood with an engine identification decal in the rear of each scoop. A 440 4-barrel decal, which was actually installed over the existing 383 decal, identified the 440 GTS.

Although Hurst accomplished the 440 engine conversion, the body data plate still called out the proper codes if one knew where to look. The bottom line of the body data plate showed an engine code of E63, which called for a 383 4-barrel V-8. The next code was D32, which was an A727 TorqueFlite, the only transmission available with the 440 engine package. The next code on line one would be LS23 for a Dart GTS two-door hardtop.

The key to identifying the 440 engine conversion package was the next code, which was M9B. The M represents a special-order V-8 in 1969. The 9 is the year and the B is the Hamtramck assembly plant. On all but some early production cars, there was also an A13 code on line three that identified the 1969 440 engine conversion package, which included 14 x 5.5–inch wheels, E70x14 red streak tires, heavy-duty suspension, 3.55:1 rear axle, and special badges and scoops. The Dart GTS 440 had a total price of about $3,650.

Although the 440 A-Body cars were not directly marketed as race cars, they were clearly intended to be available for that purpose. Quarter-mile times of 14.01 seconds at 103.8 mph were possible for the stock A-Body 440 package and stock tires, although *Car Life* was able to muster a run of 13.89 seconds at 104 mph with a similar 440 'Cuda. With some modifications, these 3,200-pound cars were very competitive in A/SA to SS/FA and were easily capable of mid 11-second ETs. There were a total of 640 Dart GTS 440s built for the 1969 model year.

## Engine Options

The engine in the 1969 Dodge Dart GTS 440 was the 440-ci RB V-8 with a 4.32 x 3.75–inch bore and stroke and a 10.1:1 compression ratio, producing 375 hp at 4,600 rpm

# THE 1969 DART GTS 440 CONTINUED

*The engine compartment for a red 1969 Dart GTS 440 was very tight, and that is why power brakes or power steering were not available. This engine has the correct orange engine color, including the valvecovers. (Angelo van Bogart Photo)*

and 480 ft-lbs of torque at 3,200 rpm. The 440 had a single Carter AVS 4-barrel carburetor mounted on a Chrysler cast-iron intake manifold. The special driver- and passenger-side cast-iron exhaust manifolds were modified significantly from a standard unit. The driver-side manifold had a severe curve to clear the steering column so the 440 engine would fit into the tight A-Body engine compartment. All 1969 440 V-8 block, heads, and valvecovers were painted 440 Engine Orange.

## Transmission Options

The only transmission available with the 1969 Dart GTS 440 was the aluminum case 3-speed A727 TorqueFlite automatic with a 2.45:1 first gear ratio. A 4-speed manual transmission was not available for a number of reasons. One was that it would have required the use of a stronger Dana 60 rear axle, which would not fit under the A-Body chassis and body width. Also, clutch linkage would have been difficult to adapt to this conversion.

## Rear Axle Options

An 8¾-inch ring gear Chrysler rear axle with a standard 3.55:1 gear ratio was used and was mounted on heavy-duty parallel leaf springs. The Dart GTS 440 had a standard center console with a chrome-handled shifter.

## Wheel and Tire Options

Standard tires were E70X14 red streak mounted on 14 x 5.5 painted steel wheels.

*The metallic-green interior on a white 1969 Dart GTS 440. Notice the GTSport badge on the door panels and the standard console and shifter.*

### *1969 Dart GTS and Swinger 340 Advertising*

One of the earliest ads for the new Scat Pack 1969 Darts appeared in *Motor Trend* in October 1968. This full-page color ad featured an overhead front photo of a red Dart Swinger 340 with a black vinyl roof and black Bumblebee stripe posed on a beach. The car was equipped with mag-wheel-type wheel covers, red line tires, and optional bumper guards. The large headline read simply, "Swinger." Beneath the headline the subhead said, "Dart Swinger 340" and was followed by smaller text detailing the features of the car.

The ad text began, "Play your cards right and three bills can put you in a whole lot of car this year." Below, details of the Dart Swinger 340 standard equipment were listed. As usual, the bottom of the page carried the slogan, "Dodge Scat Pack . . . the cars with the Bumblebee stripes." A large front-on image of an orange Bumblebee with black racing slicks was placed at the bottom of the page.

Another full-page vertical ad appeared at about the same time with the Dodge Girl dressed in a short white dress and white boots at the top of the page. Text on either side of her read, "This year, Dodge is turning up the fever." Below the girl was a driver-side rear view of a red 1969 Dart Swinger 340 with a black Bumblebee stripe and mag-type full wheel covers. Two smaller photos inside the larger one showed the black vinyl front seat and a view of the front of the car. Text below the photo stated, "Announcing Dart Swinger. For the swinger at heart . . . a brand new Dart." Two short columns of text at the bottom described features and called the car "Swinger 340 above: newest member of the Scat Pack."

A later ad appeared in the March 1969 issue of *Motor Trend*. This ad was horizontal and showed another red Dart Swinger 340, this one with a white Bumblebee stripe and

An ad, which appeared in the October 1968 issue of Motor Trend, featured a bright red 1969 Dart Swinger 340. The ad listed the standard equipment and features and prominently displayed the Scat Pack bee and slogan. (Dodge, Plymouth, and the AMC design are registered trademarks of FCA US LLC)

An earlier ad for a red 1969 Dart Swinger 340 only mentions Scat Pack in the small text at the bottom of the page. This Dart Swinger has the black Bumblebee stripe with Dart Swinger logo. (Dodge, Plymouth, and the AMC design are registered trademarks of FCA US LLC)

An early ad for a 1969 Dodge Dart Swinger 340. The Swinger 340 emphasis was its low price shown as less than $3,000 in this ad. The ad lists the standard features and equipment of the Swinger 340. (Dodge, Plymouth, and the AMC design are registered trademarks of FCA US LLC)

no vinyl roof speeding from the passenger's side toward the driver's side on a highway. This car also had the optional mag-wheel-type wheel covers. The lower half of the image was black with white lettering and a large headline that read, "6,000 rpm for less than $3,000." Below, a smaller subhead in red type said, "Dart Swinger 340," followed by even smaller text in white telling about the standard equipment and details of the Dart. The large racing Bumblebee was at the lower right of this page.

There was also advertising for the Dart GTS. A full-page example appeared that showed an overhead rear view of a green Dart GTS with a black Bumblebee stripe on a country road. Large text at the top read "Dodge GTS" and smaller red letters at the bottom stated the slogan "Run with the Scat Pack" with a large Bumblebee at the right lower corner. This Dart featured painted steel wheels with small hubcaps.

**A full-page magazine ad for a metallic-green 1969 Dart GTS does not indicate whether this Dart has a 340, 383, or 440 engine. The engine size was shown only with the hood scoop decals. "Run with the Scat Pack" was used prominently. (Dodge, Plymouth, and the AMC design are registered trademarks of FCA US LLC)**

1969 Dodge Swinger 340. A bold new member of the Dodge Scat Pack.

**For 1969, Dodge offered the new 340-powered Swinger as a less-expensive way to be a member of the Scat Pack. The 340 Swinger included a standard Bumblebee stripe on its tail and fake scoops on its hood to separate it from the economy versions of the Dart.**

66    Dodge Scat Pack and Plymouth Rapid Transit System

# CHAPTER 4

# 1970

## The Scat Pack Continues

*"The 1970 Dodge Scat Pack is Road Ready!"*

*The Scat Pack brochure cover page illustrated the image of the winning Dodges at the dragstrip. The accompanying materials told dealers how to make use of the materials and the program to enhance their business. (Dodge, Plymouth, and the AMC design are registered trademarks of FCA US LLC)*

One of the more obvious moves by Dodge at the beginning of the 1970 model year was the announcement of the new Scat Pack Club. Now, many of the magazine ads that previously had a mail-in coupon for ordering materials from Dodge at Scat Headquarters were used as an application form to join the Scat Pack Club. Special Scat Pack Club applications were also available at all Dodge dealers for salespeople to hand out to "interested people and prospective members." All buyers of new Scat Pack cars received a Scat Pack Club package soon after taking delivery of their new car. The application asked for their name, address, and age. There were even local Scat Pack Club chapters around the country.

For their $3 annual dues, the 1970 Scat Pack Club member received a full packet of goodies to enhance their already high enthusiasm for their new Dodge. Members received a high-performance parts and tune-up catalog, a wallet identification card, an embroidered jacket patch, a hard-nosed bumper sticker, and a 40-page *Guide to Auto Racing 1970*. In addition, members received a subscription to *Dodge Performance News*, a tabloid newsletter carrying the latest news of Scat Pack cars in national competition and the Dodge Scat News, an illustrated quarterly that featured local chapter news, and service and tuning tips.

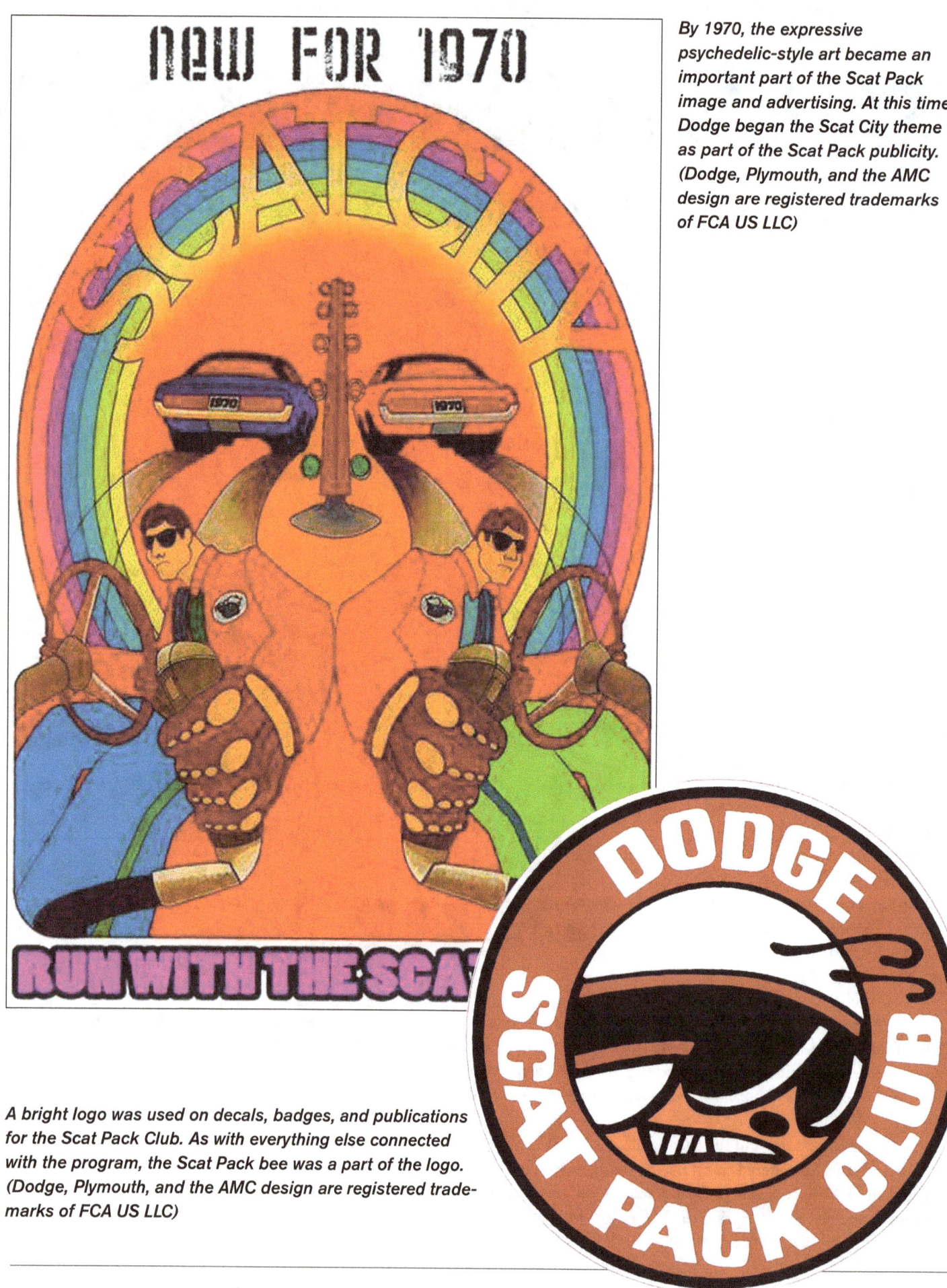

*By 1970, the expressive psychedelic-style art became an important part of the Scat Pack image and advertising. At this time, Dodge began the Scat City theme as part of the Scat Pack publicity. (Dodge, Plymouth, and the AMC design are registered trademarks of FCA US LLC)*

*A bright logo was used on decals, badges, and publications for the Scat Pack Club. As with everything else connected with the program, the Scat Pack bee was a part of the logo. (Dodge, Plymouth, and the AMC design are registered trademarks of FCA US LLC)*

*An article was published early in the 1970 model year to promote the news about the cars of the Scat Pack and what they were doing in various forms of competition, including drag racing, circle track, and road racing. Of course, there was never a 1970 Daytona, but this ad leads one to believe it was a late scratch for the next model year. (Dodge, Plymouth, and the AMC design are registered trademarks of FCA US LLC)*

*A red Scat Pack brochure was sent to dealers to explain how to make the most of the Scat Pack Club and the Scat Pack program to increase sales and exposure to the potential buyers. (Dodge, Plymouth, and the AMC design are registered trademarks of FCA US LLC)*

### Dodge Announces Scat City

Toward the end of 1969, Dodge published a detailed 8-1/2 x 11 eight-page color and black-and-white brochure titled "Dodge Announces Scat City," which provided racing news and road tests, and ended with a two-page section about the new "Scat Packages" offered by Dodge. The top of the first page featured a color photo of a red 1969 Dodge Charger Daytona with a white Bumblebee stripe in action on a race track. The driver was Bobby Isaacs and he was featured later in the publication as one of the professional racing drivers who road tested examples of all of the cars in the new 1970 Scat Pack program. The other drivers included Dick Landy, Don Garlits, Charlie Allen, and Don White.

The rest of the text on the first page of this brochure tells about the accomplishments and wins of some of the drivers featured later in the publication under the heading, "Scat City is anywhere competition is hot, keen and sanctioned." The story is about NASCAR winner Isaacs catching a plane for the Chelsea, Michigan, Proving Grounds for the Scat Pack Chargers.

Chapter 4: 1970    69

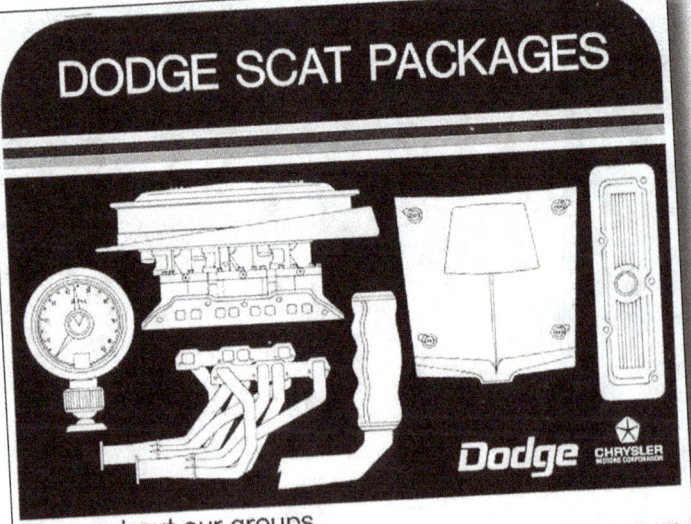

A page from the Scat Pack Club member publication describes the special parts and groups of parts offered to make the owners' cars improve their performance and appearance. (Dodge, Plymouth, and the AMC design are registered trademarks of FCA US LLC)

The next day, Isaacs was to take the "Wing Thing" Charger Daytona for a flat-out shakedown run on the track.

Next was "Big Daddy" Don Garlits, who was also catching a plane, but this one at Kennedy Airport in New York. Garlits was traveling to Michigan for a date with the "Hot new Dodge Challenger R/T." And another short story was about USAC Champion Don White who was arriving in Michigan to take a 1970 Charger R/T around the high bank circuit for a test drive. More text follows, "California Charlie Allen, the all-American boy, world's greatest Dodge Dart drag race artist showing up to smoke the new version of the swinger 340."

Last mentioned was "Dick Landy, who races for loot, puts his boot in the new Super Bee Six-Pack. Finds it sizzles and gets off the line like lightning." The piece ends with "Be a swinger and join the Scat Pack Club . . . And don't forget to keep the tach in the black." It was very clear with this type of action that Dodge was pulling no punches to place its Scat Pack of high-performance cars at the lead in every aspect of motorsports.

The last page of the brochure, headed with the title line, "Dodge Scat Packages," listed the five performance packages. The publication pointed out "New this year are prepackaged Scat Packages. They are designed to take you from dress-up-and-show to hot-and-torrid in easy stages. These named packages included performance and dress-up parts for "New and not so new

**Dodge dealer promotional kits for the 1970 Scat Pack program featured colorful illustrations of Dick Landy's pro-Stock Challenger in action. Landy was one of the most important racers in Dodge's drag racing stable for 1970. (Dodge, Plymouth, and the AMC design are registered trademarks of FCA US LLC)**

Dodges" and told customers to check the Dodge parts catalog or see your dealer.

### *Performance Packages*

The first package was The Showboat, which included a dress-up kit with chrome valve covers, oil filler cap, air cleaner, hood pins and locks, and chromed road wheels. Package number two was The Read-out. This package included a full-sweep tach: oil pressure and fuel pressure gauges to keep you filled in on what's happening.

The third package was called The Kruncher, which included a hot ring and pinion, matching speedometer pinion, and a Hurst shifter. Fourth was The Bee-Liever that offered the choice of a high-rise intake manifold and carburetor or a cam and headers. The fifth and last package was The Top Eliminator that provided a Six-Pack hood and pins, Six-Pack intake manifold, and three 2-barrel carburetors, transistorized ignition, electric fuel pump, and a cool can for the engine fuel lines. At the end of the page were a list of benefits of the Scat Pack Club and information on how to join.

*Dodge's 1970 Scat Pack Club promotional materials included order forms and a list of nine products offered to potential customers. Scat Pack items included patches, badges, catalogs, tune-up tips, and a subscription to the newsletter. (Dodge, Plymouth, and the AMC design are registered trademarks of FCA US LLC)*

*Dodge dealer Scat Pack promotional kits included a colorful program cover with artistic renditions of five 1968 Hemi Darts. The bottom of the piece featured the Dodge Scat Pack Club decal. (Dodge, Plymouth, and the AMC design are registered trademarks of FCA US LLC)*

Chapter 4: 1970    71

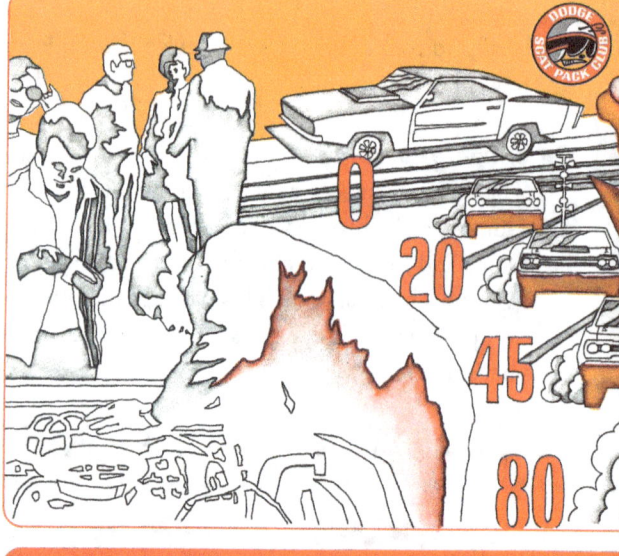

The idea of a club for young, swinging car enthusiasts... with money to spend... is not new. It is tried and proved. So is the fact that clubs sell cars. (For example, industry sources estimate that Mustang club members have each accounted for 3 new car sales a year, on the average.)

You're in business to make money. So are we. And it's obvious to both of us that the most direct way—today and tomorrow—is through performance vehicles... our Scat Pack.

Look at this: Total Scat Pack car sales are up 63% over last year and industry penetration for Dodge high performance cars has gone from 9% to 12½% for the same period.

Opportunity? You bet. What's more, in September we'll add the Challenger.

You're ready and we're ready... together we've got the cars, the parts, the working programs and the potential.

Of course, we're not the only ones who see this potential. We don't have to tell you how Ford, GM and American Motors feel about the Performance Car market. You know your local competition better than we... and you see the striped Mustangs, Camaros, Novas, Javelins, etc. drive past your door all day long.

We've been doing very well with our Scat Pack and we're going to do better. We're going to do it by making your business the center of interest for performance car buffs.

How?

With your own, exclusive, brand-new...

**dodge scat pack club**

Our club is built around you and your market. It's aimed, of course, at Scat buyers, but its purpose is to sell cars... and, certainly, parts.

This brochure explains the club, how it works, what will convince Scat owners to join, what we (the factory) are providing and how you can participate.

Read on. When you've finished, we think you'll sign up now.

**How Much Does it Cost to Become a Participating Dealer?**
$25.00.

**Is Dodge Division Deeply Committed to Performance?**
Not only Dodge, but the entire Chrysler Corporation. The performance market is already big... and growing. Today, every fifth car you and other Dodge dealers sell is a Scat Packer. With five Scat cars for 1970, we're going after an even bigger share. Commitment? We're going all the way.

**How is Dodge Backing Your Scat Club?**
First, as you probably can tell, the member materials—wallet card, embroidered patch, Scat Speaks... a quarterly bulletin of local club events, bumper sticker, etc.—cost a lot more than the 3 dollars the member is paying. Dodge is picking up the difference as an investment in your future sales.

Second, Dodge's service training programs—Master Technician, Learn to Earn and the basic service manuals—have been performance-oriented and will be continually up-dated to keep pace with the [...]

Third, the v[...] clinics—which [...] thousands of [...] dealerships al[...] again being me[...]

Fourth, the [...] will be promot[...] Managers club[...] Service Mana[...] national orga[...] Performance [...]

Fifth, the 1[...] terials... a [...] formance part[...]

## Your Club Operating Materials

Your all-new Scat Pack Club Kit is chock full of eye-catching and useful material... to help you launch and sustain your local club. Check your kit carefully—be sure everything is in good order, then put it to good use for maximum effectiveness. Don't forget, as specified on the supplemental order form provided—certain items may be purchased in additional quantities. Plan ahead now to cover your requirements for the coming year... orders are chargeable to your Parts Account.

Your Kit Contains...

**Scat Pack Club Window Poster**—This large (50" x 75") 4-color poster is designed to bring customers and prospects right in off the street... establishes your dealership as the "place to be" for performance cars, parts, service.

**Mini-Poster For Salesmen**—Four of these mini-posters are provided in each kit for use in salesmen's offices. Intended to "show & tell" what each club member gets, the posters serve to remind salesmen and act as informative "sell pieces" for consumers.

**Club Operations Manual** — Providing all you need to know to operate your own club, this manual now lists film sources available for club use, suggested scripts for radio spots, layouts for newspaper ads, films for TV advertising, ideas galore for "club paddock" and other promotional activities... plus complete club operation procedures.

**Scat Sells**—This monthly training piece provides your salesmen with the latest news about competitive activities and stresses how to sell the technical features of Dodge performance cars. Includes charts, engineering drawings and photos.

**Application Forms**—To sign walk-in Scat Pack Club membership prospects, each salesman should have a number of these forms. One 100-sheet pad per kit. Redesigned for 1971.

**IBM Prospect List**—Updated quarterly, this IBM galley listing of owners tells your salesmen who has bought a Dodge (from 1968 to date) in your trading area, who has joined the Scat Pack Club and which members are Dodge owners. Ideal "bird dog" device for locating new prospects for performance (and other) Dodge cars.

**Hustle Stuff Parts Catalog**—Chrysler Parts Division book provides performance salesmen and parts/service department personnel with a reference piece they can use... and use... and use.

**Tune-Up Tips Booklets**—Sample copies for each of the Dodge performance engines are included in each kit. Informative data for the salesman who cares enough to study. Updated for 1971.

Used Properly... Your Scat Pack Club Materials Will Sell Performance Cars, Parts and Accessories.

7

Dodge Dealer information kits explained the benefits of starting and supporting a new Scat Pack Club. Dodge told the dealers that the program was intended to stimulate performance sales and showroom traffic, but it was up to the dealer to make the program work. (Dodge, Plymouth, and the AMC design are registered trademarks of FCA US LLC)

Dodge offered dealers a detailed promotional kit that included a Scat Pack Club Operations Manual. This kit provided details for the dealer on how to start and make the most out of the benefits offered by the Scat Pack program. (Dodge, Plymouth, and the AMC design are registered trademarks of FCA US LLC)

### Scat Pack Lineup for 1970

The 1970 model year began in late fall 1969 as usual, and the Scat Pack lineup continued as before with the addition of a completely new model, essentially a new type of high-performance car for Dodge. The styling changes for 1970 were not as dramatic as those for the 1968 models, but there were enough new and distinctive features to clearly set them apart from the pack. The basic body structure was an evolution from the 1968–1969 examples, but the changes to the front and rear designs were altered

and Super Bee were given a new twin-scoop center power-bulge hood; large single simulated scoops behind each door opening further identified the R/T. The Super Bee was not available as a convertible model, but the new Power-Bulge hood was now available with optional twin functional Ramcharger scoops.

The Dart had some significant changes for the 1970 model year. The front-end styling was redesigned to have a more aerodynamic appearance by slanting back from top to bottom. The grille surround wrapped around the sides of the front fenders, giving a more rounded and modern look to the front of the car. Both the grille and chrome-plated front bumper appeared more integrated and fit closer into the body. The grille now featured a chrome vertical split in the center with small rectangular parking lights on each side. Twin hood-mounted air scoops were now available as an option.

The rear of the Dart was also slanted back from the top of the deck to the chrome bumper, which had rectangular taillights and the center license plate mounting integrated into it. Like the front, the rear bumper was wider and more closely fitted to the body, giving a subtle but noticeable aerodynamic appearance.

across all lines. All Dodge Coronet Scat Pack body types were continued for 1970 and included the two-door hardtop, coupe, and convertible. The special A12 Six-Pack package was no longer available for 1970, but the 390-hp 440 Magnum Six-Pack engine still existed as an option. The Charger R/T was still only available as a two-door hardtop, but the radical NASCAR-oriented Daytona was dropped for 1970. The 1970 Dart GTS and Swinger received significant restyling although still only available as either a two-door hardtop or convertible.

## Facelifts

The Charger received a facelift for 1970, but it was not as dramatic as the Coronet. The Charger kept its hidden headlight theme, but it was treated to a front-end concept similar to the Coronet that utilized a full-width grille opening surrounded by a continuous-loop chrome bumper. A large, rear-facing scoop at the front of each door identified the Charger R/T. The rear fascia and roofline of the Charger were carried over from 1969. The Charger 500 model was now a premium-level trim option rather than a separate NASCAR-based model.

The Coronet received the most dramatic facelift for the 1970 model year. A massive dual-loop chrome bumper that completely encircled the twin grilles dominated the front of the 1970. The design, created by Diran Yazejian, a graduate of the Art Center College of Design in California, clearly distinguished the Coronet from the Charger. The Coronet grille and bumpers were divided by a peak in the hood that sloped downward into the center of the front fascia. The Coronet R/T

## New, Wilder Colors

The 1970 model year (including some released in 1969) saw the introduction of a new line of unusually bright and attention-grabbing extra-cost body hues called "high impact or "high performance," depending on which make's brochure was being used. Each car line adopted the same or similar colors and paint code but each gave them a unique name. These acrylic enamel bright colors were a sign of the times and, as some believe, representative of the positive economic situation. Usually the optional colors were a $15 or so premium over the standard colors. The additional cost did not represent any improved quality or finish but merely the cost of producing something with less than average sales numbers. Not everyone wished to have the most eye-catching car in town.

The Plum Crazy In-Violet shade of purple, for one, had a habit of peeling off in sheets during that first year so quality was clearly not involved. This may have been a problem at a particular plant but the incidence of it was obvious. The choices included in the Dodge high-impact color charts were FC7 Plum Crazy (purple), FJ5 Sublime, EK2 Go-Mango, EV2 Hemi-Orange, and FY1 Banana. Two additional colors, FJ6 Green-Go and FM3 Panther Pink, were added at midyear. These were among the 21 different colors used on 1970 Dodge B-Body cars.

Chapter 4: 1970

## The Challenger

Totally new for 1970 was the exciting Dodge Challenger, designed on the new E-Body platform shared (except for wheelbase differences) with the Plymouth Barracuda. The Challenger, introduced on September 23, 1969, was an obvious break from the rest of the Dodge line and was directed at the so-called "Pony Car" market first made popular by the 1964 Ford Mustang (although really a latecomer following the 1964 Plymouth Barracuda fastback by weeks), and later by the 1967 Chevrolet Camaro. All four-passenger Challengers were either two-door hardtops or two-door convertibles. The new wider and bolder design and longer front end of the Challenger allowed engineers room to install the more powerful B, RB and 426 Hemi powerplants, making it the ideal new member of the Dodge Scat Pack team.

The 110-inch-wheelbase Challenger was developed following a personal luxury concept, emphasizing the upscale Mercury Cougar as its market target. Styling was directed by Harry Cheeseborough, senior vice-president of styling and product planning, based on a winning concept by Dodge design chief Bill Brownlee. The basic Challenger had a definite horizontal character line that followed the flow of the body. The Dodge Challenger front end fascia had four round headlights, setting it immediately apart from the new Plymouth Barracuda, which had two. The Challenger design gave new potential for an image of straight-line acceleration and quarter-mile performance.

## Charger R/T

The 117-inch-wheelbase 1970 XS29 Charger R/T Sport Hardtop was based on the same steel unibody platform and fastback body design as the very similar 1969 model, including its wide rear fascia and dual rectangular taillights. The 1970 Charger was immediately set apart from the previous model year by its massive and unique continuous-loop chrome-plated front bumper. The flat-black plastic mesh Charger R/T grille was deep-set and surrounded by a wide Agent Silver bezel with a full-width bright horizontal center bar. The quad round headlights were still retractable by electric solenoids and the driver-side headlight door mounted a die-cast R/T badge. Standard and unique to the 1970 Charger R/T were the large nonfunctional rear-facing fiberglass scoops

*A passenger-side front quarter view is of an original unrestored FE5 Bright Red 1970 XS29 Charger R/T with V6W white dual longitudinal stripe. This Charger has optional 15-inch Rallye wheels W21 with correct original tires and a white vinyl roof.*

*The rear-facing nonfunctional scoop with R/T badge was standard on all 1970 Charger R/Ts. This 1970 Charger R/T wears the ultra-rare color of FM3 Panther Pink.*

mounted at the front edge of the doors. Each scoop carried a die-cast R/T badge.

### Exterior Options

The 1970 Charger R/T was available in 18 acrylic enamel body colors and four optional color-coordinated vinyl roof colors of green, black, white, and green Gator-Grain. The Charger R/T was equipped with standard full-length bright roof drip-rail moldings and a unique rear end treatment featuring a black applique not used on the standard Charger.

### Body Stripe Options

The Charger R/T Bumblebee stripe at the rear quarters was now a single, wide stripe with thin stripe lines on both sides. The stripe was available in five colors of red, black, white, green, and blue, restricted by body-color combinations to ensure a complementary appearance. The R/T logo cutout offered in 1969 was no longer available. The 1970 Charger R/T had standard dual longitudinal stripes available in the same colors as the Bumblebee stripe. This stripe followed the outline of the Charger body from the front of the doors to the rear of the body.

### Interior Options

The 1970 Charger was available in a variety of all-vinyl and cloth interior trim combinations with front bucket seats and a rear bench seat for all models. The Charger R/T standard interior included front bucket seats with an optional fixed center cushion and folding center armrest. The pleated inserts were trimmed in diamond basket weave texture with Krinkle-grain skirts and bolsters available in blue, green, burnt orange, charcoal, white, and tan. The loop style carpet was color coordinated except for the white interior, which was available with blue, green, gold, red, or black carpeting. An additional standard trim was available for the Charger R/T with similar seats in charcoal cloth and vinyl.

### Special Edition

The Charger R/T was also available in a Special Edition Décor Group, Sales Code A47, which added full-foam leather and vinyl front bucket seats, wood-grain steering wheel with stainless-steel spider and vinyl-covered padded horn button, wood-grain inserts in the instrument panel, hood-mounted turn signals, pedal dress-up, deep-dish wheel covers, light package, and Special Edition nameplate. The SE interior was available in green, tan, blue, and charcoal.

### Instrument Panel

The instrument panel of the 1970 Charger was nearly identical to the 1969 except for the ignition switch, which was now mounted in the steering column. The 1970 switch included a standard antitheft steering column lock. A large, round 150-mile-per-hour speedometer was placed to the right of an identically sized optional combination tachometer and clock. To the right of the speedometer were four smaller, round bezels that contained the fuel, temperature, oil pressure, and alternator gauges. The instrument cluster was mounted in a textured flat-black background panel.

### Engine Options

The standard engine in the 1970 Charger R/T was the 440-ci V-8. The standard powerplant was a 440-ci V-8 based on the RB (raised-block) configuration. The single Carter AVS 4-barrel equipped 440 Magnum produced 375 hp at 4,600 rpm and 480 ft-lbs of torque at 3,200 rpm. The 440 had a bore and stroke of 4.32 x 3.75 inches and a compression ratio of 9.7:1, lowered from the previous year. All 1970 440 engines were 440 Engine Orange to more closely relate to the performance image of the optional 426 Hemi. The 440 Magnum single 4-barrel engine used a black crackle-finish unsilenced air cleaner.

A new engine option for the 1970 Charger R/T was the 440-ci RB-based V-8 with three 2-barrel Holley carburetors mounted on a Chrysler cast-iron intake manifold, replacing the cast-aluminum Edelbrock unit used in 1969. This engine was identified with a V-code on the VIN and E87 on the body code plate. The 440 Magnum Six-Pack engine had a 10.5:1 compression ratio and was still rated at 390 hp at 4,700 rpm and 490 ft-lbs of torque at 3,200 rpm. The 1970 engine did not have the additional special components that came standard with the 1969-1/2 A12 Six-Pack conversion engine package that was available on the Super Bee.

The only other optional engine available with the 1970 Charger R/T was the 426 Hemi V-8 rated at 425 hp at 5,000 rpm and 490 ft-lbs of torque at 4,000 rpm. The two Carter AFB 4-barrel-equipped Hemi had a bore and stroke of 4.25 x 3.75 inches and a compression ratio of 10.3:1. The major change for 1970 was the adoption of hydraulic valve lifters. The Hemi cast-iron block and heads were finished in Street Hemi Orange with a black crackle-finish air cleaner. The large, wide Hemi valve covers were also black crackle-finish. An R on the VIN and E74 on the body code plate indicated the Hemi.

### Transmission Options

The 1970 Dodge Charger R/T had a standard cast-aluminum case A727 3-speed TorqueFlite automatic transmission when equipped with the 440 V-8 engines. The TorqueFlite was operated with either a column- or console-mounted chrome shift lever, depending on the interior options. A cast-iron case A833 4-speed manual transmission with a 2.44:1 low gear was standard with the 426 Hemi and optional with the 440. The 4-speed used a Hurst shifter, which, for the first time, used a unique walnut-grain pistol grip design on a wide, flat Hurst chrome-plated handle. The chrome console-mounted shifter handle was curved to the left and back, as in the previous year, while the floor-mounted version was curved back and up. Original handles had a distinct taper in thickness toward the top. Both shifters used a pleated, black rubber boot. The Hemi was available with an optional TorqueFlite automatic transmission.

### Rear Axle Options

The standard rear axle with the 1970 Charger R/T with a 440 or 426 Hemi engine and TorqueFlite automatic transmission was the Chrysler 8¾-inch banjo-type, which was available in ratios from 2.94:1 to 3.91:1, with 3.23:1 being standard. A 1⅞-inch-diameter pinion stem was phased in during the 1969 model year, so most 1970 models will have this Casting Number 2881489 carrier. A special Performance Axle Group option (Sales Code 358) was available that provided a 3.55:1 rear axle gear ratio, special slip-drive fan, and an extra-wide high-performance radiator fan shroud. When a 4-speed transmission was ordered with the 440 or 426 Hemi engine, a 9¾-inch ring gear Dana 60 heavy-duty rear axle with a 3.54:1 gear ratio was used, with an optional 4.10:1 ratio provided when the Super Track Pak or Super Performance Axle Packages were ordered. Single-piston power front disc brakes with floating calipers were optional.

### Wheel and Tire Options

The 1970 Charger R/T was equipped with standard 14 x 6–inch stamped-steel wheels, which could be equipped with either a small hubcap or one of two new optional styled wheel covers. Optional 14-inch Magnum 500 styled Rallye road wheels with chrome-plated trim rings were available. Fifteen-inch wheels were no longer required for the 426 Hemi. All-new 15-inch Rallye wheels with F60x15 Wide Oval tires were available as an option if heavy-duty brakes and Rallye Suspension were ordered. Early in 1970 production, new 15x7–inch steel wheels became available as an option under Sales Code U84. All steel wheels were restyled for 1970 and featured a flat surface at the lug nut–mounting area.

### Production Numbers

A total of 10,337 1970 Charger R/Ts were built. And 10,337 XS29 Charger R/T two-door sport hardtops were built for the 1970 model year.

### Advertising and Publicity

One of the early magazine ads for the 1970 Charger R/T was a full-page color piece featuring a red Charger R/T SE with a white Bum-

*Implying that you could get the girl with a mean, tough car was nothing new in automotive advertising. Although a model hiking up her skirt to show a little more leg certainly could give you the impression that buying a Charger RT/SE may give you a decided advantage. (Dodge, Plymouth, and the AMC design are registered trademarks of FCA US LLC)*

*This color magazine ad featuring a Panther Pink 1970 Charger R/T was used to announce the lower price of the new Charger. Along with the new price, the ad describes the higher-performance equipment standard in the R/T. (Dodge, Plymouth, and the AMC design are registered trademarks of FCA US LLC)*

blebee stripe viewed from the rear. A beautiful young girl in a short white lace dress and long blond hair is standing at the passenger-side rear leaning on the deck lid. The large black text beneath the photo states, "Mother warned me . . . that there would be men like you driving cars like that." More enticing and alluring text ends with the logo at the bottom that reads, "Join the fun . . . catch Dodge fever." There was no mention of the Scat Pack in many of the 1970 print ads.

Another ad featuring the 1970 Charger first told everyone about the new high-impact colors and showed a wide front view of a Panther Pink Charger. The large black headline text read, "Charger is tickled pink over its new lower price." A beautiful blond Dodge girl in a flowered dress was posed by the Charger and, although it was not an R/T, the availability of the R/T option over this new lower-priced standard Charger was mentioned as part of the text.

More direct emphasis was placed on the Charger R/T in the dealer showroom brochure. A wide rear view of a Plum Crazy 1970 Charger R/T with Magnum 500 styled wheels filled two pages and placed the car in front of a colorful background of a purple-and-pink shaded sunset. The large bold text at the top of both pages read, "Charger R/T," with the face of a Dodge racing driver between those words.

### 1970 Dodge Coronet R/T

The 1970 Dodge Coronet was still based on the same 117-inch-wheelbase unibody platform but featured a dramatic new front end styling theme, making it obviously different from the 1969 model. In place of the wide horizontal single grille design used in 1969, massive dual-loop chrome bumpers that encircled the twin grilles and quad headlights dominated the 1970 Coronet front end. They clearly distinguished the Coronet from the Charger.

*All 1970 Coronet R/T two-door hardtops had a standard simulated front-opening scoop with embossed R/T badge. This R/T is finished in FE5 Bright Red and has optional Magnum 500 styled steel road wheels with trim rings.*

The Coronet grille and bumpers were divided by a peak in the hood that sloped downward into the center of the front fascia. The Coronet R/T had a new twin-scoop center power-bulge hood with a bright-red-trimmed R/T badge in the front center and was further identified by large simulated front-opening scoops behind each door opening. The Power-Bulge hood was now available with optional twin functional Ramcharger scoops with Sales Code N96.

The Coronet taillights were dramatically redesigned from those used in 1969. They were triangular in general shape with bright trim surrounding the lens. The Coronet R/T used a different taillight design from other models that added an overlay that divided it into three separate rectangular lights. The R/T used a black-accented trim panel with the Dodge name spelled out in the center and a small R/T badge centered beneath the name. All 1970 Coronets had a new W-shaped rear bumper with optional chrome bumper guards available on all models.

As in the previous year, all Coronets with the 426 Hemi

*This 1970 Coronet R/T is finished in FK5 Dark Burnt Orange Poly and is equipped with Magnum 500 styled steel wheels with bright trim rings. The R/T had a standard power-bulge hood with twin simulated scoop openings and has a black vinyl roof and a white Bumblebee stripe.*

*A page from a Dodge showroom brochure features a 1970 Coronet R/T with a black Bumblebee stripe and is finished in FJ5 Sublime high-impact paint. Smaller pictures show the Rallye wheels and other standard equipment of the R/T. (Dodge, Plymouth, and the AMC design are registered trademarks of FCA US LLC)*

engine had steel torque boxes welded in place across the frame rails in front of the rear spring front mounting. All convertibles had the same rear reinforcements plus an additional plate welded across the front body crossmember to the body side seam. Hemi cars also had a flat steel reinforcement welded in place above the rear axle pinion snubber.

### Exterior

The 1970 Coronet R/T was available as a WS23 two-door hardtop and a WS27 two-door convertible and offered 22 body colors, 7 of them high-impact, and 13 interior trim combinations. In addition to the standard painted roof shell, all Coronet hardtops, coupes, and sedans were available with an optional vinyl roof. The boar-grain vinyl roof was available in green, white, and black, and the optional Gator-Grain was available in green only. The roof color was always coordinated with the appropriate body and interior colors. All vinyl roofs had standard bright roof side drain trough moldings.

### Interior

The 1970 Coronet R/T two-door hardtop and convertible standard interior trim combinations were all-vinyl high-back bucket seats with optional center console and folding center armrest in dark blue, dark green, burnt orange, tan, gold, black, and white. All seat designs featured longitudinal pleats of Shallow Elk grain in the cushions and backs and smooth Coachman-grain skirts. Color-keyed loop-pile carpeting was standard in all combinations, but the white trim had only black carpet.

### Instrument Panel

The 1970 Coronet standard instrument panel and cluster design was similar to what was used in 1969, except that the ignition switch was combined with a steering column lock and was moved to the steering column for 1970. More padding was added to the lower portion of the 1970 panel, and the rectangular areas around the driver-side light switch panel and passenger-side wiper switch panel were recessed. Like the previous year, the 1970 panel used a rectangular cluster opening with a horizontal speedometer in the center and two smaller gauges on each side. The alternator and fuel gauges were on the left of the steering column and the temperature gauge and clock were on the right. A rocker-type headlight switch and thumbwheel panel light dimmer were recessed in the lower driver-side panel. The optional radio was mounted in the center of the instrument panel like the previous year but now had more conventional round knobs rather than the thumbwheel of 1969.

### Wheel and Tire Options

The standard steering wheel for the Coronet R/T was a three-spoke, color-keyed polypropylene wheel with a bright partial horn ring and vinyl-covered hub. A wood-grain, sports-type steering wheel with stainless-steel spider and vinyl-covered padded horn button was optional on all models. Also optional on all models was a three-spoke Rim-Blow steering wheel with a padded vinyl-covered hub.

### Engine Options

The standard engine in the 1970 Coronet R/T was the 440-ci V-8. The standard powerplant was a 440-ci V-8 based on the RB (raised-block) configuration. The single Carter AVS 4-barrel equipped 440 Magnum produced 375 hp at 4,600 rpm and 480 ft-lbs of torque at 3,200 rpm. The 440 had a bore and stroke of 4.32 x 3.75 inches and a compression ratio of 9.7:1, lowered from the previous year. All 1970 440 engines were painted Chrysler Performance Orange. The 440 Magnum single 4-barrel engine used a black crackle-finish unsilenced air cleaner.

A new engine option for the 1970 Coronet R/T was the 440-ci RB-based V-8 with three 2-barrel Holley carburetors mounted on a Chrysler cast-iron intake manifold, replacing the cast-aluminum Edelbrock unit used in 1969. This engine was identified with a V-code on the VIN and E87 on the body code plate. The 440 Magnum Six-Pack engine had a 10.5:1 compression ratio and was still rated at 390 hp at 4,700 rpm and 490 ft-lbs of torque at 3,200 rpm. The 1970 engine did not have the additional special components that came standard with the 1969-1/2 A12 Six-Pack conversion engine package.

The only other optional engine available with the 1970 Coronet R/T was the 426 Hemi V-8 rated at 425 hp at 5,000 rpm and 490 ft-lbs of torque at 4,000 rpm. The two Carter AFB 4-barrel-equipped Hemis had a bore and stroke of 4.25 x 3.75 inches and a compression ratio of 10.3:1. The major change for the Hemi in 1970 was the adoption of hydraulic valve lifters. The Hemi cast-iron and heads and cast-aluminum intake manifold were finished in Late Street Hemi Orange with a black crackle-finish air cleaner. The large, wide Hemi valve covers had a black crackle finish. An R on the VIN and E74 on the body code plate indicated the Hemi.

### Transmission Options

The 1970 Dodge Coronet R/T had a standard cast-aluminum case A727 3-speed TorqueFlite automatic transmission when equipped with the 440 V-8 engines. The TorqueFlite was operated with either a column- or console-mounted chrome shift lever, depending on the interior options. A cast-iron case A833 4-speed manual transmission with a 2.44:1 low gear was standard with the 426 Hemi and optional with the 440. The 4-speed used a Hurst shifter, which for the first time used a unique walnut-grain pistol grip design on a wide, flat Hurst chrome-plated handle. The chrome console-mounted shifter handle was curved to the left and back, as in the previous year, while the floor-mounted version was curved back and up. Original handles had a distinct taper in thickness toward the top. Both shifters used a pleated black rubber boot. The Hemi was available with an optional TorqueFlite automatic transmission.

### Rear Axle Options

The standard rear axle with the 1970 Coronet R/T with a 440 or 426 Hemi engine and TorqueFlite automatic transmission was the Chrysler 8-3/4-inch banjo-type, which was available in ratios from 2.94:1 to 3.91:1, with 3.23:1 being standard. A 1$^7$/$_8$-inch-diameter pinion stem was phased in during the 1969 model year, so most 1970 models will have this Casting Number 2881489 carrier. A special Performance Axle Group option (Sales Code 358) was available that provided a 3.55:1 rear axle gear ratio, special slip-drive fan, and an extra-wide high-performance radiator fan shroud. When a 4-speed transmission was ordered with the 440 or 426 Hemi engine, a 9¾-inch ring gear Dana 60 heavy-duty rear axle with a 3.54:1 gear ratio was used, with an optional 4.10:1 ratio provided when the Super Track Pak or Super Performance Axle Packages were ordered. Single-piston power front disc brakes with floating calipers were optional.

### Wheel and Tire Options

The 1970 Coronet R/T had standard 14 x 6–inch stamped-steel wheels, which could be equipped with either a small hubcap or one of two new optional styled wheel covers. Optional 14-inch Magnum 500 styled road wheels with chrome-plated trim rings were available. The 15-inch wheels were no longer required for the 426 Hemi. All-new 15-inch Rallye wheels with F60x15 Wide Oval tires were available as an option if heavy-duty brakes and Rallye Suspension were ordered. Early in 1970 production, new 15 x 7–inch steel wheels became available as an option under Sales Code U84. All steel wheels were restyled for 1970 and featured a flat surface at the lug nut–mounting area.

### Production Numbers

A total of 2,319 WS23 Coronet R/T two-door hardtops and 296 WS27 convertibles were built for the 1970 model year.

## 1970 Coronet Super Bee

The 1970 Coronet Super Bee continued to follow the same marketing placement as previous years, directing an image of performance and style for a relatively lower price than the R/T

*This original unrestored 1970 Coronet Super Bee is finished in EK2 Go-Mango High-Impact paint and has the standard body color painted steel wheels with small hubcaps. This Super Bee has a black Bumblebee stripe with Super Bee logo and black vinyl roof.*

*A view of a Light Green 1970 Coronet Super Bee shows the dual scoop hood and massive twin section front bumper surrounding the quad headlights. A bright Super Bee badge is mounted at the front center of the hood. (Jim Stodolka Photo)*

or other premium models in the Dodge Coronet line. The 1970 Super Bee was based on the same 117-inch-wheelbase unibody platform as the Coronet R/T but was available as the WM21 two-door coupe and the WM23 two-door hardtop only. There were no Super Bee convertibles for 1970.

The Super Bee body was almost identical to the R/T, including the black finish grille insert, a power-bulge hood, and optional functional Ramcharger hood scoops, but the Super Bee hood was equipped with a Bumblebee badge in its front center. The Super Bee did not use the front-facing simulated side scoops that were standard on the R/T. Optional chrome-plated hood pins were available with Sales Code J45. The Super Bee was available with the same standard interior trim, steering wheel, and instrument panel as the R/T. The same optional exterior body colors were also available on the Super Bee as all other Coronet models. A total of 11,540 two-door hardtop and 3,966 two-door coupe 1970 Super Bees were built.

### Body Stripe Options

Two body stripe options were available in the 1970 Coronet Super Bee. First was a standard wide Bumblebee stripe with

*A driver-side rear quarter view of a Blue Fire Poly 1970 Coronet Super Bee shows the details of V6W white side stripe and Super Bee logo. Note the optional Rallye wheels and dual exhaust with oval tips.*

*This 1970 WM23 Coronet Super Bee two-door hardtop is finished in EB5 Blue Fire Poly and is equipped with a 426 Hemi engine and a V6W white side stripe. It also has optional Rallye wheels, which were new for 1970.*

Super Bee logo cutout that wrapped around the rear quarters, similar to the 1969 version, available in white, red, and black. The second was the more dramatic "C" stripe that began at the rear of the door openings, surrounding the side scoop, and extended to the rear quarter with a round Super Bee logo cutout in the center. It was also available in red, white, and black.

### Engine Options

The standard engine for the 1970 Dodge Coronet Super Bee was a special high-performance version of the B-block–based 383-ci V-8 indicated with an E63 code on the body data plate. Dodge called the high-performance version of the single 4-barrel 383 a 383 Magnum. It had a bore and stroke of 4.25 x 3.38 inches and a compression ratio of 9.5:1, reduced from 1969, producing 335 hp at 5,200 rpm, five more than the standard single 4-barrel 383. The 383 Magnum had an unsilenced air cleaner and dual exhaust, making 425 ft-lbs of torque at 3,400 rpm. Most significant was the special high-performance camshaft used only in the 383 Magnum V-8 and its Plymouth Road Runner counterpart. This camshaft had a lift of .450 inch on the intake and .465 inch on the exhaust valve. Intake and exhaust duration was 268 degrees for the intake and 284 degrees for the exhaust, with 46 degrees of overlap. The 383 Magnum V-8 used in the 1970 Super Bee was also equipped with heavier valvesprings, a standard windage tray, and dual exhaust. Most 383 high-performance engines in 1970 were painted Chrysler Performance Orange.

A new engine option for the 1970 Coronet Super Bee was the 440-ci RB-based V-8 with three 2-barrel Holley carburetors mounted on a Chrysler cast-iron intake manifold, replacing the cast-aluminum Edelbrock unit used in 1969. This engine was identified with a V-code on the VIN and E87 on the body code plate. The 440 Magnum Six-Pack engine had a 10.5:1 compression ratio and was still rated at 390 hp at 4,700 rpm and 490 ft-lbs of torque at 3,200 rpm. The 1970 engine did not have the additional special components that came standard with the 1969-1/2 A12 Six-Pack conversion engine package.

*The driver-side taillight of an EB5 Blue Fire Poly 1970 Coronet Super Bee hardtop. Note the brushed silver finish on the rear deck panel and wedge-shaped bright taillight housing.*

*The optional 426 Hemi engine resides under this hood, which features the standard twin hood scoops with bright Hemi badges and functional Ramcharger fresh air system. Note the bright-rimmed side-marker lights.*

*This engine compartment of a blue 1970 Coronet Super Bee has the optional 426 Hemi engine. The Hemi had a standard Ramcharger fresh air intake system. The black rubber insert is intended to clear the Hemi brake booster. Note the correct red battery caps.*

Chapter 4: 1970   81

The only optional engine offered other than the 440-6 with the 1970 Dodge Super Bee was the impressive 426 Hemi V-8 producing 425 hp at 5,000 rpm and 490 ft-lbs of torque at 4,000 rpm. The Hemi, indicated by E74 on the body data plate, still had the same 10.3:1 compression ratio used in previous years. The 426 Hemi for 1970 had a camshaft with hydraulic valve lifters and a lift of .490 inch on the intake valves and .480 inch on the exhaust, with 284 degrees of duration on both. The Hemi was equipped with a cast-aluminum intake manifold that mounted two Carter AFB 4-barrel carburetors. Low-restriction cast-iron headers and dual pipes handled the exhaust. Of course, like all 1966–1971 Street Hemi engines, this one was equipped with the iconic distinctive black crackle-finish valvecovers and was painted Street Hemi Orange.

### Transmission Options

Newly available and standard for the 1970 Super Bee with the 383 4-barrel V-8 only was the less expensive cast-iron case 3-speed manual transmission. The 3-speed was fully synchronized in all forward speeds, so you could downshift to low gear while the car was still moving. The 3-speed manual was available column-mounted, floor-mounted, and console-mounted, depending on the model.

The optional manual transmission on the 1970 Dodge Super Bee was the super strong cast-iron case Chrysler New Process A833 4-speed manual with a chrome-handled Hurst floor-mounted shifter with a wood-grained pistol grip. The cast-iron case A833 had a standard 2.47:1 low-gear ratio with the 383 engine and a 2.44:1 with the 440 or Hemi to help with hard launches and quick acceleration. The 440 or Hemi transmission had a stronger input shaft to handle the additional torque and power.

The only other optional transmission was the aluminum case A727 Chrysler TorqueFlite 3-speed automatic with a 2.45:1 low gear. A special small-diameter (11-inch) and high-stall-speed torque converter was standard equipment with the Super Bee.

### Rear Axle Options

The standard rear axle with the TorqueFlite or 383 with the 4-speed manual transmission was the Chrysler 8¾-inch banjo-type unit with a standard 3.23:1 gear ratio. When the 426 Hemi and a 4-speed transmission were ordered, a stronger 9¾-inch ring gear Dana 60 axle with a 3.54:1 ratio was installed with its standard Sure Grip. Both axles were supported with the standard and very effective Chrysler-designed heavy-duty longitudinal leaf springs.

### Wheel and Tire Options

Standard tires on the 383 Coronet Super Bee were F70x14–inch white sidewall that were only available with the heavy-duty suspension and power disc brakes that came with the Super Bee. Standard wheels were 14 x 6 pressed steel. When equipped with the optional 426 Hemi engine or heavy-duty brakes and suspension, standard tires were F60x15–inch raised white-letters mounted on painted pressed-steel wheels.

### 1970 Coronet R/T and Super Bee Advertising and Publicity

One of the first color magazine ads for a 1970 Coronet Super Bee featured a front view of a Sublime Poly Super Bee accelerating past the Christmas tree at a dragstrip with an attentive driver at the wheel. The headline of small white text to the right of the picture stated, "Dodge introduces a new model Super Bee at a new lower price. $3,074." The remainder of the text explained that the reason the Super Bee was $64 cheaper was that a 3-speed manual transmission was now

*When a bench seat was ordered in a 1970 Super Bee, the Hurst Pistol Grip shifter became even more impressive. The long, curved handle and wood-grained grip may not have been the best for racing, but for the street the driver felt positively in control. No other manufacturer had anything like this.*

*A period magazine ad shows an FJ5 Sublime 1970 Coronet Super Bee two-door hardtop posed at the line on a dragstrip. This ad promotes the new lower price of the Super Bee compared to the 1968 model. (Dodge, Plymouth, and the AMC design are registered trademarks of FCA US LLC)*

standard equipment rather than a more expensive 4-speed manual or TorqueFlite automatic. An aggressive-looking Super Bee logo with "Dodge Scat Pack" beneath it appeared to the lower left of the ad.

### 1970 Dodge Challenger

New for the 1970 model year was the exciting E-Body Challenger, Dodge's late but impressive entry into the Pony Car field, competing with the Chevrolet Camaro and Ford Mustang. The new Challenger was based on a 110-inch-wheelbase E-Body platform that was designed wide enough not only to improve handling and ride, but also to easily adapt to the larger and more powerful B, RB, and 426 Hemi V-8 engines. Even the Challenger firewall structure was based on the larger B-Body. The Challenger was a ready and willing new member of the Scat Pack Club.

The front and rear chassis design was much like the rest of the Scat Pack line with a steel K-member and dual torsion bars in front supporting the engine, and independent front suspension and asymmetrical parallel rear leaf springs holding up the rear axle. The front track width was 59.7 inches like the B-Body platform, but the rear was a bit wider at 60.7 inches. The great difference was in the overall height, which was about 2 inches lower than the B-Body cars. This gave the new Challenger a low and lean stance.

*The 1970 Challenger R/T convertible body differs from the hardtop in that it has an internal reinforcement between the rear wheel wells. This R/T is finished in FC7 Plum Crazy with a white R/T stripe and has 14-inch Rallye wheels.*

Chapter 4: 1970    83

*This original unrestored 1970 Challenger R/T convertible is finished in FC7 Plum Crazy and has a white convertible top and a V9Y Top Banana Bumblebee stripe. It is also equipped with optional Rallye wheels and raised white-letter tires.*

*A 1970 Challenger R/T SE equipped with the distinctive SE black vinyl roof with a smaller rear window and SE badge. This car has the unusual combination of EK2 Go-Mango paint and a V9Y Top Banana Bumblebee stripe.*

### 1970 Dodge Challenger R/T

The 1970 Challenger R/T was available in three types, all using the same basic shell and doors: JS23 two-door hardtop, JS27 convertible (with appropriate modifications and reinforcements), and JS29 SE two-door hardtop. The Challenger body was immediately identified by its distinctive front-end design that incorporated a wide, oval, deep-set grille opening, a narrow chrome bumper, and quad round headlights. The grille opening was outlined with a narrow stainless steel trim molding on all models. The dark square mesh grille was inset into the center of the recessed black surround and included a bright Challenger script and a red-filled bright die-cast R/T badge. A Challenger R/T nameplate and badge also appeared on the passenger-side rear of the deck lid to identify it.

#### Hood Options

Two different hoods were used on the 1970 Challenger R/T, both different from the standard flat steel hood used on a standard Challenger. The standard steel performance hood for the Challenger R/T had a raised center power bulge with twin simulated scoops. The Challenger R/T with multiple carburetors was also available with the optional Shaker fresh air hood. The Shaker fresh air hood had an opening in the center to allow the carburetor-mounted Shaker air cleaner and scoop assembly to protrude. The opening was trimmed with a raised molding assembly.

The N96 Shaker hood option was not available on the Challenger until January 1970, and then only for the 440 Six-Pack and Hemi engines. It later became available as an option on the Challenger 340 with the 340 Performance Package. The Shaker dome was painted Rallye Red when that body color was ordered, but it was initially available only in Organosol Black for all other body colors. By the end of the 1970 model year, the Shaker dome was offered in FE5 red, EB5 blue (red and blue were available only with matching body colors), DA1 Astrotone Argent Silver, and 5X8 black.

#### Exterior Options

The 1970 Challenger was available in 18 body colors. Standard finishes included Light Blue Metallic, Bright Blue Metallic, Dark Blue Metallic, Rallye Red, Light and Dark Green Metallic, Dark Burnt Orange, Beige, Dark Tan Metallic, white, black, cream, and Light Gold Metallic. There were also five special extra-cost "High-Performance" colors: FC7 Plum

Crazy, FJ5 Sublime, EK2 Go-Mango, EV2 Hemi Orange, and FY1 Top Banana. Two additional High-Performance colors of FJ6 Green Go and FM3 Panther Pink were made available after February 24, 1970. The 1970 Challenger was available in four vinyl-top colors complemented by the large selection of body colors. A total of 42,625 Dodge Challengers were built for the 1970 model year.

### Body Striping Options

To accent the variety of body color schemes available in 1970, the Challenger had a standard painted Bumblebee stripe, so-called because it wrapped around the rear portion of the deck. The Bumblebee stripe consisted of two parts. The rear portion was 5¼ inches wide and the front part was 1/4 inch wide, with a 5/16-inch space between them. The Bumblebee stripe was offered in six colors: V9W White, V9X Black, V9R Bright Red, V9B Bright Blue, V9Y Yellow, and V9F Green. The original stripe color codes appear on the body data plate on the driver-side inner fenderwell. If the Bumblebee stripe was deleted and no other stripe was ordered, a V98 code appears. The Challenger R/T was also available with a no-cost optional body side tape stripe with the R/T stencil cut into the tape on the rear of the front fender. The tape stripe was available in V6X Black, V6W White, V6B Blue, V6F Green, and V6R Red. V6J Light Green and V6M Pink were added after March 9, 1970. The Challenger T/A had a distinctive tape stripe, indicated by a V6H code on the body data plate. This stripe ran from the front edge of the front fender and continued over the door and to the forward portion of the rear quarter panels, ending just below the quarter window opening. There were two variations of the door portion of the stripe, depending upon which optional side mirror was used.

### Interior Options

The 1970 Challenger R/T and T/A had standard full-foam high-back vinyl bucket seats with integrated head restraints in nine interior trim combinations. The Regal or Coachman-grain vinyl bucket seats were available in black, Bright Blue, dark green, Burnt Orange, red, or dark tan. The pattern consisted of small lateral pleats that extended to each side of the seat cushion. The lateral pleats were accented by a lengthwise seam about one-quarter of the way from each edge.

The Challenger Special Edition had standard high-back pleated leather cushion front bucket seats with Coachman-grain vinyl bolsters. The SE rear seat was all Coachman-grain vinyl. The SE interior was available in dark tan, Burnt Orange, and black. The Challenger R/T and SE were also available with cloth and vinyl bucket seats in Burnt Orange, black, dark tan, or dark green as a credit option.

### Instrument Panel Options

The Challenger instrument panel was finished in a color matching the interior trim and was standard with an upper pad. The standard instrument cluster had a black textured finish. A Challenger nameplate was placed on the upper passenger-side side of the pad. The Challenger R/T had a standard Rallye instrument cluster. The Challenger had a standard three-spoke wood-grain steering wheel. All steering columns had a pleated collapsible design.

### Engine Options

The standard engine in a 1970 Dodge Challenger R/T was a 383-ci B-block Magnum V-8 with a single 4-barrel carburetor, a bore and stroke of 4.25 x 3.38 inches, and a compression ratio of 9.5:1, producing 335 hp at 5,200 rpm. The 383 Magnum was equipped with an unsilenced air cleaner and dual exhaust, making 425 ft-lbs of torque at 3,400 rpm. Most significant was the special high-performance camshaft used only in the 383 Magnum V-8. This camshaft had a lift of .450 inch on the intake and .465 inch on the exhaust valve. Intake and exhaust duration was 268 degrees for the intake and 284 degrees for the exhaust with 46 degrees of overlap. The 383 Magnum V-8 used in the 1970 Challenger was also equipped with heavier valve springs, a standard windage tray, and dual exhaust. Most 383 high-performance engines in 1970 were painted Chrysler Performance Orange.

The single Carter AVS 4-barrel-equipped 440 Magnum produced 375 hp at 4,600 rpm and 480 ft-lbs of torque at 3,200 rpm. The 440 had a bore and stroke of 4.32 x 3.75 inches and a compression ratio of 9.7:1, lowered from the previous year. All 1970 440 engines were painted Chrysler Performance Orange. The 440 Magnum single 4-barrel engine used a black crackle-finish unsilenced air cleaner.

The third engine option in the 1970 Challenger R/T was the 440-ci RB-based V-8 with three 2-barrel Holley carburetors mounted on a Chrysler cast-iron intake manifold, replacing the cast-aluminum Edelbrock unit used in 1969. This engine was identified with a V-code on the VIN and E87 on the body code plate. The 440 Magnum Six-Pack engine had a 10.5:1 compression ratio and was still rated at 390 hp at 4,700 rpm and 490 ft-lbs of torque at 3,200 rpm.

The fourth engine available with the 1970 Challenger R/T was the 426 Hemi V-8 rated at 425 hp at 5,000 rpm and 490 ft-lbs of torque at 4,000 rpm. The two Carter AFB 4-barrel-equipped Hemi had a bore and stroke of 4.25 x 3.75 inches and a compression ratio of 10.3:1. The major change for the Hemi in 1970 was the adoption of hydraulic valve lifters. The Hemi cast-iron and heads and cast-aluminum intake manifold were finished in Late Street Hemi Orange with a black crackle-finish air cleaner. The large, wide Hemi valve covers had a black crackle finish. An R on the VIN and E74 on the body code plate indicated the Hemi.

### Transmission Options

The 1970 Dodge Challenger R/T had a standard cast-aluminum case A727 3-speed TorqueFlite automatic transmission when equipped with the 440 V-8 engines. The TorqueFlite was operated with either a column- or console-mounted chrome shift lever, depending on the interior options. A cast-iron case A833 4-speed manual transmission with a 2.44:1 low gear was standard with the 426 Hemi and optional with the 440. The 4-speed used a Hurst shifter with a unique walnut-grain pistol grip design on a wide, flat Hurst chrome-plated handle. The chrome-plated console-mounted shifter handle was curved to the left and back, as in the previous year, while the floor-mounted version was curved back and up. Original handles had a distinct taper in thickness toward the top. Both shifters used a pleated black rubber boot. The Hemi was available with an optional TorqueFlite automatic transmission.

### Rear Axle Options

The standard rear axle with the 1970 Challenger R/T with a 440 or 426 Hemi engine and TorqueFlite automatic transmission was the Chrysler 8¾-inch banjo-type, which was available in ratios from 2.76:1 to 3.91:1, with 3.23:1 being standard. A 1⅞-inch pinion stem was phased in during the 1969 model year, so most 1970 models will have a carrier with Casting Number 2881489. A special Performance Axle Group option (Sales Code 358) was available that provided a 3.55:1 rear axle gear ratio, special slip-drive fan, and an extra-wide high-performance radiator fan shroud. When a 4-speed transmission was ordered with the 440 or 426 Hemi engine, a 9¾-inch ring gear Dana 60 heavy-duty rear axle with a 3.54:1 gear ratio was used. An optional 4.10:1 ratio provided when the Super Track Pak or Super Performance Axle Packages were ordered. Single-piston power front disc brakes with floating calipers were optional.

### Wheel and Tire Options

The 1970 Challenger R/T was equipped with standard 14 x 6–inch stamped-steel wheels, which could be equipped with either a small hubcap or one of two new optional styled wheel covers. Optional 14-inch Magnum 500 styled road wheels with chrome-plated trim rings were available. Because of the redesigned standard wheels, 15-inch wheels were no longer required for the 426 Hemi. All-new 15-inch Rallye wheels with F60x15 Wide Oval tires were available as an option if heavy-duty brakes and Rallye Suspension were ordered. Early in 1970 production, new 15 x 7–inch steel wheels became available as an option under Sales Code U84. All steel wheels were restyled for 1970 and featured a flat surface at the lug nut-mounting area.

### Performance

Performance evaluations and road tests for a 1970 Challenger were many for the car's first year. Most every automobile enthusiast publication made sure that they were provided with at least one to report their finds to the anxious public and potential buyers. *Sports Car Graphic* tested a new 1970 Challenger R/T with the 440 Magnum engine in November 1969 and recorded impressive results.

The Challenger was equipped with a 3-speed TorqueFlite automatic transmission connected to the 8¾-inch ring gear rear axle with a 3.55:1 ratio. The 4,080-pound Challenger produced a 0-60–mph time of 6.4 seconds, admirable for the times. A quarter-mile time of 14.8 seconds at 95 mph supported this performance.

Another test was accomplished by *Road Test* in June 1970 using a 1970 Challenger R/T with the 426 Hemi. This particular 3,800-pound Challenger had the $235.65 Super Trac Pak option with a 4.10:1 ratio Dana 60 rear axle plus the A833 4-speed transmission. The low-axle ratio increased acceleration capabilities but greatly reduced fuel mileage, which was probably not a consideration of a Hemi owner. The 425 hp of the Hemi produced 0-60–mph times of 6.8 to 7.1 seconds and a quarter-mile best time of 14 seconds at 104 mph.

## 1970 Challenger T/A

The Challenger T/A, or Trans-Am package, was only available as a two-door hardtop and was identified by Sales Code A53 on the body data plate. The Challenger T/A was a

*A 1970 Challenger T/A finished in EK2 Go-Mango with a black stripe and a flat-black fiberglass hood with T/A scoop. This T/A has the optional Rallye wheels.*

*An original unrestored 1970 Challenger T/A finished in FK5 Dark Burnt Orange with the standard black T/A stripe, black rear spoiler, and 340 Six-Pak callout. This T/A also has an optional black vinyl roof and 15-inch Rallye wheels.*

1970-only model and the standard engine was a 290-hp 340-ci LA-based Six-Pak V-8 with standard 4-speed manual transmission. No optional engines were available. The T/A package included a unique exhaust system with chrome-plated pipes exiting from side outlets in front of the rear wheel openings.

The Challenger T/A used a flat-black painted fiberglass hood with a molded-in distinctive raised scoop and chrome front hood hold-down pins. The T/A hood required special edge molding and lighter-tension springs. The scoop opening had a center divider and was raised off the surface of the hood to provide higher airflow capabilities over all other types of scoops. The T/A hood was used on some standard Challengers ordered with a Shaker hood when Shaker hood stocks ran short. The 1970 Challenger T/A had no identifying grille badge.

### Engine Options

The standard and only engine available with the 1970 Challenger T/A was an LA-based 340-ci high-performance V-8 that developed 290 hp at 5,000 rpm and 340 ft-lbs of torque at 3,200 rpm, with a 10.5:1 compression ratio. The 340 Six-Pak engine had three Holley 2-barrel carburetors on a Chrysler-designed Edelbrock aluminum intake manifold. The large oval air cleaner was orange and had a soft black rubber hood seal around its circumference. This engine can be noted by the letter J on the VIN plate and was used only in the 1970 Challenger T/A and Plymouth 'Cuda AAR.

The cast-iron block differs from the standard 340 in that it was stress-relieved with additional material added to the main bearing bores. The engine had specially machined cast-iron heads with offset pushrods to allow for larger ports. The engine was also equipped with offset, cast-iron, adjustable rocker arms and special rocker arm shafts. The 340 three 2-barrel engines were painted Street Hemi Orange.

### Transmission Options

The T/A was available with either an A727 TorqueFlite 3-speed automatic or an A833 4-speed manual transmission.

### Rear Axle Options

The 1970 Challenger T/A was equipped with a standard 8¾-inch ring gear rear axle with Sure Grip and a standard 3.55:1 axle ratio. A lower 3.91:1 ratio was available as an option.

### K-Member

The T/A used the same basic steel unibody construction as the Challenger R/T, except for improvements in handling, suspension, and brakes more closely related to the specialized track racing duty for which the T/A was designed. First, the T/A used a unique K-member with Part Number 3583952, identified by a small metal tag welded to the lower side of the K-member. The tag has the numbers 52 (the last two digits of the part number) stamped on its face from the reverse side. As with all Challengers, the K-member was painted semi-gloss black, known as OEM Black.

*The H6E4 red interior trim combination on a 1970 Challenger R/T includes a red carpet and matching red ABS door panels and instrument panel pad. This car is also equipped with an optional 4-speed transmission and console-mounted Hurst shifter with pistol grip.*

### Steering and Suspension

The Challenger T/A front suspension used a .94-inch-diameter anti-sway bar. The T/A was available with race-directed optional quick-ratio (12:1) power steering, accomplished by the addition of a longer pitman arm. The wider arc of the longer steering arm quickened steering response without actually changing the standard ratio of the power steering gear. Because less travel was required, the steering gear was modified to limit internal gear travel and avoid damage to the mechanism.

### Wheel and Tire Options

Standard brakes for a 1970 Challenger R/T were 11 x 3–inch front drums and 11 x 2-1/2–inch rear drums, but the T/A used 10.7-inch power-assisted front discs and 11 x 2-1/2–inch rear drums as standard equipment. The T/A came with standard gloss-black painted 15 x 7–inch steel wheels mounted with E60x15 Goodyear Polyglas GT tires on the front and G60x15 tires on the rear. The black painted 15-inch wheel had a standard hubcap and bright trim ring.

### 1970 Challenger R/T and T/A Advertising

The 1970 Dodge Challenger color dealer showroom brochure featured the R/T prominently. A full horizontal page spread showed a Go-Mango 1970 Challenger R/T with the optional 440 SixPack engine and red Shaker hood scoop posed with a young couple, including a man wearing a red Scat Pack Club jacket with black racing stripe and badge. The large headline read, "The Six-pack. It snarls, it quivers, it leaps vast prairies at a single bound." Small text provided details of the car starting with, "Three two-barrel carburetors, special intake, Daytona-type four-speed transmission and Rallye Suspension, molded around a race-ready 440 V-8." Four color images

*A full-page vertical magazine ad featuring a red 1970 Challenger R/T two-door hardtop with optional hood pins and a black vinyl roof. The blonde model shows a great example of 1970 style. (Dodge, Plymouth, and the AMC design are registered trademarks of FCA US LLC)*

below the text showed details of the Shaker hood scoop, front seat and door panel, wood-grained steering wheel, and rear fascia.

*A red 1970 Challenger R/T is featured in a showroom brochure and is equipped with a 440 Six-Pack engine and shaker hood scoop. This Challenger is also equipped with Magnum 500 styled road wheels and trim rings. (Dodge, Plymouth, and the AMC design are registered trademarks of FCA US LLC)*

*An unusual ad features details of the 1970 Challenger T/A and lists its standard equipment. Like most ads of the time, the Scat Pack bee and "Run with the Dodge Scat Pack" slogan are featured prominently. (Dodge, Plymouth, and the AMC design are registered trademarks of FCA US LLC)*

An early vertical full-page ad for the Challenger showed a red 1970 Challenger R/T. A young blond-haired girl in a bright minidress sat invitingly and gracefully on the driver-side front fender. The headline read, "America's only all-new car is here! New Dodge Challenger. See it this week!" There was only one small line of text at the bottom that read, "Dodge Challenger R/T 2-door hardtop. If you want all the 'news' for '70 . . . you could be DODGE MATERIAL."

Only one promotional or advertising piece was produced for the 1970 Challenger T/A. It is not clear whether this early black-and-white horizontal ad was for a dealer brochure or for an outside publication. The left side of the ad featured a large image at the top of the right front of a Challenger T/A in action on a wet road surface. A Dodge and Chrysler logo appeared at the bottom of the photo. Below that photo were four smaller photos of the driver's side, passenger-side rear, hood scoop, and unique chrome exhaust pipe.

The right half of the ad had a black background and a large headline in white that read, "Challenger T/A. This car has never raced, yet it has more firsts than any other car in its class." Beneath the headline was a list of the special features of the Challenger T/A, including its "Small-block engine with Six Pak carburetion, and air scoop borrowed from a pursuit plane." and its "Daytona rake for extra stability." At the bottom was another small wide-angle photo of a T/A and to its right, a "Run with the Dodge Scat Pack" logo and Bumblebee.

The ad that cemented Dodge Challenger as a member of the Scat Pack showcased a red shaker-equipped car encompassing nearly 75 percent of the page with a tagline reading, "This Pony has Horses . . . 1970 Dodge Challenger R\T." Subtly in the lower left-hand corner next to the Dodge Scat Pack logo read, "Dodge Scat Pack . . . the cars with the Bumblebee stripes." This acknowledgment concluded that if you have a Bumblebee stripe, you're a full-fledged Scat Pack member.

### 1970 Dodge Dart Swinger 340

The 1970 Dart was still based on the 111-inch-wheelbase A-Body platform used since 1967, but the Dart body was updated with significant body design changes. Front-end styling was redesigned to have a more aerodynamic appearance by slanting back from top to bottom. The bright grille and headlight surround wrapped noticeably around the sides of the front fenders, giving

*An enthusiast magazine ad features a front view of a red 1970 Challenger R/T posed at a racetrack. This Challenger has the optional Shaker hood scoop that was standard with the 426 Hemi and optional with the other available engines. (Dodge, Plymouth, and the AMC design are registered trademarks of FCA US LLC)*

This original unrestored 1970 Dart Swinger 340 is finished in FE5 Rallye Red and equipped with optional Rallye wheels and optional twin Ramcharger hood scoops. This Dart also has an optional black vinyl roof and a black Bumblebee stripe.

This 1970 Dart Swinger 340 is finished in FM3 Panther Pink with a white Bumblebee stripe and a white vinyl roof. The Dart also has optional Rallye wheels, hood pins, and raised white-letter Goodyear Polyglas tires. (Kori Alexander Photo)

a more modern look to the front of the car. Both the grille and chrome-plated front bumper were more integrated and fit closer into the body. The new grille featured a bright vertical divider in the center with small rectangular parking lights on each side. Twin hood-mounted air scoops were available as an option on the Dart Swinger but were not available with the functional Ramcharger fresh air system used on the Super Bee. The performance hood with twin scoops was available with an optional flat-black paint treatment (Sales Code V21) to add to the sporty appearance.

The rear of the Dart was also slanted back from the top of the deck to the chrome bumper, which had rectangular taillights and the center license plate mounting integrated into it. The rear bumper was wider and more closely fitted to the body, giving a more, but still subtle, aerodynamic appearance. Wide rectangular taillights were now mounted into each end of the chrome-plated rear bumper rather than the body, giving a smoother appearance to the rear view of the Dart. A full vinyl roof was offered in green, white, and black. The vinyl roof included a standard bright molding around the lower edge of the rear quarter and roof drip rail.

### Interior Options

Interior trim options were similar to those available in 1969. The standard interior trim in the Dart Swinger 340 was an all-vinyl bench seat. Available colors were blue and black with a black rubber floor mat. Carpeting was provided when the 4-speed transmission was ordered because the rubber mat could not be fitted around the shifter hump in the floor. An extra-cost option in the Dart Swinger 340 two-door hardtop was pleated all-vinyl trim in green, tan, blue, and black, also as a bench seat design. Also optional at extra cost were full-foam all-vinyl bucket seats in tan, black, and green. An optional center console was available at extra cost. The Swinger 340 included custom door trim panels, carpeting, and rear quarter armrest and ashtray. Interior trim colors had recommendations for appropriate body color combinations, but any color could be ordered with any interior trim. Exterior stripe and Bumblebee stripe colors were also listed in a chart with recommendations coordinated with interior trim colors.

### 383 and 440 Dropped

Performance offerings based on the Dart were reduced for the 1970 model year as the Dart GT and GTS were dropped from the line. For 1970, the standard Dart Swinger was available in non-high–performance mode. This left the LL23 Dart Swinger 340 two-door hardtop as the only performance-oriented compact Dodge available. Losing the GTS also meant that the powerful 383 and 440 high-performance V-8 engine options were no longer available, leaving only the 340-ci LA-based engine for performance fans. The Dart Swinger 340 had standard Rallye suspension, front disc brakes, and E70x14 fiberglass-belted bias-ply tires on 14x5.5J steel wheels. Optional 14-inch Rallye wheels were available, along with chrome wire wheel covers.

The price of the Dart Swinger 340 was reduced from 1969 with the use of a standard 3-speed manual transmission. The 4-speed and TorqueFlite transmissions were optional. The Swinger 340 was still a valid member of the Scat Pack Club and popular with enthusiasts. A total of 13,785 Dart Swinger 340 hardtops were made for the 1970 model year.

### Engine Options

The standard and only engine available for the 1970 Dart Swinger 340 was the LA-series-based 340-ci V-8, identical to

*This is a detail view of one of the optional twin nonfunctional hood scoops on a Panther Pink 1970 Dart Swinger 340. The scoops are neatly trimmed in chrome-edge moldings and include an engine callout badge. (Kori Alexander Photo)*

that used in the 1969 model. The rear-mounted distributor identified the 340. The 340 was rated at 275 hp at 5,000 rpm and 340 pounds of torque at 3,200 rpm. The 340 V-8 had a bore of 4.04 inches and stroke of 3.31 inches, and had a single Carter Thermo-Quad 4-barrel carburetor. The 340 had a 10.5:1 compression ratio so premium fuel was required. All 340 V-8 engines had hydraulic valve lifters and dual exhausts with chrome tips.

### Transmission Options

The standard transmission for the 1970 Dart Swinger 340 was the less expensive cast-iron case 3-speed manual transmission. The 3-speed was fully synchronized in all forward speeds, so you could downshift to low gear while the car was still moving. The 3-speed manual transmission was available column-mounted, floor-mounted, and console-mounted, depending on the model. The shifter used a round chrome handle with a round black plastic knob.

The optional transmission on the 1970 Dart Swinger 340 was the cast-iron case Chrysler New Process A833 4-speed manual with a 2.66:1 low-gear ratio. A Hurst Performance floor shift was used with the 4-speed, but unlike the B- and E-Body Dodges, the A-Body Dart did not use the familiar flat Hurst handle with pistol grip. The Dart used a round chrome-plated handle with a round wood-grained shift knob. The super strong aluminum case A727 TorqueFlite 3-speed automatic was optional and was equipped with a 2.45:1 low gear. Both transmissions were extra cost.

### Rear Axle Options

The standard rear axle with the TorqueFlite or 4-speed manual transmission was the Chrysler 8¾-inch banjo-type unit with a standard 3.23:1 gear ratio. Sure Grip limited-slip was optional with the 3.23:1 gears. The rear axle was supported by Chrysler-designed heavy-duty longitudinal parallel leaf springs.

### Wheels, Tires, and Brakes

The 1970 Dart Swinger 340 brakes were up to the performance levels of the car. It was equipped with 10-inch rear drums and 10.79-inch power disc brakes on the front. Standard tires on the 1970 Dart Swinger 340 were E70x14 fiberglass-belted bias-ply mounted on 14 x 5.5–inch steel wheels. Sales Code W15 full wire-type wheel covers were also available as an extra-cost option but only with the E70x14 tires. Sales Code W21 styled 14-inch Rallye road wheels were also available.

### Advertising

Advertising material for the 1970 Dart Swinger 340 two-door hardtop included a full-color ad very similar to one used in 1969. It showed a red Dart with a black vinyl roof and black Bumblebee stripe accelerating on what appears to be a track location. The text in white letters beneath the front of the car reads, "1970 Dart Swinger 340. If you can find a hotter performance car for less than $2,808, buy it." A more detailed but smaller text block beneath reads in part, "Lots of luck. Try

*An original magazine ad features a red 1970 Dart Swinger 340 during a road test. This Dart Swinger has a black Bumblebee stripe and an optional black vinyl roof. (Dodge, Plymouth, and the AMC design are registered trademarks of FCA US LLC)*

*A page from a Dodge showroom brochure shows a red Dart Swinger 340 with an optional black vinyl roof and black Bumble Bee stripe on a beach. This Dart is equipped with the twin non-functional hood scoops. (Dodge, Plymouth, and the AMC design are registered trademarks of FCA US LLC)*

laying down less than three G's anywhere else." The remainder of the text describes the standard and optional equipment offered with the Dart Swinger 340. The lower right side of the ad carries the familiar bee logo and ad line, "Dodge Scat Pack... the cars with the Bumblebee stripes."

One of the images used in the 1970 Dart color dealer showroom brochure showed a front view of a red 1970 Dart Swinger 340 with a couple posing on the far side of the car. The headline read, "Dart Swinger 340" and it featured five smaller images of the wood-grained steering wheel and instrument panel, wood-grain shift knob, a close-up of the Swinger badge, hood scoop with 340 badge, and a rear view of the car with the black Bumblebee stripe clearly visible. The car was equipped with Rallye sport wheels. A paragraph of text above the images began with, "The Dart that gives you a head start." More small text below provided details of the standard features and options available on the 1970 Swinger 340. The bottom line ended with "You could be Dodge Material," but no mention was made of the Scat Pack program.

### Winding Down the 1970 Model Year

As usual, regular production ended sometime around July and August and after a longer-than-usual changeover shutdown period, the new 1971 models began rolling down the assembly lines in ever-increasing numbers. The shutdown was longer than usual for the B-Body lines because of the dramatic changes made for the 1971 model year. In some cases, additional assembly line management personnel were hired to assist with the changeover. Although any mention of the Scat Pack program had been greatly reduced toward the end of the model year, the program and Scat Pack Club still existed and would see more emphasis in the showroom and in advertising and publicity as the new models were introduced toward the end of 1970.

*Some of Dodge's promotional materials for 1970 featured actual performance tests of Scat Pack cars driven by famous race car drivers. This one shows Charlie Allen driving a 1970 Dart Swinger 340.*

# CHAPTER 5

# 1971

## BOLD NEW DESIGNS

*"If you want more run for your money...join the Pack."*

The Dodge Scat Pack Club and Scat Pack Program were alive and well at the beginning of 1971. For the first year anniversary of the club, Dodge published a full-page promotional piece with an application to join the Scat Pack Club. The bold headline read, "Join one of the fastest growing performance car clubs. Dodge Scat Pack Club." The first line of text told enthusiasts, "Dodge Scat Pack Club. Quickly getting to be the 'in' performance car club." The rest of the page listed the contents of the benefits package a member received upon sending in his application and $5.95 fee.

These included:
- Illustrated tune-up tips four-page folder
- Hustle Stuff Parts catalog
- Pocket-Pack all-weather racing jacket
- Official club blazer patch
- "Scat Packers Unite!" bumper sticker
- Official club identifier folder
- Dodge Scat Pack Club decal
- Wallet-sized membership card
- *Scat Speaks* illustrated quarterly newsletter
- 1971 Auto Racing Guide
- Four-page monthly Dodge *Performance News*. At the end of the 1970 calendar year, Dodge published the anniversary issue of *Scat Speaks*, Volume 1, Number 4. It was the quarterly newsletter for Scat Pack owners and club members. The newsletter, with its bright orange background and bold black logo, mentioned that, "The

*This 1971 Charger R/T is finished in FC7 Plum Crazy high-impact paint and is equipped with the standard 440 Magnum V-8 engine. The louvers on the door panel are standard with the R/T. Note the original equipment dual white stripe tires and optional Magnum 500 styled wheels.*

resounding call to arms has resulted in a membership of over 14,000 Dodge fans throughout the country." The text also pointed out that "2,008 Dodge dealers who have joined up to promote the Dodge name and its fine stable of high-performance machinery."

The 1971 Hustle Stuff catalog was based on the catalog first produced by Chrysler in 1969 and provided enthusiasts with a 32-page list of available parts and equipment to modify their Dodge and Plymouth performance vehicles. Many of these performance parts were the same ones used on Dodge and Plymouth factory-supported drag racing cars that were winning races around the country.

This Dodge Scat Pack Club jacket was available from the Scat Pack Club in 1971. (Kyle Banachard Photo)

The 1971 Chrysler Hustle Stuff catalog featured parts and accessories for all Dodge and Plymouth high-performance and racing vehicles. The cover image was a generic stylized image of the Sox & Martin Pro-Stock Hemi `Cuda. (Dodge, Plymouth, and the AMC design are registered trademarks of FCA US LLC)

### Scat Pack Lineup for 1971

The 1971 model year was a year not only of dramatic changes in styling themes for Dodge but in the basic model lineup. Charger as a separate body type was dropped for 1971 and kept only as a model consolidated into the Coronet intermediate line. The Coronet was now only available as a four-door sedan and station wagon, leaving all two-door hardtop models as variations of the new Charger theme. The Challenger was much the same as the 1970 model with updates to the grille design and bodies of the R/T limited to two-door hardtop only. The A-Body Dart design was carried over almost unchanged from 1970, but

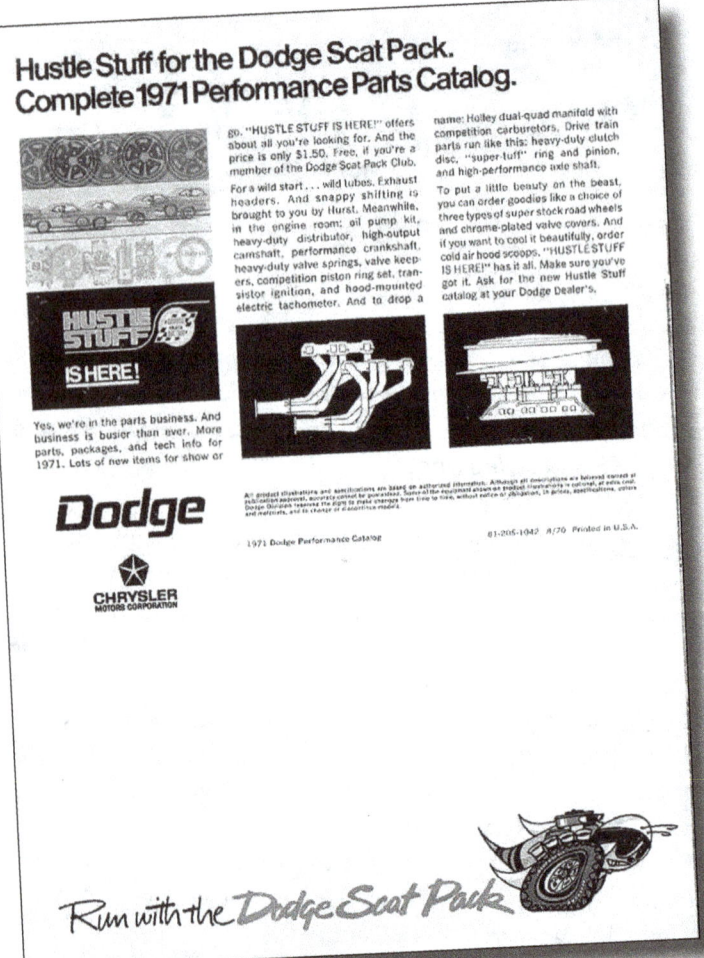

This page from the 1971 Scat Pack Club package lists the performance parts available through the 1971 Hustle Stuff catalog available from Dodge. This information was published late in 1970. (Dodge, Plymouth, and the AMC design are registered trademarks of FCA US LLC)

*An example of some of the Scat Pack Club information with an application to join the club. This piece lists the materials a club member received after joining the club. (Dodge, Plymouth, and the AMC design are registered trademarks of FCA US LLC)*

*The cover from the Scat Pack materials package sent to Dodge dealers to explain the Scat Pack Club and how it could increase sales and traffic at the showroom. (Dodge, Plymouth, and the AMC design are registered trademarks of FCA US LLC)*

it was handily moved out of the Scat Pack Club for 1971 and replaced with the aggressively named Dodge Demon 340 two-door coupe.

### 1971 Dodge Charger R/T and Super Bee

The utilitarian 1971 Dodge Coronet four-door sedan and station wagon were now a separate and unique model series built on a much longer 118-inch-wheelbase platform, although still using the standard Chrysler-designed unibody construction with a steel front K-member and longitudinal parallel rear leaf spring suspension. The Coronet design featured more rounded styling than the 1970 model, accentuated by a full-width grille opening with quad round headlights and a large chrome-plated surround serving double duty as the front bumper. A bright Tri-Star Dodge badge was mounted in the center of the grille. The Coronet series was offered as a Coronet, Coronet Custom, and Coronet Brougham; none

*Hemi Orange 1971 Charger R/T with a black vinyl roof, standard black body stripe, and Rallye wheels. The 1971 body appears longer and heavier than the previous model, but it is actually shorter with differences only in front and rear overhang. (Kori Alexander Photo)*

*This 1971 Charger Super Bee is finished in Hemi orange and has the optional retractable headlights. Notice the difference in grille design with the previous red Charger. This Super Bee has a flat-black Super Bee hood decal and optional bright hood pins.*

*The Ramcharger fresh air intake system opens by a switch on the instrument panel and allows forced cold air into the intake system and air cleaner. This Super Bee is equipped with the 383 Magnum V-8 engine.*

*A view of the retractable optional headlights on a Plum Crazy 1971 Charger R/T. The headlights are operated by a vacuum solenoid system. This Charger is also equipped with optional headlamp washers.*

were considered performance models. Concealed headlamps that were standard on a Charger SE were optional on the WS23 Charger R/T and WP23 Super Bee only.

The performance-oriented intermediate Dodges were in the Charger line, all on a wheelbase shortened to 115 inches for 1971. Although the overall length of the Charger was shortened from 208.5 to 205.4 inches, it appeared longer due to a shortened rear overhang and lengthened front overhang. The width of the body was increased from 73.4 to 75.9 inches, all adding to the perceived appearance of a much larger car. The Charger's shipping weight still ranged from 3,764 to 4,083 pounds, so it was not lighter.

### Exterior

The Charger two-door hardtop and coupe body lines were more flowing and streamlined than the 1970 models and the rear window was now flush with the fastback-style roof C-pillar on all models. The Charger was available in three models: the Charger; Charger 500, which included the Super Bee and SE; and the Charger R/T. Overall styling was similar for all, but the Charger Super Bee and R/T had a standard power bulge hood and the R/T had simulated dual vertical vents on the doors. The Charger R/T power bulge hood had standard louvers and both the R/T and Super Bee were available with the optional functional Ramcharger fresh air hood, standard when the 426 Hemi engine was ordered. The Charger R/T came with all of the standard luxury features of the Charger 500. Of course, the Charger Super Bee and Charger R/T were ready and willing members of the Dodge Scat Pack Club.

The full-width grille with quad round headlamps and chrome-plated bumper/surround had a large vertical center divider on the Charger. The front and rear bumpers of the Charger R/T and Super Bee were available with an optional color bumper group, not available with the concealed headlamps. The colored bumpers were created by spraying unchromed

*The flat-black vinyl decal on the hood of a Hemi Orange 1971 Charger Super Bee. The Scat Pack bee takes a prominent place in the center of the graphic design.*

*This is the optional J81 black rear deck spoiler on a Dark Bronze Metallic 1971 Charger Super Bee. Note the distinctive Scat Pack bee on the passenger's side of the deck lid.*

*This is an overhead view of an EV2 Hemi Orange 1971 Charger R/T with an optional black vinyl roof, Rallye wheels, and standard black stripe. (Kori Alexander Photo)*

The optional grille with retractable headlights and headlight washers on a Plum Crazy 1971 Charger R/T gave the nose a clean look. This R/T has an optional white vinyl roof, dual white stripe tires, and Magnum 500 wheels.

The headlight washer and retractable headlight mechanism of a Plum Crazy 1971 Charger R/T. Note the extra hood bumper attachment threaded hole that was changed later in production.

steel bumpers with a layer of urethane that was then painted in limited body colors. The Charger R/T and Super Bee colored bumpers were only available in Bright Orange, Citron Yella, Hemi Orange, Go Green Go, Plum Crazy, and Dark Green. The 1971 Charger R/T and Charger Super Bee were available in 24 color schemes, including the extra-cost High-Performance shades of C7 Plum Crazy, J6 Green Go, V2 Hemi Orange, and Y3 Citron Yella.

### Interior

Standard interior trim in the Charger R/T and optional in the Super Bee consisted of full-foam all-vinyl high-back bucket seats with integral head restraints. A fixed center cushion and folding front center armrest were optional at extra cost. The bucket seat interior was available in blue, green, tan, black, gunmetal, white, and gold. The Charger R/T and Super Bee were also available with an optional trim scheme of cloth and vinyl high-back bucket seats with integral head restraints in green, black, and orange/black.

A total of 3,118 Charger R/T and 5,054 Charger Super Bee two-door hardtops were built for the 1971 model year.

This is the standard black vinyl interior trim with pleated bucket seats in a 1971 Charger R/T. The center console and armrest are optional equipment. The sports-type Rallye instrument panel was standard on the R/T.

This Plum Crazy 1971 Charger R/T has an optional chrome-plated N91 rear deck luggage rack. A rear spoiler was not available when the luggage rack was ordered. This Charger also has an optional white vinyl roof.

## 1971 Charger R/T Engine options

The standard engine in the 1971 Charger R/T was a 440-ci raised-block Magnum V-8 rated at 370 hp at 4,600 rpm and 380 ft-lbs of torque at 3,200 rpm. The 440 Magnum was equipped with a single Carter AVS 4-barrel carburetor and still had the same 4.32 x 3.75–inch bore and stroke as previous years. The 440 Magnum V-8 was also available as an option in the 1971 Charger SE.

An optional engine for the 1971 Charger R/T was the 440 RB V-8 with three Holley 2-barrel carburetors. The 440 Six-Pack engine had a 10.2:1 compression ratio and produced 390 hp at 4,700 rpm and 490 ft-lbs of torque at 3,200 rpm.

Just 178 Charger R/Ts were built with the 440 Six-Pack option in the 1971 model year.

The second optional engine available in the 1971 Charger R/T was the 426-ci Hemi V-8. This was the last year for the Hemi, which finally succumbed to emissions and fuel mileage concerns. The 1971 version of the Hemi produced 425 hp at 4,600 rpm and 490 ft-lbs of torque at 4,000 with a 10.2:1 compression ratio. The Hemi was still equipped with two Carter AFB 4-barrel carburetors and its iconic wide black crackle-finish valvecovers. The Hemi was painted Hemi Orange.

Only 63 1971 Charger R/T hardtops were equipped with a 426 Hemi engine in 1971.

## 1971 Charger Super Bee Engine Options

The standard engine in a 1971 Charger Super Bee was a 383-ci Magnum B-block V-8 with a bore and stroke of 4.25 x 3.75 inches. The 383 Magnum had a compression ratio of 8.5:1 and produced 300 hp at 4,800 rpm and 410 ft-lbs of torque at 3,400 rpm. The 383 Magnum had a single 4-barrel carburetor.

The second optional engine in the 1971 Charger Super Bee was the small-block 340-ci V-8. The 340 developed 275 hp and 340 ft-lbs of torque with a 10.3:1 compression ratio. Horsepower ratings changed for the 1971 model year from the previous gross to net horsepower so they cannot be directly compared. The old gross system measured the engine with no accessories, but the new net system reduced the horsepower ratings by rating the engines with all normal accessories. This change would serve to reduce the insurance surcharges based

*Another view of a 1971 Charger 440 Magnum V-8 engine. This Charger is equipped with optional factory air conditioning. Note the mounting of the A/C condenser in front of the radiator.*

**The engine compartment of a Dark Bronze Metallic 1971 Charger Super Bee with the optional 426 Hemi engine was even a tight fit for B-Bodies. The Hemi was not available with air conditioning.**

*This is a detail view of the bright 426 Hemi engine callout badge on the hood of a Dark Bronze Metallic 1971 Charger Super Bee. This Hemi-powered Super Bee has the standard Ramcharger fresh air system in the hood.*

on horsepower.

One of the optional engines for the 1971 Charger Super Bee was the same 440-ci V-8 with three 2-barrel carburetors that was offered in the Charger R/T. Like the R/T version, the Six-Pack Super Bee had a 10.2:1 compression ratio and produced 390 hp at 4,700 rpm and 490 ft-lbs of torque at 3,200 rpm. Only 99 Super Bee hardtops were produced with the 440 Six-Pack option.

The next engine option for the 1971 Charger Super Bee was the 426 Hemi V-8, producing 425 hp at 4,600 rpm and 490 ft-lbs of torque at 4,000 rpm with a 10.2:1 compression ratio. The Super Bee Hemi had two Carter AFB 4-barrel carburetors and was identical to the engine used in the 1971 Charger R/T.

### Transmission Options

The 1971 Dodge Charger R/T had a standard cast-aluminum case A727 3-speed TorqueFlite automatic transmission when equipped with the 440 V-8 engines. The TorqueFlite was operated with either a column- or console-mounted chrome shift lever, depending on the interior options. The 1971 Super Bee with the 383 4-barrel V-8 only was the less expensive cast-iron case 3-speed manual transmission. The 3-speed was fully synchronized in all forward speeds, so you could downshift to low gear while the car was still moving. The 3-speed manual was available column-mounted, floor-mounted, and console-mounted, depending on the model. The A727 TorqueFlite was optional with the Super Bee 383 V-8. A special small-diameter (11-inch) torque converter with a high-stall speed was standard with the Super Bee.

A cast-iron case A833 4-speed manual transmission with a 2.44:1 low gear was standard with the 426 Hemi and 440 and optional with a 2.47:1 low gear with the 383. The 4-speed used a Hurst shifter, which for the first time used a unique walnut-grain pistol grip design on a wide, flat Hurst chrome-plated handle. The chrome console-mounted shifter handle was curved to the left and back, as in the previous year, while the floor-mounted version was curved back and up. Original handles had a distinct taper in thickness toward the top. Both shifters used a pleated black rubber boot. The Hemi was available with an optional TorqueFlite automatic transmission.

### Rear Axle Options

The standard rear axle with the 1971 Charger R/T with a 383, 440, or 426 Hemi engine and TorqueFlite automatic transmission was the Chrysler 8¾-inch banjo-type, which was available in ratios from 2.94:1 to 3.91:1, with 3.23:1 being standard. A 1⅞-inch-diameter pinion stem differential used a carrier with Casting Number 2881489. A special Performance Axle Group option (Sales Code 358) was available that provided a 3.55:1 rear axle gear ratio, special slip-drive fan, and an extra-wide high-performance radiator fan shroud. When a 4-speed transmission was ordered with the 440 or 426 Hemi engine, a 9¾-inch ring gear Dana 60 heavy-duty rear axle with a 3.54:1 gear ratio was used, with an optional 4.10:1 ratio provided when the Super Track Pak or Super Performance Axle Packages were ordered. Single-piston power front disc brakes with floating calipers were optional. Both axles were supported with Chrysler-designed heavy-duty longitudinal parallel leaf springs.

### Wheel and Tire Options

The 1971 Charger R/T was equipped with standard 14 x 6–inch stamped-steel wheels, which could be equipped with either a small hubcap or one of two new optional styled wheel covers. Optional 14-inch Magnum 500 styled Rallye road wheels with chrome trim rings were available. All-new 15-inch Rallye wheels with F60x15 Wide Oval tires were available as an option if heavy-duty brakes and Rallye Suspension were ordered.

Standard tires on the 383-powered Super Bee were F70 x 14–inch white sidewalls that were only available with the heavy-duty suspension and power disc brakes that came with the Super Bee. Standard wheels were 14x6 painted pressed steel.

*These dual white stripe tires and Magnum 500 styled wheels with trim rings were optional equipment on this FC7 Plum Crazy 1971 Charger R/T. These are original stock tires from 1971.*

### Advertising and Publicity

Charger R/T and Super Bee advertising and publicity was toned down a bit from the 1970 model. More emphasis was placed on the showroom brochure illustrations, and fewer magazine ads featured the Scat Pack line. One of the more

This vertical ad shows a red 1971 Charger R/T with body painted front bumper, Ramcharger fresh air system, and Magnum 500 styled wheels. Detailed images below show the features of the R/T. (Dodge, Plymouth, and the AMC design are registered trademarks of FCA US LLC)

This is an early ad promoting the 1971 Dodge Scat Pack showing a red Charger Super Bee with body color front bumper and a blue Demon 340. (Dodge, Plymouth, and the AMC design are registered trademarks of FCA US LL)

This 1971 ad shows both a red 1971 Charger Super Bee and a smaller photo of a green 1971 Charger R/T with optional white vinyl roof. A "Run with the Dodge Scat Pack" slogan is prominently featured. (Dodge, Plymouth, and the AMC design are registered trademarks of FCA US LLC)

Chapter 5: 1971   101

*A red 1971 Charger Super Bee with a body-color painted front bumper and an optional white vinyl roof is featured in a 1971 ad. This ad promotes the standard 383 Magnum V-8 engine and its use of regular fuel. To the right is a 1971 Charger R/T finished in red with an optional black vinyl roof and optional body-painted rear bumper. The text describes the standard equipment and features of the R/T and implies that the R/T is for adults. (Dodge, Plymouth, and the AMC design are registered trademarks of FCA US LLC)*

colorful magazine illustrations appeared in the October 1970 issue of *Motor Trend*. It was part of a six-page insert and featured a blond-haired Dodge girl posing in front of a blue 1971 Demon 340 and a red Charger Super Bee, both with optional vinyl roofs. The right rear pocket of her bright white jeans hosted a round, bright-red Scat Pack Club patch. The headline shouted, "If you want more run for your money . . . join the Pack. . . . The 1971 Dodge Scat Pack."

Another colorful page was in a showroom brochure and featured a bright-red 1971 Charger R/T with a black hood graphic and optional Ramcharger fresh air hood scoop. The headline read, "R/T. When this one snarls . . . they listen."

Dodge was clearly promoting the Scat Pack idea and performance image.

Another full-page vertical ad was run in a number of enthusiast magazines that showed a red 1971 Charger Super Bee at the top of the page in a desert location. It had a flat-black hood graphic and the optional Ramcharger fresh air hood scoop. Across the bottom of the page was a lime-green 1971 Charger R/T with a white vinyl roof in a full passenger-side view. The center of the colorful page had an image of the iconic Dodge Scat Pack Bee to the right.

Two more full-page ads were from the same six-page insert in the October 1970 *Motor Trend*. The first showed a front view of a red 1971 Charger Super Bee with line images below it of some of the special features of the Super Bee. The next page was a rear view of a red 1971 Charger R/T and below it were images of the wheel and tire, hood scoop, and tachometer available in the R/T.

### 1971 Dodge Challenger R/T

The 110-inch-wheelbase E-Body Challenger two-door hardtop was continued into the 1971 model with few changes. Most obvious was the grille, which now had two distinct rectangular bright-trimmed openings with a Dodge badge on the driver's side. The grille was not recessed into the front fascia as much as the 1970 model. The 1971 Challenger still had quad round headlights and broad bright-trim molding around the top of the fenders and hood edge. The convertible body type was dropped for the 1971 model year, but the Challenger R/T two-door hardtop models were still part of the lineup. The A93 coupe package, introduced in late 1970, replacing the roll-down quarter windows, was still offered on all but the R/T. A total of 4,630 Challenger R/T two-door hardtops were built for the 1971 model year.

*An original unrestored GY9 Dark Gold Metallic 1971 Challenger R/T. This car is equipped with a 426 Hemi engine, 4-speed transmission, and standard painted steel wheels. Note the correct F60x15 Goodyear Polyglas GT tires and black R/T tape stripe.*

#### Engine Options

The standard engine in a 1971 Dodge Challenger R/T was a 383-ci B-block Magnum V-8 with a single 4-barrel carburetor, a bore and stroke of 4.25 x 3.38 inches, and a compression ratio of 8.5:1, producing 250 hp (net) at 4,800 rpm. The 383 Magnum had an unsilenced air cleaner and dual exhaust, making 325 ft-lbs (net) of torque at 3,400 rpm. Most significant was the special high-performance camshaft used only in the 383 Magnum V-8. This camshaft had a lift of .450 inch on the intake and .465 inch on the exhaust valve. Intake and exhaust duration was 268 degrees for the intake and 284 degrees for the exhaust, with 46 degrees of overlap. The 383 Magnum V-8 used in the 1971 Challenger was also equipped with heavier valve springs, a standard windage tray, and dual exhaust. The 383 Magnum V-8 was equipped with a single Holley 4160 carburetor with vacuum-operated secondaries. Most 383 high-performance engines

*A driver-side rear quarter view shows a 1971 Challenger R/T finished in GA4 Light Gunmetal Metallic with a black vinyl roof and Rallye wheels. It also has chrome racing mirrors and the black R/T tape stripe.*

*This original, unrestored GB5 Bright Blue Metallic Challenger R/T convertible shows the redesign of the grille and front bumper for 1971. This Challenger has the optional white tape stripe and shaker hood scoop. It has optional Rallye wheels and raised white-letter Goodyear tires.*

*The 1971 Dodge Challenger R/T with a 340 engine was available with optional air conditioning and power disc front brakes. The 1971 models were now standard with electronic ignition and a modern transistorized voltage regulator.*

in 1971 were painted Chrysler Performance Orange, but some 1971 engines may have been finished in Chrysler Engine Medium Blue.

The first optional engine in the 1971 Dodge Challenger R/T was the LA-series V-8 with 340 ci that developed 235 hp and 310 ft-lbs of torque. Horsepower ratings changed for the 1971 model year from the previous gross to net horsepower, so they cannot be directly compared. The old standard BHP system measured the engine with no accessories, but the new net system reduced the horsepower ratings by rating the engines with all normal accessories. This change would serve to reduce the insurance surcharges based on horsepower.

The 340 V-8, indicated by an H on the VIN plate and a code of E55 on the fender data plate, had the same 4.04-inch bore and 3.31-inch stroke as the previous year. The 340 was equipped with a Carter Thermo-Quad 4-barrel carburetor that used a large, unsilenced air cleaner like the 1970 version. The air cleaner was finished in black crackle-finish with a painted metal insert that read "340 4-barrel." The 340 engine was painted Street Hemi Orange until April 1971, when the finish was changed to Chrysler Engine Blue.

The third engine option in the 1971 Challenger R/T was the 440-ci RB-based V-8 with three 2300 series 2-barrel Holley carburetors mounted on a Chrysler cast-iron intake manifold. This engine was identified with a V-code on the VIN and E87 on the body code plate. The 440 Magnum Six-Pack engine had a 10.3:1 compression ratio and was now rated at 330 hp (net) at 4,700 rpm and 410 ft-lbs (net) of torque at 3,200 rpm. A V in the VIN and a sales code of E87 on the fender data plate indicated the 440 Six-Pack.

The fourth engine option available with the 1971 Challenger R/T was the 426 Hemi V-8 rated at 425 gross hp at 5,000 rpm and 490 ft-lbs of gross torque at 4,000 rpm. The new net horsepower was rated at 350 at 5,000 rpm with net torque at 390 ft-lbs at 5,000 rpm. The two Carter AFB 4-barrel Hemi had a bore and stroke of 4.25 x 3.75 inches and a compression ratio of 10.3:1. The Hemi cast-iron and heads and cast-aluminum intake manifold were finished in Late Street Hemi Orange with a black crackle-finish air cleaner. The large, wide Hemi valvecovers had a black crackle finish. An R on the VIN and E74 on the body code plate indicated the Hemi. This was the final year for the Hemi.

### Transmission Options

The 1971 Dodge Challenger R/T had a standard cast-aluminum case A727 3-speed TorqueFlite automatic transmission when equipped with the 440 V-8 engines. The TorqueFlite was operated with either a column or console-mounted chrome shift lever, depending on the interior

*The 440 Six-Pack V-8 was available as an option in the 1971 Challenger R/T. The three Holley Six-Pack carburetors were topped with an open element air cleaner and distinctive decal.*

options. A cast-iron case A833 4-speed manual transmission with a 2.44:1 low gear was standard with the 426 Hemi and optional with the 440. The 4-speed used a Hurst shifter with a unique walnut-grain pistol grip design on a wide, flat Hurst chrome-plated handle. The chrome-plated console-mounted shifter handle was curved to the left and back, as in the previous year, while the floor-mounted version was curved back and up. Original handles had a distinct taper in thickness toward the top. Both shifters used a pleated black rubber boot. The Hemi was available with an optional TorqueFlite automatic transmission.

### Rear Axle Options

The standard rear axle with the 1971 Challenger R/T with a 440 or 426 Hemi engine and TorqueFlite automatic transmission was the Chrysler 8¾-inch banjo-type, which was available in ratios from 2.76:1 to 3.91:1, with 3.23:1 being standard. A 1⅞-inch-diameter pinion stem was used on all 1971 models, so they will have a carrier with Casting Number 2881489. A special Performance Axle Group option (Sales Code 358) was available that provided a 3.55:1 rear axle gear ratio, special slip-drive fan, and an extra-wide high-performance radiator fan shroud. When a 4-speed transmission was ordered with the 440 or 426 Hemi engine, a 9¾-inch ring gear Dana 60 heavy-duty rear axle with a 3.54:1 gear ratio was used. An optional 4.10:1 ratio was provided when the Super Track Pak or Super Performance Axle Packages were ordered. Single-piston power front disc brakes with floating calipers were optional.

### Wheel and Tire Options

The 1971 Challenger R/T was equipped with standard 14 x 6–inch stamped-steel wheels, which could be equipped with either a small hubcap or one of two new optional styled wheel covers. Optional 14-inch Magnum 500 styled road wheels with chrome trim rings were available. Because of the redesigned standard wheels, 15-inch wheels were no longer required for the 426 Hemi. All-new 15-inch Rallye wheels with F60x15

*A 1971 Challenger R/T hardtop with a black vinyl roof, Rallye wheels, and raised white-letter tires. The text lists the standard equipment and features of the Challenger R/T. (Dodge, Plymouth, and the AMC design are registered trademarks of FCA US LLC)*

*An unusual ad shows a pre-production 1971 Challenger T/A that was never built. The car has the black fiberglass hood and scoop and all of the T/A features, but it never really existed for sale. (Dodge, Plymouth, and the AMC design are registered trademarks of FCA US LLC)*

Wide Oval tires were available as an option if heavy-duty brakes and Rallye Suspension were ordered. All steel wheels were restyled for 1971 and featured a flat surface at the lug nut–mounting area.

### Advertising and Publicity

The 1971 Challenger R/T did not receive a lot of print advertising exposure, but it was included in the multi-page series that was published in a number of popular enthusiast magazines. The page for the Challenger featured a purple Challenger R/T placed in a desert setting with a young man posing alongside. The headline read, "It ain't Attila the Hun, but it ain't Mary Mild either." The text of the ad emphasizes its use of regular gasoline and its standard 383-ci V-8. Rather than pushing the winning dragstrip capabilities of the previous year, the Challenger is now touted as being perfectly suitable for driving to work "without blowing your budget." At the bottom of the page, line drawings showed images of some of the standard equipment and options available, such as a trunk rack, tachometer, quick-fill gas filler, and Rallye wheels.

The other page in this multi-page series displayed a yellow 1971 Challenger T/A with its flat-black hood panel and T/A hood scoop. The publication of this ad is strange because there never was a 1971 T/A. The people who produced the advertising were apparently not privy to the fact that no T/A Challenger was being built for the 1971 model year. The text read "End of the road for the Do-It-Yourself Kit," but it was, in fact, already the end of the road for the Challenger T/A by the end of the 1970 model year.

### 1971 Dodge Demon 340

For 1971, the Dodge Dart became a line of standard models, called the Dart, Dart Swinger, and Dart Custom, in two-door hardtop, special two-door hardtop, and four-door sedan, none of which were marketed or intended for high-performance purposes. Replacing the Dart was the entirely

*New for the 1971 model year was the Dodge Demon, based on the Plymouth Duster two-door sport coupe. The Demon was available with styled steel road wheels and optional vinyl roof. (Kurt Mann Photo)*

*The 1971 Dodge Demon was available with optional twin hood scoops, vinyl roof, full-length stripes, and flat-black hood graphic panels. This Demon is also equipped with a black rear deck spoiler. (Kurt Mann Photo)*

new 1971 Dodge LM29 Demon 340 two-door coupe, a body type based on the successful Plymouth 1970 Duster, both built on the same 108-inch wheelbase. It was considered a coupe rather than a hardtop because the quarter windows folded out rather than rolled down. The Demon name came with some controversy and included a small figure of a mischievous demon with a pitchfork as an identifying image on the car.

The Demon had smoother flowing rear body lines than the Dart due to the fastback styling and more integrated rear fascia, blended smoothly into the quarter panels. Six narrow vertical slots on each side of the rear deck lower panel represented the taillights. The front-end treatment of the Demon was identical to that of the Dart, and everything inside and out forward of the firewall was shared between the two. The 1971 Demon was available in 18 color schemes, including 3 high-impact shades. A total of 10,098 Demon 340s were made for the 1971 model year.

On March 1, 1971, near the middle of the model year, a new trim package was introduced for the Demon. It was called the Sizzler and, according to advertising material, was directed at those "buyers who, for one reason or another, can't afford the real hot machines." The Sizzler offered the trim and appearance options of the demon, such as the hood treatment and decals of the 340, but without the engine itself. The Sizzler was not an official part of the Scat Pack, but provided some buyers the same image for less cost. The Sizzler was identified by large red "Sizzler" decals.

## Engine Options

The standard engine in the 1971 Dodge Demon 340 was the LA-series V-8 with 340 ci that developed 235 hp and 310 ft-lbs of torque. Horsepower ratings changed for the 1971 model year from the previous gross to net horsepower, so they cannot be directly compared. The old standard brake horsepower system measured the engine with no accessories, but the new net system reduced the advertised horsepower by rating the engines with all normal accessories. This change would serve to reduce the insurance surcharges based on horsepower.

The 340 V-8, indicated by an H on the VIN plate and a code of E55 on the fender data plate, had a 4.04-inch bore and 3.31-inch stroke. The 340 had a 10.3:1 compression ratio and had a Carter Thermo-Quad 4-barrel carburetor that used a large, unsilenced air cleaner. Of course, premium fuel was required. The air cleaner was finished in black crackle finish with painted metal insert that read "340 4-barrel." The 340 engine was painted Street Hemi Orange until April 1971, when the finish was changed to Chrysler Engine Blue. Dual exhaust was standard with the Demon 340.

*The 1971 Dodge Demon 340 V-8 was finished in High-Performance Engine Orange and was topped with a Carter Thermo-Quad four-barrel carburetor. The black crackle-finish round air cleaner had a "Pie-Plate" that identified the 340 4-barrel engine that was standard equipment in the Demon. (Lindsey Fisher Photo)*

## Transmission Options

The 1971 Dodge Demon was equipped with a standard fully synchronized 3-speed manual shift transmission with a floor shift. An A-833 cast-iron case 4-speed manual transmission with a floor-mounted shifter was optional. A Torque-Flite 3-speed automatic transmission was also optional in the Demon 340.

## Rear Axle Options

The standard rear axle was a Chrysler 8¾-inch ring gear with a number of optional gear ratios. A 3.23:1 economy ratio was standard equipment, but lower gear ratios of 3.55:1 and 3.91:1 could be ordered for increased acceleration. The standard Rallye suspension was supported with heavy-duty front torsion bars, Firm-Ride shock absorbers, anti-sway bar, and heavy-duty rear longitudinal parallel leaf springs.

## Wheel and Tire Options

Standard brakes were 10 x 2¼–inch front and 10 x 1³⁄₂–inch rear brake drums. Power brakes and power disc brakes were optional on the Demon 340. Standard tires were E70x14 Fiberglass-belted mounted on 14x5.5J steel wheels. Rallye and styled road wheels were available as options.

### Advertising and Publicity

Advertising for the Demon was limited for the 1971 model year, but a full page showing a yellow Demon 340 was included in the multi-page section published in a number of popular enthusiast magazines. The Demon 340 coupe was shown parked in a remote desert location on a rocky surface and at the bottom of the ad were line images of the gauges, hood scoops, rear deck spoiler, and "Tuff" steering wheel available on the Demon 340. The text pointed out "the performance is a lot more than painted on."

The *1971* Scat Pack Club Operations Manual *and kit included a list of detailed materials that helped a dealer start and operate the club. The dealer received a prospect list, Hustle Stuff catalog, posters, and tune-up tips booklets. (Dodge, Plymouth, and the AMC design are registered trademarks of FCA US LLC)*

### The End of the Scat Pack

The end of the 1971 model year was clearly the end for the Dodge Scat Pack program and the Scat Pack Club. Most publicity and advertising for the 1972 model year concentrated on fuel economy, style, and low cost. Although the performance-oriented 383, 440 4-barrel, and 440 Six-Pack engines (only a select few Chargers received the 440-6), along with their related chassis equipment upgrades, were still available, they were merely a small note in the ads and order information, and it was obvious that Dodge and Chrysler were not interested in emphasizing these attributes to their buying public. The pressure from the government, fuel prices, and insurance companies had spelled out the end of the American performance car, as we knew it at the time.

*This ad shows a yellow 1971 Dodge Demon 340 Sport coupe equipped with an optional flat-black hood and twin hood nonfunctional scoops. The ad lists the standard and available features and equipment of the Demon 340. (Dodge, Plymouth, and the AMC design are registered trademarks of FCA US LLC)*

## CHAPTER 6

# 1968–1969

## TOWARD THE PLYMOUTH RAPID TRANSIT SYSTEM

*"The Plymouth Win-You-Over Beat Goes On."*

Although the actual Plymouth Rapid Transit System advertising and marketing program did not begin officially until the 1970 model year, the ideas, psychedelic artwork, and publicity began much earlier. By December 1967, print advertising was already showing up with the award-winning psychedelic art and marketing materials that would identify the program. Premier creative commercial artists such as Paul Williams, N. Dale Dalton, and David Bradesku produced wild and colorful artwork that would be remembered for years and helped create one of the most successful ad campaigns in history. The Rapid Transit System had not yet appeared but the familiar Plymouth slogan "The Plymouth Win-You-Over Beat Goes On," and the red heart still appeared on every ad and poster.

### Plymouth Performance for 1968

*A colorful poster shows a lineup of the red Road Runner, a green `Cuda, and a yellow GTX lined up, followed by billowing smoke. The bottom reads, "Motion by Plymouth, Volume II." (Dodge, Plymouth, and the AMC design are registered trademarks of FCA US LLC)*

Of course, the big news for Plymouth performance products in 1968 was the introduction of the Road Runner. The GTX, introduced for the 1967 model year, was a premium performance model of the Belvedere, but the Road Runner was a completely new idea based on offering high-performance at a lower price and without the premium frills for the young and/or entry-level buyer. The Road Runner was also the obvious choice for those who wanted performance over fluff and had no interest in the premium-line trim or options. The Barracuda line was carried over from the 1967 model year with few changes, but its performance image was enhanced forever by the announcement in early 1968 of the 1970 Hemi-powered Barracuda Super Stock package cars.

### 1968 Plymouth Belvedere GTX

The 1968 Plymouth Belvedere GTX, like all of the Dodge and Plymouth B-Body line, was a completely new and dramatic design for 1968. Gone were straight and angular lines

This 1968 RS23 Plymouth Belvedere GTX is finished in GG1 Forest Green Poly with a 304 Light Green vinyl roof. Note the distinctive dark GTX grille and performance hood and optional Magnum 500 styled steel wheels and red streak tires.

This passenger-side front quarter view shows an original, unrestored 1968 Plymouth RM21 Road Runner coupe finished in FF1 Mist Green Poly with a green (304) vinyl roof. This Road Runner is equipped with a 383 4-barrel engine, optional Magnum 500 styled chrome wheels (580), and red streak tires.

of 1967, replaced with a smoother and more modern styling theme with rounded and flowing sides and a completely new roof concept. The upper sides of the front fenders and rear quarters used a sculptured horizontal crease to accentuate the lines of the body. The Belvedere was still based on the same 116-inch-wheelbase unibody chassis as the 1967 models, but the bodies were up to 3 inches longer than the equivalent 1967 models. The GTX was available as either an RS23 two-door hardtop or an RS27 convertible.

### 1968 Plymouth Road Runner

The big news for Plymouth for the 1968 model year was the announcement of the Road Runner. The concept for the 1968 Road Runner came out of the very creative mind of Jack Smith, manager of the newly formed Plymouth midsized (B-Body) Product Planning Group. As one of his first assignments, Jack had been responsible for the highly successful 1967 Belvedere GTX program. By the spring of 1967, Plymouth vice president Robert S. Anderson decided that the company had to make a conscious effort to go after the 18- to 20+- year-old youth market. The first job was to change Plymouth's historically stodgy image. To accomplish this, the goal had to be to produce an attractive, high-performance car based on a less expensive low-line, low-cost, midsized model such as the Belvedere I two-door sedan. This enormous responsibility fell into the hands of Jack Smith.

Smith and his assistant, Gordon Cherry, developed the idea based on the 1968 RL21 Belvedere two-door coupe, but the choice of the name was supposed to be left to Plymouth's new advertising firm of Young & Rubicam. As with many plans and ideas, they don't always work out the way they were planned. Cherry happened to be watching a Warner Brothers Road Runner and Coyote cartoon one Saturday and the idea came to him that this was the right image for their new performance car. Smith agreed with Cherry that the Road Runner "was hot off the line, it was fast, it never got beaten, and could stop on a dime." The choice was obvious.

The next challenge was to get the new model developed and into production in time for the regular new model release in September 1967, less than six months away. Early in the project it was clear that something would have to be done to negotiate arrangements with Warner Brothers to secure permission to use images of the Road Runner on the car and in its advertising and publicity materials. The first step was to quickly have the name registered with the Automobile Manufacturer's Association, reserving it for exclusive use by Chrysler Corporation. The name itself was public domain, generic, so that was not a problem. The image of the bird was another story entirely and that image was critical to the success of the product.

One six-hour conference call between Smith and the powers at Warner Brothers completed the necessary negotiations and the agreement was complete. Smith recalled in a recent interview that the price for the use of the Road Runner image was between $40,000 and $50,000. Chrysler's styling director Dick Macadam was totally against placing any decal of a cartoon bird on one of his cars, so it took some bit of trickery on the part of Smith to get that done. Smith invited some important dealers to the unveiling and managed to place the new decals on the show car. When Chrysler executives saw the dealers' positive reactions to the name and the bird logo, that closed the deal and the Road Runner image was born.

### 1968 Plymouth Barracuda

The 1968 Barracuda looked very much like the 1967 model except for the small, round bright-rimmed side markers at the front and rear quarters and minor trim changes to the grille and badging. The new side markers were required and standard on all cars, according to new 1968 Federal automobile safety regulations. The new Barracuda was still based on the same 108-inch-wheelbase unibody platform and was available in three body types: BH29 two-door fastback BH23 sport hardtop, two-door sport coupe, and BH27 two-door convertible.

The performance package available with the 1968 Barracuda was called the "Formula S" and offered a high-performance 340 ($212) or 383 ($251) V-8, 4-speed manual transmission, heavy-duty clutch and suspension, and dual exhaust. A special TorqueFlite 3-speed automatic transmission was optional.

### Advertising

One of the first ads to appear was in the November 1967 issue of *Popular Hot Rodding*, which showed the driver-side front of a light green 1968 Plymouth GTX with a dragstrip Christmas tree with a green light lit and clouds of orange, pink, and purple smoke coming off the back of the car as it accelerates away from a starting line. Large block text above the car states, "GTX. That's short for Adios!" Smaller text at the top of the page describes the long list of special features and details of the 440-ci V-8 that powers the GTX. At the end of the text is the slogan "the Plymouth win-you-over beat goes on." Because no artist's name is visible, it is hard to tell, but this may be a Paul Williams' illustration by the style of the drawing.

Another early piece was a December 1967 ad in *Hot Rod* that featured a David Bradesku illustration of a bright-blue 1968 Plymouth Road Runner with the front wheels leaping off the ground with the car followed by willowing clouds of orange, red, green, purple, and yellow curling up behind the rear of the car. As in most of his ads for Plymouth, Bradesku managed to always sneak his signature last name along the lines of one of the smoke clouds, barely visible unless one was looking for it.

In its January 1968 issue, *Hot Rod* featured a vertical ad with a front view of a red 1968 Barracuda launching itself past a dragstrip Christmas tree on an obvious black strip surface. Colorful headers from beneath the car billowed smoke in bright orange, purple, and tan that followed in large wispy clouds behind the car. Bold text above the car said only, "Shortcut." Smaller text at the top of the page described the 340 and 383 V-8 engines in detail. The smaller line beneath the text told the reader where a 24 x 17–inch cartoon poster of the ad could be ordered by sending one dollar to the address provided. Bradesku's last name was just barely visible in the lower-left tan smoke cloud.

A two-page spread appeared in the same issue of *Hot Rod* that showed a large side view image of a blue 1968 Road Runner with the light-blue Road Runner bird standing at its left rear holding a white racing helmet. The car was an artistic rendition posed against a white background with mountains in the background and a small "Salt Flats" sign posted. A two-tone brown and tan smoke trail billowed out into the distance from behind the car. Text telling about the details was at the lower

*This wildly psychedelic ad showing a 1968 GTX was an opening shot at the beginning of what would later become the Rapid Transit System for Plymouth. The headline, "GTX. That's short for 'Adios!'," was the lead that hinted of what was to come over the next few years. (Dodge, Plymouth, and the AMC design are registered trademarks of FCA US LLC)*

Chapter 6: 1968–1969

Artist David Bradesku created this large piece of psychedelic art. It was one of the more-unique ads that Plymouth used in 1968. Bradesku, like some of the other Plymouth advertising artists, found a way to hide his name in his artwork so it would not be forgotten. (Dodge, Plymouth, and the AMC design are registered trademarks of FCA US LLC)

left and larger black letters of "Beep-Beep!" were at the lower left. A Plymouth and Chrysler logo were printed at the lower right side of the page. An artist's signature was not visible on the illustration.

The February 1968 issue of *Hot Rod* featured a full-page color ad with a psychedelic illustration of a rear view of an orange 426 Street Hemi engine and silver 4-speed transmission with yellow, orange, and purple smoke billowing from the header collectors. Inside one of the purple smoke clouds the

This colorful Plymouth Barracuda ad was another great example of the artwork of David Bradesku, who produced a lot of the psychedelic style of art during this era, some similar to the work done by German-born artist Peter Max. This ad appeared in the January 1968 issue of *Hot Rod*. (Dodge, Plymouth, and the AMC design are registered trademarks of FCA US LLC)

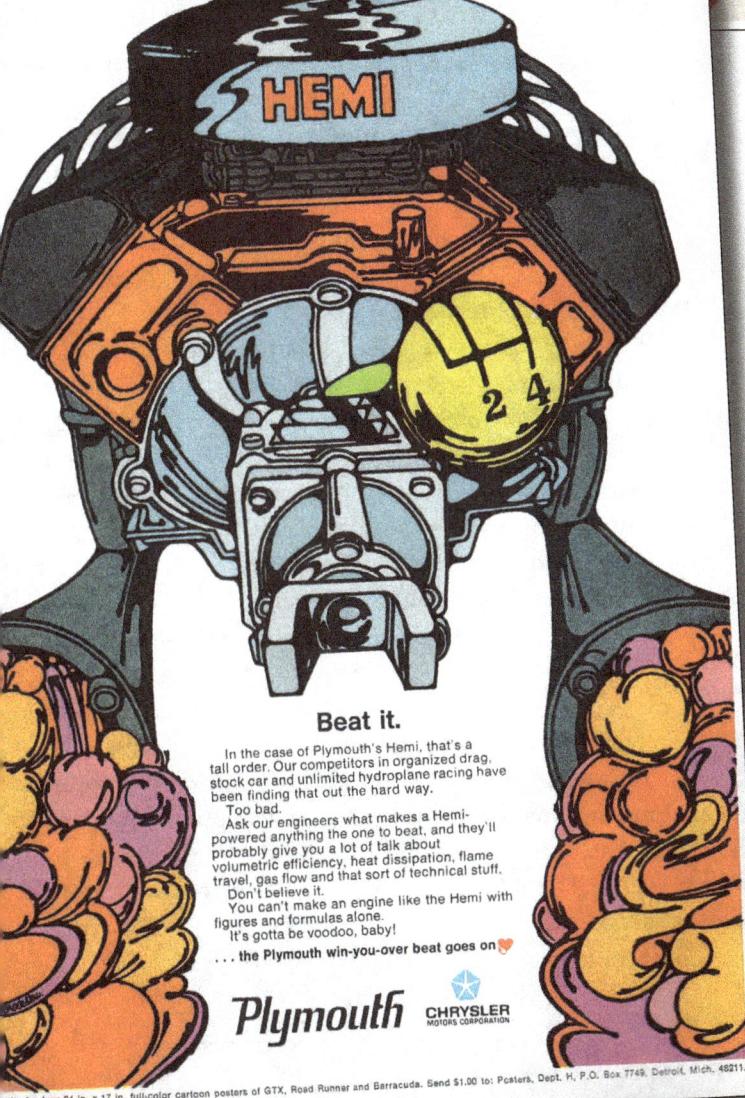

*A two-page ad based on the psychedelic artwork that identified Plymouth's aggressive advertising program of 1968 through 1971. This ad portrays a bright blue 1968 Road Runner in the desert with the iconic Road Runner just arriving from the Salt Flats, presumably for attaining land speed records. (Dodge, Plymouth, and the AMC design are registered trademarks of FCA US LLC)*

artist Dave Bradesku's name could just barely be read. Just beneath the rear of the transmission output shaft were the words "Beat it" in bold black letters. Beneath that line the smaller text continued, "In the case of Plymouth's Hemi, that's a tall order." This was followed by more text telling the reader about the engineering development and competition experience of the hemispherical combustion chamber powerplant. The bottom of the ad listed the ordering information for the four 24x17 full-color cartoon posters of the GTX, Road Runner, and Barracuda that could be purchased for $1.

*David Bradesku's psychedelic-style color ad was published in the February 1968 issue of Hot Rod and portrays the power and winning accomplishments of Plymouth's 426 Hemi engine. (Dodge, Plymouth, and the AMC design are registered trademarks of FCA US LLC)*

Chapter 6: 1968–1969

### 1969 High-Performance Plymouths

The Plymouth lineup for 1969 was much like that of 1968. Obvious changes across the lineup included updates from small, round side markers to larger rectangular pieces, as required by federal regulations. Cosmetic model changes to the grille and tail panel assembly differentiated 1968 models from the 1969 models in the B-Body Road Runner, GTX, and A-Body 'Cuda and Barracuda S.

#### 1969 Plymouth Belvedere GTX

GTX's third time through the sale brochure saw it maintain its top billing as Plymouth's B-Body luxury and performance car. Standard again was the 440, producing 375 hp with the lone engine option being the 426 Hemi. With 1968 being the high watermark for GTX production, 1969 saw a slight dip in sales to 14,902 units, as Road Runners continued to eat into the sales of the GTX.

**Shown here is the driver-side front quarter of an original, unrestored 1969 Road Runner RM23 two-door hardtop with optional 14-inch sport wheel covers and white sidewall tires. This Road Runner is finished in a special-order (99) Bahama Yellow color with a black vinyl roof.**

**This is the driver-side view of a 1969 Belvedere GTX two-door hardtop finished in BB1 Black with a black vinyl roof and optional Magnum 500 styled steel wheels with brushed trim rings. This GTX has a red interior and optional chrome fender-mounted turn signals.**

#### 1969 Road Runner and A12 6-Barrel Package

The sophomore campaign added a convertible model to the already potent Road Runner lineup. Sales nearly doubled from 1968 as more than 86,000 Road Runners traversed the assembly lines at Lynch Road, St. Louis, and Los Angeles. Road Runner had established itself as a budget-conscious supercar.

A new and exciting model option was announced midyear 1969 for the Road Runner. After February 1969, Plymouth offered the Sales Code A12 1969-1/2 Six-Barrel engine conversion package to the Road Runner (and on its Dodge Super Bee cousin). The package was priced at $462.80 more than the cost of a standard Road Runner 116-inch-wheelbase WM21 coupe and WM23 two-door hardtop. Although its primary position was the replacement of the standard 383 4-barrel V-8, the package included a substantial list of unique components. The standard engine in the 1969 Road Runner was the 383 4-barrel with the 426 Hemi as the only option.

The 440 4-barrel V-8 was normally only available as the standard powerplant in the GTX, so the VIN on the A12 package will always show an "M" code, indicating a special-order V-8. The body code plate will always show the E63 engine code for a 383 4-barrel V-8 at the bottom line and a 999 on the top line to indicate a special order V-8. The special package was indicated by the A12 code on the third line of the plate.

#### 1969 Plymouth Barracuda

The 1969 Barracuda looked very much like the 1967 and 1968 models, except for minor trim changes to the grille and badging. The most obvious change was the use of rectangular side markers, replacing the small, round ones used in 1968. The new Barracuda was still based on the same 108-inch-wheelbase unibody platform and was still available in three body types: BH29 two-door fastback BH23 sport hardtop, two-door sport coupe, and BH27 two-door convertible.

The performance package available with the 1969 Barracuda was called the 'Cuda and offered a high-performance A-block 340 or B-block 383 V-8, 4-speed manual transmission, heavy-duty clutch and suspension, and dual exhaust. A special TorqueFlite 3-speed automatic transmission was optional. Because in 1969 the 'Cuda was a specific option group on the Barracuda, there was no breakout of production figures.

A total of 12,757 BH23 Barracuda two-door hardtops, 17,788 Barracuda two-door fastbacks, and 1,442 Barracuda convertibles were built for the 1969 model year.

*This yellow 1969 Plymouth `Cuda 340 has an optional and very rare Mod Top vinyl roof. This `Cuda has the optional black tape stripe, red streak tires, and full wheel covers. This is an original, unrestored low-mileage `Cuda. The interior trim was designed to complement the roof.*

*This is a red 1969 `Cuda fastback sport coupe with standard painted steel wheels, small hubcaps, and red streak tires. The original, unrestored `Cuda has red vinyl interior trim.*

## 1969 `Cuda

An addition to the 1969 engine lineup was the special RB-based 440-ci V-8 powered `Cuda. The 440 was rated at 375 hp and had special cast-iron exhaust manifolds modified to clear the chassis and steering gear. The 440 was available only with a TorqueFlite transmission and 3.55:1 rear axle gears. A 4-speed with the 440 V-8 would have required the heavy-duty Dana 60 rear axle, which was not readily adaptable to the A-Body platform tread width. These cars were built on the line coded as a 383 and then sent to Hurst to have the 440 engine and related parts installed. The body code plate will show an "M" code identifying a special order engine and an "A13" 440 engine conversion package code that was available on both Coupe and Fastback body styles.

## Advertising

Some of the earliest images of the new 1969 Plymouth line appeared in the factory dealer brochures. Rather than rely on artistic illustrations, these catalogs and brochures used accurate real color photographs, posed in attractive outdoor settings. The GTX was shown in metallic green with a green vinyl roof, redline tires, and Magnum styled wheels. A young father and his son were posed happily behind the passenger-side front fender. The headline at the upper left said, "GTX. Reverent racing men have long called it The Boss. This year it'll be 'Boss Sir.'" The remainder of the small text described the details and special available features of the car to attract sales.

In the same brochure, a red 1969 Road Runner hardtop with wide dual black racing stripes on its hood was posed in a hazy desert setting with Monument Valley peaks in the background. The headline stated, "You'll like the sound of a lot of things, including the "'Beep-Beep!'" The end of the text pointed out that, "It all adds up to a clean, unfrilled performance car that a young guy can afford." Another page in the brochure showed a yellow Road Runner hardtop and the rear of a green Road Runner convertible in the same desert setting. Its text read, "Pity the poor coyote. Now he's up against another bird."

Print advertising for the 1969 Performance Plymouths early in the model year featured more of the large psychedelic art posters and double-page magazine spreads similar to those offered the previous year. These included wild and colorful artwork by Young & Rubicam agency artist Paul Williams. Williams' art took on a different style and colors than those of David Bradesku and are immediately identifiable. His work seems to be always signed somewhere in the illustration. There was also emphasis on the recent selection by *Motor Trend* of the Road Runner as the Car of the Year for 1969.

One of the more significant ads depicting the *Motor Trend* award was a two-page spread showing a red 1969 383 Road Runner posed in a side view in the desert similar to a 1968 ad but with the car facing to the right rather than to the left. The purple Road Runner bird posed at the driver-side rear and a yellow smoke trail led off to the distance with orange and blue mountains behind the car. The artwork is by Paul Williams and his signature appears at the upper left just below the mountains. The car has a black vinyl roof and Magnum styled wheels, an effort to portray the options Plymouth suggested to order with the car. Most important, the top of the spread featured a headline that said, "*Motor Trend* tells it like it is . . . Plymouth Road Runner named Car of the Year." Four columns of small text beneath the headline detailed the equipment, features, and options available with the Road Runner. Of course, the bottom of the page had the Plymouth logo on the left and a Warner Brothers-Seven Arts Copyright notice at lower right.

One of the layouts that appeared in *Hot Rod* featured a dark brown GTX shown in a large, purposely distorted front view. The tires were extra wide and the car was passing a dragstrip Christmas tree with a cheering crowd off to the left of the illustration. In the background, large clouds of billowing green, blue, and purple smoke filled the sky. The large letters at the bottom of the pages noted, "Plymouth Tells It Like It Is." Above the large text, smaller writing told, "1969 'BOSS' makes first timed runs—NHRA mans the clocks." At the lower right another note said, "See test results, page 119." Another page in the same magazine provided information on the performance runs and capability of the GTX to readers.

Ads for the introduction of the new 1969-1/2 Road Runner A12 Six-Barrel came a little later in the model year. One interesting ad appeared in the July 1969 Issue of *Car Craft*. This vertical full-page ad featured the artistic portrayal of a front-end view

*A number of Plymouth posters featured notice that the 1969 Road Runner had been awarded Car of the Year by* Motor Trend. *This poster featured the iconic Road Runner bird holding the award next to a red Road Runner in the desert. (Dodge, Plymouth, and the AMC design are registered trademarks of FCA US LLC)*

*A poster with psychedelic artwork signed by artist Paul Williams featured a blue Hemi Road Runner accelerating at the dragstrip with blasts of flames exiting its header pipes. The Motor Trend* Car of the Year *award was the prominent message. (Dodge, Plymouth, and the AMC design are registered trademarks of FCA US LLC)*

*This signed Paul Williams poster shows an orange 1969 GTX charging off the line at a dragstrip with smoke billowing out from the rear tires. The headline announces that the "Boss" makes first timed runs. (Dodge, Plymouth, and the AMC design are registered trademarks of FCA US LLC)*

An 11 x 17–inch promotional poster features a green 1969 'Cuda 340 with optional black stripes and twin hood scoops shown in signed psychedelic artwork by artist Paul Williams. (Dodge, Plymouth, and the AMC design are registered trademarks of FCA US LLC)

One of Plymouth Division's promotional posters features an overhead view of a red 1969-1/2 Road Runner A12 440 Six-Barrel with the throats of the three carburetors showing through the scoop opening. (Dodge, Plymouth, and the AMC design are registered trademarks of FCA US LLC)

of a bright orange Road Runner Six-Barrel with its aggressive functional scoop and flat-black fiberglass hood. Rather than the smoke usually shown in these ads, this one used radiating black lines from the center of the roof against a gray background to emphasize the impact of the car. A Plymouth badge showed up clearly against the black hood held closed by chrome hood pins and cables. No artist signature is visible, but the work appears to be from Paul Williams. Small text beneath the illustration says, "ETs and specs on our newest Road Runner: 440 cubes, Glass hood and (Heh-Heh!) Three Holleys!" Large text announces the Plymouth slogan of "Plymouth Tells It Like It Is." The rest of the page lists the details of the equipment and options on the Six-Barrel Road Runner.

Another unusual and very artistic Paul Williams' two-page layout appeared in a different issue of *Hot Rod* and showed an aggressive front-end view of a green 'Cuda 340 launching from the starting line of a dragstrip with the starting line Christmas tree in the background. The 'Cuda is equipped with the twin hood scoops and dual black racing stripes and its header outlets are blowing heavy red and purple smoke, filling the background. The large black letters at the bottom of the page stated, "Plymouth Tells It Like It Is." Above that line was smaller text that read, "Cuda 340 storms the quarter right in front of NHRA and everybody." A small line at the lower right told readers to "See test results, page 150." This ad also told readers how and where to order a copy of Plymouth's wild new high-performance car catalog for 50 cents.

### The Slot Car World

One of the more popular pastimes for enthusiasts of all ages in 1969 was the sport of slot car racing. This exciting activity consisted of racing model cars on a track with a slot that held the car in the center of the track. An electric motor provided power, propelling it around the circuit at scale high speeds. Chrysler, Plymouth, and other manufacturers saw this as an opportunity to capture the interest of the young fans who might become future buyers of performance products. In 1969, Plymouth offered "Shutdown! Plymouths electric drag race game."

Posters and ads for the game were distributed and published everywhere and your attention was captured immediately by the lead headline that read, "RRRRRev up with

Shutdown." The text said, "Shutdown your friends. Shutdown your kids. Plymouth's new shift-for-yourself Super Stock racing set." The set was available through Plymouth dealers who supplied order forms to send your $14.95 to Plymouth to get a set for yourself. It was clear that promoting Plymouth performance and racing were big priorities during this era.

The box for the set pictured one of the now-familiar colorful psychedelic illustrations by David Bradesku of two powerful Plymouth racers lunging at you in red, orange, green, and yellow clouds of billowing tire smoke. On the left was a 1969 GTX with a front license plate that read, "The Boss," referring, of course, to Ronnie Sox, the winningest and most popular member of Chrysler's drag racing teams. On the right was a similar red and blue 1969 Plymouth, but this one was a Road Runner driven by the always-winning Road Runner bird himself leaning out the driver's side window.

The colorful cover artwork for the Shut Down Plymouth Super Stock Racing Set. The image shows a Road Runner and a GTX racing each other at a dragstrip. They represent the actual Plymouth drag race cars driven by Ronnie Sox around the country. (Dodge, Plymouth, and the AMC design are registered trademarks of FCA US LLC)

The cover of a promotional kit sent to Plymouth dealers to instruct them on the advantages of the Motor Trend Car of the Year Award concerning their sales and traffic. (Dodge, Plymouth, and the AMC design are registered trademarks of FCA US LLC)

# CHAPTER 7
# THE RAPID TRANSIT SYSTEM IS BORN

*"As the name implies, it's a system; a total concept in transportation that goes far beyond eight pistons and a steering wheel."*

Although the ideas and purpose of Plymouth's amazing new advertising program began at the beginning of the 1970 model year, the evolution of that program developed by increments over the two previous years. The emphasis on performance came out of the needs of the car-buying public of the time, driven by the peak of the Baby Boomer's desire for speed, power, and style. No one wanted their car to be like everyone else's and a person's means of transportation had to be a direct reflection of their own personality and life. The Plymouth Division and the advertising genius behind it would direct them into an entirely new realm of artistic expression and excitement for 1970.

Model year new car announcements came on September 19, 1969, and along with them came Plymouth's new Rapid Transit System. As Plymouth marketing put it, "We now have a system . . . it's a total concept in high-performance transportation which combines the lessons learned in competition, an information network, people who understand high-performance, trick parts and great products." They continued with: "The Rapid Transit System is years of racing experience . . . The Rapid Transit System is information . . . the System is high-performance parts." They ended with, "Above all, the Rapid Transit System is the product, everything from

*A colorful Plymouth Rapid Transit System logo was used on much of its advertising for the 1970 model year. Note the stylized illustrations of the five Plymouth models in the program. (Dodge, Plymouth, and the AMC design are registered trademarks of FCA US LLC)*

a 'sleeper' with a 340, to a giant 440-ci, all the way up to a Hemi-Cuda with a Quivering Exposed."

It was clear at the beginning of the model year that the product was indeed what the Rapid Transit System was about

One of the first Rapid Transit System ads published for the 1970 model year. This ad is a two-page spread that features a caricature of all of the famous people involved with Plymouth performance, racing, and publicity such as Ronnie Sox, Buddy Martin, Tom Hoover, and many more. (Dodge, Plymouth, and the AMC design are registered trademarks of FCA US LLC)

and that line of products from Plymouth expanded for the 1970 model year. The creative advertising and marketing program was exciting, artistic, and different but the cars were what made the difference to the public. In addition to the standard line from 1969, the Plymouth stable now included a new A-Body Valiant Duster and a completely new E-Body 'Cuda, all the way up to the massive but powerful C-Body Sport Fury GT, a product that had not been previously marketed as a performance car.

### 1970 Rapid Transit System Lineup

The 1970 model year saw a new and enlarged lineup for Plymouth high-performance products, and the Rapid Transit

A two-page spread was used extensively in advertising and showroom brochures to show all of the high-performance 1970 Plymouth models included in the new Rapid Transit System program. (Dodge, Plymouth, and the AMC design are registered trademarks of FCA US LLC)

System program identified them and supported them in great detail. The intention was that all levels and ages of performance enthusiasts would have their desires met and become lifelong buyers. Each of the line of Plymouth models offered a special performance version directly marketed to the youthful buyers interested in displaying their identity through their car.

## B-Body Styling

The styling changes for the 1970 B-Body Plymouth were not as dramatic as the 1968 model, but there were enough new and distinctive features to set them apart from the pack. The body structures were an evolution of the 1968 and 1969 bodies, but the changes to the front and rear designs were altered across all lines. All performance Belvedere body types were continued for 1970 and included the two-door hardtop, coupe, and convertible.

## Exterior

The front end of the Belvedere GTX and Road Runner, like the rest of the B-Body Plymouth line, received more subtle changes than its Coronet stablemate, but the body shell was modified from the 1969 version. The horizontal creases at the top edge of the front fenders and rear quarters were eliminated, which gave the body a smoother, cleaner appearance. Rather than the "dog bone" shape of 1969, the new quad-headlight Plymouth grille presented a more horizontal image with a B shape. Round parking and turn-signal lamps were integrated into the chrome front bumper. Taillights were also redesigned and were changed into rounded rectangles on each side of the rear lower deck panel.

## 1970 GTX

The 1970 Plymouth RS23 GTX was based on the two-door hardtop Belvedere body and styling with subtle changes that emphasized the performance potential of the GTX. The GTX was not available as a convertible in 1970 for the first time in its production life. Most noticeable was the bright GTX badge on either side of the rear quarters. The badge was placed on the simulated air scoops centered on the front of the rear quarters just behind the door openings. These were identical to the scoops used on the 1970 Road Runner. The dark mesh quad headlight front grille was identical to that used on the Road Runner, except for the large, bright GTX badge in its center. A total of 7,748 GTX two-door hardtops were built for the 1970 model year. A total of 678 of them were equipped with the 440 Six-Barrel and 76 with the 426 Hemi engine.

*A driver-side front quarter view of an original unrestored black 1970 GTX two-door hardtop with optional flat-black tape stripe, Rallye wheels, and raised white-letter Goodyear Polyglas tires.*

*Note the distinctive bright-rimmed flat-black GTX rear deck lower trim panel and small GTX badge on the passenger's side of the deck lid.*

*This GTX has the optional Air Grabber system, black hood stripes, and hood pins.*

Chapter 7: The Rapid Transit System Is Born 121

*A driver-side rear quarter view shows the optional flat-black rear deck spoiler and black rear deck lower panel of this Limelight 1970 GTX two-door hardtop.*

*The engine compartment of a 1970 GTX two-door hardtop equipped with a 440 Six-Barrel engine and Air Grabber fresh air intake system. Note the correct battery and red battery caps.*

*The driver-side rear view of the rare optional V1G black Gator Grain vinyl roof on a W1 White 1970 GTX two-door hardtop.*

### Engine Options

The standard engine in the 1970 Plymouth GTX was the 440-ci V-8. The standard powerplant was a 440-ci V-8 based on the RB (raised-block) configuration. The single Carter AVS 4-barrel 440 Commando produced 375 hp at 4,600 rpm and 480 ft-lbs of torque at 3,200 rpm. The 440 had a bore and stroke of 4.32 x 3.75 inches and a compression ratio of 9.7:1, lowered from the previous year. All 1970 440 engines were painted Chrysler Performance Orange. The 440 Commando single 4-barrel engine used a black crackle-finish unsilenced air cleaner.

A new engine option for the 1970 GTX was the 440-ci RB-based V-8 with three 2-barrel Holley carburetors mounted on a Chrysler cast-iron intake manifold, replacing the cast-aluminum Edelbrock unit used in 1969. This engine was identified with a V-code on the VIN and E87 on the body code plate. The 440 Super Commando Six-Barrel engine had a 10.5:1 compression ratio and was still rated at 390 hp at 4,700 rpm and 490 ft-lbs of torque at 3,200 rpm. The 1970 engine did not have the additional special components that came standard with the 1969-1/2 A12 Six-Barrel conversion engine package.

The only other optional engine available with the 1970 GTX was the 426 Hemi V-8 still rated at 425 hp at 5,000 rpm and 490 ft-lbs of torque at 4,000 rpm. The two Carter AFB 4-barrel Hemis had a bore and stroke of 4.25 x 3.75 inches and a compression ratio of 10.3:1. The major change for the Hemi in 1970 was the adoption of hydraulic valve lifters. The Hemi cast-iron and heads and cast-aluminum intake manifold were finished in Late Street Hemi Orange with a black crackle-finish air cleaner. The large, wide Hemi valve covers had a black crackle finish. An R on the VIN and E74 on the body code plate indicated the Hemi.

### Transmission Options

The standard equipment transmission for the 1970 GTX with the 440 single 4-barrel engine was the aluminum case A727 3-speed TorqueFlite automatic. The only optional trans-

*The interior of a white 1970 GTX two-door hardtop. The interior is P6XY Gold and black vinyl with bucket seats and a center console and Hurst pistol grip shifter for the 4-speed manual transmission.*

mission was the fully synchronized cast-iron A833 4-speed manual with a short-stroke Hurst floor shifter and unique Pistol grip handle. When equipped with the 440 Six-Barrel or 426 Hemi engine, there was a choice of either the 4-speed or the TorqueFlite, as neither was standard.

### Rear Axle Options

The standard rear axle for the 1970 GTX with the 440 or 426 engine and TorqueFlite automatic transmission was the Chrysler-designed 8¾-inch ring gear banjo-type with a 3.23:1 gear ratio. The optional Performance Axle Package offered a 3.55:1 ratio and the High-Performance axle package a 3.91:1 ratio, both with heavy-duty Sure Grip limited-slip differential. The 4-speed GTX had a standard Dana 60 rear axle with a standard 3.55:1 gear ratio, but an optional ratio of 4.10:1 was provided with the A34 Super Track Pak and A32 Super Performance Axle packages, both with a Sure Grip limited-slip differential.

### Wheel and Tire Options

The 1970 Plymouth GTX standard wheels were 5.5 x 14-inch painted steel with small hubcaps and optional sport wheel covers or wire spoke wheel cover. The optional wheels were 14-inch stamped-steel Magnum-type with chrome trim rings or 14- or 15-inch stamped-steel Rallye wheels with chrome trim rings. Standard GTX tires were white-stripe F70x14 fiberglass-belted. F70x14 fiberglass-belted raised white-letter or F60x15 raised white-letter tires were optional.

### Production Numbers

A total of 7,748 GTX two-door hardtops were built for the 1970 model year. A total of 678 of them were equipped with the 440 Six-Barrel and 76 with the 426 Hemi engine.

### Advertising and Publicity

The 1970 GTX was featured prominently in two large two-page spreads announcing the new Rapid Transit System at the beginning of the model year. Both were based on a single image of the five models in the RTS program and showed a straight-on low-angle shot of the `Cuda, Road Runner, Sport Fury GT, GTX, and Duster 340 against a background view of a banked race track. The cars were shown in a variety of colors with the GTX in Lemon Twist, a high-performance color for 1970. One version of the ad that was used in magazines featured the lineup in black and white with the heading, "The Rapid Transit System Announced" and a column of the features of each model listed beneath their illustration.

The second version was in color and was used in the factory brochures and possibly in some magazines. This ad also listed the equipment and specifications of each model beneath the pictures. Another and more artistic piece of advertising for 1970 featured a colorful psychedelic art illustration of all five of the 1970 Plymouth models in a two-page spread. Among the images of the cars were face caricatures of many of the important people involved with Plymouth racing and high-performance such as Sox & Martin, Don Prudhomme, Tom Hoover, Don Grotheer, Tom McEwen, and more. The heading read, "Everybody offers a car. Only Plymouth offers a system." The center of the ad emphasized the RTS and the supercar clinic.

### 1970 Plymouth Road Runner and Road Runner Superbird

The performance-oriented Road Runner was based on the Belvedere but included a standard performance engine and heavy-duty suspension and brakes. The Road Runner was available as an RM21 two-door coupe, RM23 two-door hardtop, and RM27 convertible, all with a power-bulge hood center section. The Road Runner was available with a standard 383 4-barrel Road Runner V-8 and optional 440 Six-Barrel and 426 Hemi V-8. The 1970 Road Runner was available in 20 standard body color schemes, complemented by three colors of Boar Grain and one of Gator Grain vinyl roof. The Road Runner interior was available in 13 trim combinations, all with a standard carpet.

The Road Runner Superbird was a totally new model for 1970. It was based on the same concept as the similar winged 1969 Charger Daytona, but it used all different components for its wing and nose. Plymouth developed the Superbird to satisfy Richard Petty, who had moved over to Ford in 1968 because he did not have a winged car to drive such as the Dodge Daytona. Plymouth knew they needed Petty back in the fold so they

*The grille, hood, and front bumper of an FE5 Rallye Red 1970 Plymouth Road Runner with flat-black performance hood paint and optional Air-Grabber fresh air intake system.*

*Rear view of a Rallye Red 1970 WM23 Road Runner two-door hardtop with black tape stripes. Note the Road Runner decal on the passenger's side of the rear fender and the Road Runner cutout on the passenger's side of the deck lid.*

*A 1970 Road Runner Superbird RM23 finished in red with optional Rallye wheels and 440 Six-Barrel engine. The black vinyl roof is standard equipment to cover the rear window bodywork on the Superbird.*

*The driver-side front fender of a 1970 Road Runner finished in FM3 Moulin Rouge, a midyear high-performance color. The tape stripe is the distinctive Road Runner V6Y Gold Dust trail, which extends the full length of the body. (Kori Alexander Photo)*

*The steel front aerodynamic nose shown here is on a 1970 Road Runner Superbird. Note the standard equipment hood pins and Superbird decal on the driver-side headlight cover.*

took the idea from Dodge and produced their own specially built winged warrior. The Superbird carried the same RM23 VIN as a standard Road Runner, but the body code plate indicated the package with an A13 code. The Superbird did not have a standard grille or front bumper, but it had a body-color 18-inch aerodynamic steel nose cone assembly. The assembly included four decals, one on each retractable headlamp door and one surrounding the headlamp housing. The decals were black or white, depending upon the body color, and the left one had a Road Runner bird decal.

*The passenger-side rear quarter of a red 1970 Road Runner Superbird with black vinyl roof and white lettering. The large Plymouth lettering was only available in white or black.*

*An original unrestored FJ5 Limelight Poly 1970 RM23 Road runner Superbird two-door hardtop. The Superbird was an A13 accessory code on a Road Runner hardtop, and all were scheduled for building on September 30, 1969.*

### Engine Options

The standard engine for the 1970 Plymouth Road Runner was a special high-performance version of the B-block–based 383-ci V-8 indicated with an E63 code on the body data plate. The high-performance version of the single 4-barrel 383 was called a 383 4-barrel by Plymouth. It had a bore and stroke of 4.25 x 3.38 inches and a compression ratio of 9.5:1, reduced from 1969, producing 335 hp at 5,200 rpm, five more than the standard single 4-barrel 383. The Road Runner 383 was equipped with an unsilenced air cleaner and dual exhaust, making 425 ft-lbs of torque at 3,400 rpm. Most significant was the special high-performance camshaft used only in the Plymouth Road Runner 383 and its Dodge 383 Magnum V-8 counterpart. This camshaft had a lift of .450 inch on the intake and .465 inch on the exhaust valve. Intake and exhaust duration was 268 degrees for the intake and 284 degrees for the exhaust with 46 degrees of overlap. The standard 383 V-8 used in the 1970 Road Runner was also equipped with heavier valve springs, a standard windage tray, and dual exhaust. Most 383 high-performance engines in 1970 were painted Chrysler Performance Orange.

The Road Runner Superbird was virtually identical to the standard Road Runner hardtops, except that the GTX-type 440 engine and corresponding driveline and suspension was standard equipment with the 440-6 and 426 Hemi as the only optional engines.

A new engine option for the 1970 Road Runner was the 440-ci RB-based V-8 with three 2-barrel Holley carburetors mounted on a Chrysler cast-iron intake manifold, replacing the cast-aluminum Edelbrock unit used in 1969. This engine was identified with a V-code on the VIN and E87 on the body code plate. The 440 Six-Barrel engine had a 10.5:1 compression ratio and was still rated at 390 hp at 4,700 rpm and 490 ft-lbs of torque at 3,200 rpm. The 1970 engine did not have the additional special components that came standard with the 1969-1/2 A12 Six-Pack/Six-Barrel conversion engine package.

The third optional engine offered with the 1970 Plymouth Road Runner was the impressive 426 Hemi V-8, producing 425 hp at 5,000 rpm and 490 ft-lbs of torque at 4,000 rpm. The Hemi, indicated by E74 on the body data plate, still had the same 10.3:1 compression ratio used in previous years. The 426 Hemi for 1970 had a camshaft with hydraulic valve lifters and a net valve lift of .490 inch on the intake valves and .480 inch on the exhaust, with 284 degrees of duration on both. The Hemi was equipped with a cast-aluminum intake manifold that mounted two Carter AFB 4-barrel carburetors. Low-restriction cast-iron headers and dual pipes handled the exhaust. Of course, like all 1966–1971 Street Hemi engines, this one had the iconic distinctive black crackle-finish valve covers and the block, heads, and water pump were painted Street Hemi Orange.

### Transmission Options

The standard transmission with the 1970 Road Runner with the 383 4-barrel engine was the 3-speed manual with floor shifter. A 4-speed manual or 3-speed TorqueFlite were optional. When the 440 Six-Barrel or 426 Hemi was ordered, either a 4-speed manual or TorqueFlite automatic could be ordered as standard equipment.

### Rear Axle Options

The standard rear axle was a Chrysler-designed heavy-duty 8¾-inch ring gear axle with a standard 3.23:1 ratio. Optional ratios with Sure Grip were available in the Performance Axle Package in 3.55:1, the High-Performance Axle Package in 3.91:1, and the Super-Performance Axle package in 4.10:1 ratio with heavy-duty Sure Grip and a Dana 60 rear axle. The Super-Performance Axle package was available with either the 440 6-barrel or Hemi with TorqueFlite. When the 440-6 or Hemi were ordered with a 4-speed, the Track Pak rear axle package was available with 3.54: gears, Heavy-duty Sure Grip, and a Dana 60 rear axle. In addition, a Super Track Pak package was available with the 440-6 and Hemi that included 4.10:1 gears, heavy-duty Sure Grip, and a Dana 60 axle.

### Wheel and Tire Options

The standard wheels for the 1970 Plymouth Road Runner when equipped with the standard 383 V-8 were 14-inch steel wheels with small hubcaps but with optional sport or chrome wire wheel covers. Optional wheels were styled steel Rallye wheels with chrome trim rings and stamped-steel Magnum 500-type road wheels with chrome trim rings. Standard tires on the Road Runner were F70x14 white streak fiberglass-belted with F70x14 raised white-letter tires optional. The 1970 Road

Runner was also available with optional 15 x 7–inch Rallye wheels and F60x15 raised white-letter tires.

### Production Numbers

A total of 15,716 Road Runner two-door coupes, 24,944 two-door hardtops, and 824 convertibles were built for the 1970 model year. Just over 1,900 Superbirds were constructed to meet NASCAR homologation requirements.

### Advertising and Publicity

Advertising for the 1970 model year was sparse compared to 1969, but there were a couple of interesting ads for the 1970 Road Runner. One of the most familiar was a two-page spread in colorful caricature art that was also featured as a large poster for the Rapid Transit System. This ad showed (in artistic form) all of the important people who were involved with the Plymouth Division success. They included Sox & Martin, Tom Hoover, Tom McEwen, Don Prudhomme, Don Grotheer, and many more. In the forefront of the illustration were the five Plymouth high-performance vehicles that were part of the RTS program in 1970. The center of the ad showed a large sign that said "Plymouth Mtrs R.T.S. Super Car Clinic."

The second most visible and unusual ad for the 1970 Road Runner was a single-page vertical layout with an actual photo of a yellow Road Runner in an open desert with a large head of the iconic Road Runner bird sticking up out of the Air-Grabber hood scoop. Beneath the picture were the line, "The loved bird," the slogan "Plymouth makes it," and the red heart.

Another promotional image seen in a number of Plymouth promotional materials was a large and very colorful page with a black background and large red letters that blared "The Rapid Transit System" and below that in a yellow blaze, an outlined image of the five RTS Plymouths and the slogan "Plymouth makes it" in bold black letters.

## 1970 Plymouth Barracuda

The Plymouth Barracuda was an entirely restyled and re-engineered model for 1970 and based on a new E-Body platform. The Barracuda was similar to the Dodge E-Body Challenger but had a shorter 108-inch wheelbase, the same as the earlier model A-Body Barracuda. Like the Challenger, the new Barracuda was Chrysler Corporation's body entry into the "pony car" world.

There were a variety of reasons for the new Barracuda. Not only was its new design directed toward the pony car theme, the wider and longer front end allowed engineers room to install the more powerful B, RB, and 426 Hemi powerplants in addition to the existing small-block LA-series engines. The dramatic increase in horsepower and torque capability gave the new car potential for a new image that emphasized straight-line acceleration and quarter-mile performance.

Development of the new Barracuda was accomplished in Chrysler's Advanced Styling Studio under designer Cliff Voss's direction. The concept was a complete change from the previous 1964–1969 A-Body platform. The old wheelbase was maintained, but the width was increased more than 5 inches and the front and rear track increased 3 inches. The appearance and purpose of the car illustrated the muscle-car theme that was replacing the sports car influences of the past.

Although the steel unibody chassis was similar to the Dodge Challenger, the styling was significantly different. The Barracuda had two headlights, while the challenger had four. The Challenger body had a definite character line following the flow of the body, while the Barracuda was smoother and devoid of any sharp lines or angles. The Barracuda had a more distinct kick up to its short deck, giving it a more

**This full-page Road Runner ad is unusual in that it combines a cartoon Road Runner character with a photo of a real 1970 Road Runner finished in FY1 Lemon Twist, a high-performance color for 1970. The Road Runner has an optional 440 Six-Barrel engine, black hood stripe, and Air Grabber. (Dodge, Plymouth, and the AMC design are registered trademarks of FCA US LLC)**

aggressive look than the Challenger. Few external components were shared.

The clean, smoothly rounded lines, short rear deck, and long, flat hood line immediately identify the 1970 Barracuda. The Barracuda differed from the Challenger in that it had no outside quarter-panel-mounted fuel filler. The filler was mounted in the rear behind the license plate. The grille had an Argent Silver finish, a vertical center divider, and a bright chrome surround. The Barracuda upper grille opening in the body had no chrome molding and was part of the painted body shell. The lower edge of the grille was bordered by the bumper, which had a standard chrome-plated finish but was optionally available in various body-color Elastomeric configurations.

The rear deck lower panel of the Barracuda featured rectangular taillights on either side of the opening. Three chrome horizontal bars accented each of the taillight lenses. The rear bumper bordered the lower edge of the rear deck lower panel and came in chrome or optional Elastomeric colors. The Elastomeric bumper option was always accompanied by matching body color outside mirrors.

The 1970 Barracuda was offered in three basic series. The standard Barracuda was available as a BH23 hardtop or BH27 convertible in 6-cylinder or V-8 versions. There was also an optional A93 coupe package that included fixed quarter windows and a lower level of trim. The coupe package was introduced in the middle of the model year. Some coupes used a BH21 body-type code.

The BP23 Gran Coupe was the most luxurious version of the Barracuda and offered a higher level of trim, a chrome body sill, and wheel lip moldings. Distinctive Gran Coupe badges were mounted on the center side of each front fender and a distinctive identifying emblem was strategically placed to cover the deck lid lock. The Gran Coupe was also offered as a BP27 convertible.

## 1970 Plymouth `Cuda

The performance version of the 1970 Barracuda and Rapid Transit System member was simply called the `Cuda and was available as either a BS23 hardtop or a BS27 convertible. The `Cuda was available only with V-8 power and was identified by distinctive body badges and trim and a distinctive interior motif. The `Cuda was also equipped with an upgraded Rallye suspension package that included heavier springs, heavier torsion bars, and front and rear anti-sway bars (with 340 and 383 engine). The `Cuda was available with the 335-horsepower 383 4-barrel. Optional engines included the 275-horsepower 340, 375-horsepower 440 4-barrel, 390-horsepower 440 Six-Barrel, and the 425-hp 426 Hemi with two 4-barrel carburetors. When

*This original, unrestored 1970 `Cuda is TX9 Black Velvet with a V1X black vinyl roof. It is equipped with the 390-hp 440 Six-Barrel engine and N96 Shaker Hood. It has 15-inch Rallye wheels and hood pins.*

equipped with the 426 Hemi engine, the `Cuda name was changed to "Hemi-Cuda" on the hood badging.

### Exterior

The 1970 `Cuda was available in 18 exterior body hues. The standard list of colors included:

- Ice Blue Metallic
- Blue Fire Metallic
- Jamaica Blue Metallic
- Rallye Red
- Lime Green Metallic
- Ivy Green Metallic
- Deep Burnt Orange Metallic
- Sandpebble Beige
- Burnt Tan metallic
- Alpine White
- Black Velvet
- Yellow Gold
- Citron Mist Metallic

*This 1970 `Cuda AAR is finished in extra-cost FY1 Lemon Twist, one of the high-performance colors offered in 1970. Note the black strobe stripe, unique to the AAR. The bright lower sill molding is incorrect for an AAR, which should have no sill molding.*

Five extra-cost high-impact colors included:
- In Violet
- Lime Light
- Vitamin C Orange
- Tor-Red
- Lemon Twist

After February 24, 1970, the two additional high-impact colors of Sassy Grass Green and Moulin Rouge were made available.

The body colors were complemented by 12 interior trim combinations and 6 vinyl roof colors. Vinyl roof options included Gator Grain and standard Boar Grain texture.

There were also two Mod-Top options in Yellow Floral and Blue-Green Floral. The Mod-Top options included a Mod-Top decal on the rear window.

A total of 18,880 'Cuda two-door hardtops, 685 'Cuda convertibles, and 2,724 'Cuda AARs were built for the 1970 model year.

## 'Cuda Engine Options

The standard engine in a 1970 Plymouth 'Cuda was a 383-ci B-block V-8 with a single 4-barrel carburetor, a bore and stroke of 4.25 x 3.38 inches, and a compression ratio of 9.5:1, producing 335 hp at 5,200 rpm. The 383 4-barrel was equipped with an unsilenced air cleaner and dual exhaust, making 425 ft-lbs of torque at 3,400 rpm. Most significant was the special high-performance camshaft used only in the 383 4-barrel V-8. This camshaft had a lift of .450 inch on the intake and .465 inch on the exhaust valve. Intake and exhaust duration was 268 degrees for the intake and 284 degrees for the exhaust, with 46 degrees of overlap. The 383 V-8 used in the 1970 'Cuda was also equipped with heavier valve springs, a standard windage tray, and dual exhaust. Most 383 high-performance engines in 1970 were painted Chrysler Performance Orange.

The first optional engine in the 1970 'Cuda was the LA-series V-8 with 340 ci that developed 275 hp and 340 ft-lbs of torque. The 340 V-8, indicated by an H on the VIN plate and a code of E55 on the fender data plate, had the same 4.04-inch bore and 3.31-inch stroke as the previous year. The 340 had a single Carter AVS 4-barrel carburetor that used a large, unsilenced air cleaner. The air cleaner was finished in black crackle finish with painted metal insert that read "340 4-barrel." The 340 engine was painted Street Hemi Orange.

The 340 V-8, indicated by an H on the VIN plate and a code of E55 on the fender data plate, had the same 4.04-inch bore and 3.31-inch stroke as the previous year. The 340 was equipped with a Carter Thermo-Quad 4-barrel carburetor that used a large, unsilenced air cleaner like the 1970 version. The air cleaner was finished in black crackle finish with painted metal insert that read "340 4-barrel." The 340 engine was painted Street Hemi Orange until April 1971, when the finish was changed to Chrysler Engine Blue.

The second optional engine in the 1970 'Cuda was the 440-ci V-8 based on the RB (raised-block) configuration. The single Carter AVS 4-barrel 440 produced 375 hp at 4,600 rpm and 480 ft-lbs of torque at 3,200 rpm. The 440 had a bore and stroke of 4.32x3.75 inches and a compression ratio of 9.7:1, lowered from the previous year. All 1970 440 engines were painted Chrysler Performance Orange. The 440 single 4-barrel engine used a black crackle-finish unsilenced air cleaner.

The third engine option in the 1970 'Cuda was the 440-ci RB-based V-8 with three 2-barrel Holley carburetors mounted on a Chrysler cast-iron intake manifold, replacing the cast-aluminum Edelbrock unit used in 1969. This engine was identified with a V-code on the VIN and E87 on the body code plate. The 440 Six-Barrel engine had a 10.5:1 compression ratio and was still rated at 390 hp at 4,700 rpm and 490 ft-lbs of torque at 3,200 rpm.

The fourth engine option available with the 1970 'Cuda was the 426 Hemi V-8 rated at 425 hp at 5,000 rpm and 490 ft-lbs of torque at 4,000 rpm. The two Carter AFB 4-barrel Hemi had a bore and stroke of 4.25x3.75 inches and a compression ratio of 10.3:1. The major change for the Hemi in 1970 was the adoption of hydraulic valve lifters. The Hemi cast-iron and heads and cast-aluminum intake manifold were finished in Late Street Hemi Orange with a black crackle-finish air cleaner. The large, wide Hemi valve covers had a black crackle finish. An R on the VIN and E74 on the body code plate indicated the Hemi. The car was marketed as a "Hemi-Cuda" when equipped with the big Hemi engine.

## 'Cuda 340, 383, and Hemi-Cuda Performance

Some of the more interesting tests and reviews of the 'Cuda performance line were performed by Plymouth team drag racers Ronnie Sox and Buddy Martin, and their results were published in directed publicity pieces available in advertising and dealer promotional materials at the Sox & Martin Supercar Clinics. The road tests were conducted at Willow Springs International Raceway in Rosamond, California, and the dragstrip trials were under the rules and supervision of the NHRA.

## Transmission Options

The 1970 Plymouth 'Cuda had a standard cast-aluminum case A727 3-speed TorqueFlite automatic transmission when equipped with the 440 V-8 engines. The TorqueFlite was operated with either a column- or console-mounted chrome shift lever, depending on the interior options. A cast-iron case A833 4-speed manual transmission with a 2.44:1 low gear was standard with the 426 Hemi and optional with the 440.

The 4-speed used a Hurst shifter with a unique walnut-grain pistol grip design on a wide, flat Hurst chrome-plated handle. The chrome-plated console-mounted shifter handle was curved to the left and back, as in the previous year, while the floor-mounted version was curved back and up. Original handles had a distinct taper in thickness toward the top. Both shifters used a pleated black rubber boot. The Hemi was available with an optional TorqueFlite automatic transmission.

### Rear Axle Options

The standard rear axle with the 1970 'Cuda equipped with a 440 or 426 Hemi engine and TorqueFlite automatic transmission was the Chrysler 8¾-inch banjo-type, which was available in ratios from 2.76:1 to 3.91:1, with 3.23:1 being standard. A 1⅞-inch pinion stem was phased in during the 1969 model year so most 1970 models will have a carrier with Casting Number 2881489. A special Performance Axle Group option (Sales Code 358) was available that provided a 3.55:1 rear axle gear ratio, special slip-drive fan, and an extra-wide high-performance radiator fan shroud.

When a 4-speed transmission was ordered with the 440 or 426 Hemi engine, a 9¾-inch ring gear Dana 60 heavy-duty rear axle with a 3.54:1 gear ratio was used. An optional 4.10:1 ratio provided when the Super Track Pak or Super Performance Axle Packages were ordered. Single-piston power front disc brakes with floating calipers were optional.

### Wheel and Tire Options

The 1970 'Cuda with was equipped with standard 14 x 6-inch stamped-steel wheels, which could be equipped with either a small hubcap or one of two new optional styled wheel covers. Optional 14-inch Magnum 500 styled Rallye road wheels with chrome trim rings were available. Because of the redesigned standard wheels, 15-inch wheels were no longer required for the 426 Hemi. All-new 15-inch Rallye wheels with F60x15 Wide Oval tires were available as an option if heavy-duty brakes and Rallye Suspension were ordered. Early in 1970 production, new 15 x 7-inch steel wheels became available as an option under Sales Code U84. All steel wheels were restyled for 1970 and featured a flat surface at the lug nut-mounting area.

*A two-page magazine psychedelic-type advertising spread showing an orange 1970 'Cuda spewing flames from its hood scoop. This particular ad emphasizes the Rapid Transit System program and cars. This ad seems to be unsigned by an artist. (Dodge, Plymouth, and the AMC design are registered trademarks of FCA US LLC)*

*Highly stylized versions of 1970 Plymouth models appeared in Rapid Transit System promotional materials that did not appear in regular print advertising. This red 1970 'Cuda appeared at the top of an order form for 1970 Rapid Transit System goodies and also as a banner in dealerships. (Dodge, Plymouth, and the AMC design are registered trademarks of FCA US LLC)*

## `Cuda Advertising and Publicity

Like the Scat Pack Challenger R/T and T/A, the new `Cuda and `Cuda AAR were part of Plymouth's Rapid Transit System program. Advertising included the new high-performance E-Body contributions to the list of other cars in the Plymouth performance lineup and promoted them with bright colors and splashes of art. Although most of the advertising pieces promoted the entire Rapid Transit System lineup, the 1970 `Cuda and `Cuda AAR had a number of their own unique ads and unique promotional materials.

Plymouth dealers were provided with detailed materials on promoting the new Rapid Transit System program for 1970. The program was enhanced by the sales of new options and accessories intended to enhance the youth and performance market.

### 1970 Plymouth `Cuda AAR

There was a midyear variation of the `Cuda called the AAR (sales code A53), which, like the Challenger T/A, was developed for Trans-Am racing. The name AAR was derived from Dan Gurney's All-American Racers team. The AAR, which carried the BS23 code as the standard `Cuda hardtop, had a standard 290-horsepower 340 Six-Barrel engine with standard 4-speed transmission (TorqueFlite optional). The AAR was available only as a hardtop and had a distinctive flat-black fiberglass hood, black grille, fresh air scoop, and chrome side-exiting exhaust.

Only 2,724 AAR `Cudas were built.

### Engine Options

The standard and only engine available with the 1970 `Cuda AAR was an LA-based 340-ci high-performance V-8 that developed 290 hp at 5,000 rpm and 340 ft-lbs of

An original, unrestored 1970 Hemi `Cuda finished in FY1 Lemon Twist high-performance paint with a black "Hockey Stick" rear stripe. This `Cuda is also equipped with Rallye wheels and Goodyear Polyglas raised white-letter tires.

A detailed view of the 340 V-8 with three 2-barrel carburetors with the air cleaner removed as used in a 1970 `Cuda AAR. Note the black painted upper cowl panel used only in early 1970 cars. This `Cuda has an incorrect later electronic ignition module on the firewall.

torque at 3,200 rpm with a 10.5:1 compression ratio. The 340 Six-Barrel engine had three Holley 2-barrel carburetors on a Chrysler-designed Edelbrock aluminum intake manifold. The large oval air cleaner was orange and had a soft black rubber hood seal around its circumference. This engine can be noted by the letter J on the VIN plate and was used only in the 1970 Challenger T/A and Plymouth `Cuda AAR.

The cast-iron LA block differs from the standard 340 in that it was stress-relieved with additional material added to the main bearing bores. The engine was equipped with specially machined cast-iron heads with offset pushrods to allow for larger ports. The engine was also equipped with offset, cast-iron adjustable rocker arms and special rocker arm shafts. The 340 three 2-barrel engines were painted Street Hemi Orange.

### Transmission Options

The AAR used the same basic steel unibody construction as the `Cuda except for improvements in handling, suspension, and brakes more closely related to the specialized track racing duty for which the AAR was designed. First, the AAR used a unique K-member with Part Number 3583952, identified by a small metal tag welded to the lower side of the K-member. The tag has the numbers 52 (the last two digits of the part number) stamped on its face from the reverse side. As with all Barracudas, the K-member was painted semi-gloss black, known as OEM Black.

### Rear Axle Options

The 1970 `Cuda AAR had a standard 8¾-inch ring gear rear axle with Sure Grip and a standard 3.55:1 axle ratio. A lower 3.91:1 ratio was available as an option.

### Wheels and Tires

The AAR came with standard gloss-black painted 15 x 7–inch steel wheels mounted with E60x15 Goodyear Polyglas GT tires on the front and G60x15 tires on the rear. The black painted 15-inch wheel had a standard hubcap and bright trim ring. The AAR was available with either an A727 TorqueFlite 3-speed automatic or an A833 cast-iron case 4-speed manual transmission.

### Suspension and Brakes

The `Cuda AAR front suspension used a .94-inch-diameter anti-sway bar. Like its Challenger T/A brother, the AAR was available with race-directed optional quick-ratio (12:1) power steering, accomplished by the addition of a longer pitman arm. The wider arc of the longer steering arm quickened steering response without actually changing the standard ratio of the power steering gear. Because less travel was required, the steering gear was modified to limit internal gear travel and avoid damage to the mechanism.

Standard brakes for a 1970 `Cuda AAR were 11 x 3–inch front drums and 11 x 2-1/2–inch rear drums, but the AAR used 10.7-inch power-assisted front discs and 11 x 2-1/2–inch rear drums as standard equipment.

### 1970 Plymouth Duster

In addition to the E-Body Barracuda and `Cuda, another new model added to the 1970 Plymouth lineup was the entirely new A-Body Duster. The sporty Duster was based on the Plymouth Valiant compact and featured a fastback roof design and sloped rear deck. Although the front of the Duster from the cowl forward was identical to the standard Valiant, from the windshield back the look was a bit more aerodynamic and

*An original, unrestored 1970 Plymouth Duster 340 finished in white with a black vinyl roof. This Duster has a black body stripe, Rallye wheels, and Goodyear Polyglas raised white-letter tires.*

*An unrestored, original 1970 Plymouth Duster 340 is finished in the mid-year high-performance color of FM3 Moulin Rouge, which is the same as Panther Pink on a Dodge. This Duster has a body side bright molding and optional Rallye wheels with Goodyear Polyglas raised white-letter tires.*

unique. The successful design was carried out from the beginning sketches to the final clay model stages by designer Neal Walling, under the direction of vice president of Plymouth Styling Dick Macadam.

The 1970 Plymouth Duster was based on the same 108-inch-wheelbase unibody platform as the Valiant. The Duster was available as only a two-door hardtop coupe in two different models. The base model VL29 Duster with either a 125 hp 198-ci Slant Six or a 230-hp 318-ci LA-series V-8. The Duster model destined for the Plymouth Rapid Transit System program was the VS29 Duster 340, which had a standard 275-hp 340-ci LA-series V-8. The 340 Duster had a shipping weight of 3,110 pounds, which gave it a power-to-weight ratio offering the potential for performance-level acceleration and handling. Quarter-mile times into the 14-second ET bracket were a prerequisite for the Rapid Transit System team and the 340 Duster made the grade.

### Exterior

The 1970 Duster 340 was available in seven standard body colors and eight interior trim schemes with an optional vinyl roof available in complementary colors.

### Interior

The interior was available with a standard bench seat or optional bucket seat and center console configuration. A pistol-grip floor shifter accompanied the optional 4-speed transmission and an optional 8,000-rpm tachometer was available with the center console. A 3-speed manual transmission was standard with a 3-speed TorqueFlite automatic optional. The Duster was equipped with standard front disc brakes and E70x14 tires mounted on 14 x 5–1.2 Rallye wheels. A total of 24,817 Duster 340s were built for the 1970 model year.

In addition to the production 1970 Duster 340, the Plymouth Rapid Transit System was well represented by 426 Hemi-powered Dusters used in the new NHRA Pro-Stock drag racing class around the country. Professional drag racing teams such as Sox & Martin, Don Grotheer, Arlen Vanke, and many others competed at a number of events across the country. In addition to drag racing events, Sox & Martin and Don Grotheer also displayed their cars and educated drag racing fans at Plymouth dealer–sponsored Supercar Clinics at selected dealers from coast to coast. Fans were able to connect the image of their own cars with the super-high-performance racing members of the Rapid Transit System team.

### Engine Options

The standard and only engine available for the 1970 Plymouth Duster 340 was the LA-series-based Commando 340-ci V-8, identical to that used in the 1969 model Barracuda. The

*The 1970 Plymouth Duster 340 was available with optional air-conditioning and power disc front brakes. The LA-based 340 Duster engine was painted Performance Orange with a black crackle-finish air cleaner housing with a distinctive aluminum "pie-plate" identification on top.*

rear-mounted distributor identified the 340. The 340 was rated at 275 hp at 5,000 rpm and 340 ft-lbs of torque at 3,200 rpm. The 340 V-8 had a bore of 4.04 inches and stroke of 3.31 inches and was equipped with a single Carter Thermo-Quad 4-barrel carburetor. The 340 had a 10.5:1 compression ratio so premium fuel was required. All 340 V-8 engines had hydraulic valve lifters and dual exhausts with chrome tips.

### Transmission Options

The standard transmission for the 1970 Duster 340 was the less-expensive cast-iron case 3-speed manual transmission. The 3-speed was fully synchronized in all forward speeds, so you could downshift to low gear while the car was still moving. The 3-speed manual transmission was available column-mounted, floor-mounted, and console-mounted, depending on the model. The shifter used a round chrome handle with a round black plastic knob.

The optional transmission on the 1970 Duster 340 was the cast-iron case Chrysler New Process A833 4-speed manual with a 2.66:1 low-gear ratio. A Hurst Performance shifter with a flat chrome-plated handle and wood-grain pistol grip was standard. The super strong aluminum case A727 TorqueFlite 3-speed automatic was optional and had a 2.45:1 low gear. The console-mounted TorqueFlite shifter was the new "Slap Stick" from Chrysler. The "Slap Shift" allowed easy manual upshifts without the risk of going into a higher gear each time it was pushed. Both transmissions were extra cost.

## Rear Axle Options

The standard rear axle with the TorqueFlite or 4-speed manual transmission was the Chrysler 8¾-inch banjo-type unit with a standard 3.23:1 gear ratio. Sure Grip limited-slip was optional with the 3.23:1 gears. The rear axle was supported by Chrysler-designed heavy-duty longitudinal parallel leaf springs included in the heavy-duty suspension package.

## Wheel and Tire Options

The 1970 Duster 340 brakes were up to the performance levels of the car. It was equipped with 10-inch rear drums and 10.79-inch power disc brakes on the front. Standard tires on the 1970 Duster 340 were E70x14 fiberglass-belted bias-ply mounted on Sales Code W21 styled 14-inch Rallye road wheels. Sales Code W15 full wire-type wheel covers were also available as an extra-cost option but only with the E70x14 tires, and 14x5.5-inch steel wheels were also available.

## Advertising and Publicity

There were a number of road tests and articles about the performance capabilities of the 1970 Duster 340, but some of the more interesting were among the series of tests and reviews published by the famous drag racing team of Ronnie Sox and Buddy Martin. These tests and reviews, published by Plymouth, gave enthusiasts a respected opinion and evaluation of the performance potential of the Duster. The acceleration trials were conducted at a dragstrip and supervised and certified by the NHRA.

The 3,265-pound 1970 340 Duster tested was finished in Vitamin C Orange and had a 4-speed transmission, front disc brakes, Performance Axle Package with 3.91: rear axle gears, E70x14 tires, and power steering. This Duster had 669 miles on the odometer when subjected to the testing.

*A page from a 1970 Plymouth showroom brochure shows an FY1 Lemon Twist Duster 340 equipped with optional Rallye wheels and Goodyear Polyglas raised white-letter tires. (Dodge, Plymouth, and the AMC design are registered trademarks of FCA US LLC)*

*This page from a 1970 Plymouth showroom brochure shows a red 1970 Duster 340 equipped with white sidewall tires and full wheel covers. Note the distinctive Duster image on the rear deck lower panel. (Dodge, Plymouth, and the AMC design are registered trademarks of FCA US LLC)*

Both Ronnie and Buddy drove the cars in the various tests and commented afterward on their experience to the readers. They said that the Duster was maneuverable and they liked the way you can hang the tail out. Braking distance was 146.3 feet at 60 mph to 0, which was admirable at the time. Quarter-mile acceleration registered an average of 14.07 seconds at 100.9 mph after 10 runs.

## 1970 Fury

An entirely new member of Plymouth's performance family and member of the Rapid Transit System was the massive C-Body Fury. The 1970 Plymouth Fury was available in six separate models all based on the same 120-inch-wheelbase unibody platform for hardtops, convertibles, and sedans and 122-inch-wheelbase for station wagons. Although shorter and smaller than the Chrysler line, the Fury was still considerably larger, wider, and heavier than the B-Body offerings and not normally considered to be a performance choice.

The base Fury was called Fury I and offered the basic, but still relatively luxurious, large Plymouth, with a standard 225-ci Slant Six engine. Next was the Fury II with the same equipment plus the addition of integral backup lamps and taillights in the rear bumper, 120-mph speedometer, heater control, and carpets. The Fury III had all of these plus body side moldings, side markers, deluxe steering wheel, door-frame trim, larger tires, and trunk lights. The highest line was the Sport Fury, offering everything in the first three models plus hidden headlights, red, white, and blue grille badge, deck lid medallion, and wheelhouse moldings. The Fury III coupe and the Sport Fury deleted the ventipanes standard on the Fury I and II. Optional 318 to 440-ci V-8 engines were available in all models.

### Fury S23

Two additional performance-oriented Fury models were offered for 1970, both based on the Fury two-door hardtop. First was the Fury S23, which included a standard 230-hp 318-ci V-8 and two optional 383 V8s and the 440 4-barrel V-8. The S23 package interior included a cloth and vinyl or all-vinyl bench seat or optional all-vinyl bucket seats with available center console. The S23 Sport Fury exterior featured hidden headlights, dual power bulges on the hood, and dual longitudinal stripes in white, black, or burnt orange. A badge on the rear of the deck lid identified the S23 package, along with reflective strobe stripes on the sides and deck lid.

Only 689 Sport Fury S23 models were produced for the 1970 model year.

### Sport Fury GT

The second and highest-performance model was the 1970 Plymouth Sport Fury with GT package. The PP23 1970 Sport Fury GT was the ideal if not obvious candidate for the Rapid Transit System. The standard powerplant was a 350-hp 440-ci wedge V-8. The Fury GT 440 engine had a single 4-barrel carburetor, high-flow heads and intake manifold, and high-performance dual exhaust with 2½-inch pipes from the engine manifolds. The Sport Fury GT was also available with an optional 390-hp 440 Six-Barrel V-8 with three Holley 2-barrel carburetors.

To handle this horsepower, the Sport Fury GT was equipped with heavy-duty suspension, heavy-duty driveshaft and brakes, and 6-inch-wide steel road wheels mounted with Polyglas-belted H70 x 15–inch tires. To identify the Fury GT, the hood had dual power bulges with bright 440 engine badges and pin stripes on both sides of the hood, in addition to special stripes on the body sides.

### Exterior

The 1970 Plymouth Fury was available in seven basic body types. First was a four-door sedan available in the Fury I, Fury II, Fury III, and Sport Fury. Next was a two-door sedan available with the Fury I, Fury II, and Fury Gran Coupe. A four-door station wagon version was available with the Fury II, Fury III, and Sport Fury. All station wagons were offered in six- and nine-passenger configurations. A two-door hardtop coupe was available with the Fury III, Sport Fury, and Sport Fury GT. A four-door hardtop sedan was offered with the Fury III and Sport Fury. A fastback two-door coupe was available in the Fury III and Sport Fury series. Last, a two-door convertible was available in the Fury III only.

The modern body styling of the 1970 Fury was similar to its 1969 predecessor with subtle curves on the upper rear quarters. Long horizontal lines and trim on the lower body sides accentuated the length and width of the Fury. A massive wraparound chrome-plated bumper surrounding the bright grille and quad headlights dominated the front end. The styling was differentiated among the low and higher line models by hidden retractable units in the Sport Fury. All 1970 Fury hoods had a lengthened and swept-up rear edge that provided for more aerodynamic hidden windshield wipers. The hood had dual power bulges and twin tape runners in white, black, and Burnt Orange. The rear fascia also had a wide horizontal theme with wide rectangular taillights on either side of a wide chrome-plated bumper that wrapped around the body sides.

Only 2,672 Sport Fury GTs were built for the 1970 model year.

## Interior Options

The 1970 Plymouth Sport Fury GT was available with a standard all-vinyl bench seat with fold-down center armrest or optional Brougham interior trim available with all-vinyl or cloth and vinyl bucket seats. The interior trim was available in Satin Black, Baltic Blue, Chestnut Tan, Bayou Green, and Regatta Red.

One of the interior trim choices for a 1970 Plymouth Sport Fury GT was Bayou Green pleated vinyl. The wide two-spoke steering wheel remained black and fronted the attractive rectangular gauge cluster and rocker switches. This Sport Fury has a center console and floor shifter for the TorqueFlite automatic transmission. (Dave Carson Photo)

## Engine Options

The standard powerplant of the 1970 Plymouth Sport Fury GT was the 440-ci Commando V-8 based on the RB wedge combustion chamber design. The 440 Commando engine had a single 4-barrel carburetor and a 9.7:1 compression ratio that produced 350 hp at 4,400 rpm and 480 ft-lbs of torque at 2,800 rpm. The horsepower and torque at lower RPMs than the higher-performance versions of the 440 were needed to move the heavier Fury down the road with vigor. The 440 V-8 had a bore of 4.32 inches and a stroke of 3.75 inches. The air cleaner was a dual snorkel design that provided more efficient airflow for the large displacement engine. The 440 V-8 in the Fury required premium fuel to prevent knock.

The only optional engine in the 1970 Sport Fury GT was the 440 Super Commando Six-Barrel V-8, with a special intake manifold and three Holley 2-barrel carburetors. The Six-Barrel engine used the same basic cast-iron block as the Commando V-8 but had a 10.5:1 compression ratio producing 390 hp at 4,700 rpm and 490 ft-lbs of torque at 3,200 rpm. This was the same engine available as an option on the 1970 Plymouth `Cuda and the GTX. Both 440 engines had "high-lift, long duration, high-overlap camshafts" (276/292/54 degrees), according to Plymouth advertising materials. Both also were equipped with low-restriction dual exhaust with high-flow mufflers and chrome-plated tips. The 440 Six-Barrel required premium fuel only.

## Transmission Options

The 1970 Plymouth Fury GT standard equipment transmission was what Plymouth referred to as a High-Upshift A727 TorqueFlite 3-speed automatic. There were no optional transmissions available. The driveline was attached to an extra-heavy-duty Dana built 9¾-inch ring gear rear axle by a 3.25-inch-diameter driveshaft with heavy-duty 7290 universal joints.

## Rear Axle Options

The standard rear axle gear ratio was 3.23:1 with 2.76:1 optional. A Chrysler Sure Grip limited-slip differential was optional with all axle ratios.

The optional 440 Six-Barrel V-8 in the 1970 Sport Fury was covered with a large, orange, oval-shaped air cleaner sporting a "440 Six-Barrel" decal and an open element air filter. The engine was finished in Orange. Note the unique finned exhaust manifold used on the Sport Fury engine. (Dave Carson Photo)

A Plymouth showroom brochure page features a blue 1970 Sport Fury GT, one of the more unexpected Rapid Transit System members for 1970. This Fury has optional Rallye wheels. Note the distinctive "power bulges" on the hood. The Sport Fury GT was available with a 440 Six-Barrel engine. (Dodge, Plymouth, and the AMC design are registered trademarks of FCA US LLC)

## Suspension Options

Sport Fury GT suspension was heavy-duty and included .98-inch-diameter torsion bars, heavy-duty shock absorbers, a .94-inch-diameter front anti-sway bar, and heavy-duty six-leaf rear springs. Standard brakes were 11-inch drums with self-adjusting 3-inch-wide shoes in the front and 2½-inch-wide shoes in the rear. Power disc front brakes with full-floating calipers were optional.

## Wheel and Tire Options

Sport Fury GT standard steel wheels were 15 x 6–inch with H-70x15 Polyglas-belted Wide Oval white-lettered tires. The Sport Fury GT was also available with optional 15-inch styled steel road wheels with chrome trim rings.

## Advertising and Publicity

There were very few road tests on the 1970 Sport Fury, but one of the most complete tests was presented by *Road Test* in its May 1970 issue. The test and accompanying article was performed on a cream-colored 1970 Sport Fury GT Brougham hardtop with a black vinyl roof. This Fury was equipped with the optional 390-hp 440 Six-Barrel engine and standard 3-speed TorqueFlite automatic transmission. The package included a luxurious interior with bucket seats, chrome-plated road wheels, power steering, and power brakes (with front discs), all options on the base sport Fury. This list of extras brought the price to over $5,125, quite a step above the base Sport Fury price of $3,898.

The reviewers in 1970 found that the big Sport Fury was a competent highway cruiser with a smooth ride and easy handling, mostly due to its size and weight. Cornering ability on secondary roads was limited by the Fury's tread width, forcing the driver to slow down just to maneuver the curves safely and stay between the ditches. Slight understeer and body roll were among the descriptions used. It was clear that the Sport Fury was never intended to handle like a sports car, but its stable manners on the road put it a cut above many of its size and price competitors. Its standing start quarter-mile performance did not put it firmly into the Rapid Transit System requirements, but it was adequate with a best run of 92.5 mph at 16.01-second ET.

*A Plymouth showroom brochure page uses the iconic and colorful 1970 psychedelic art style to draw attention to the "Plymouth makes it" slogan used in its advertising. The Rapid Transit System is not mentioned. (Dodge, Plymouth and the AMC design are registered trademarks of FCA US LLC)*

*The cover of the 14-page dealer promotional kit for the 1970 Rapid Transit System program made it very clear that the marketing direction was for the youth high-performance buyer, and Plymouth was offering everything the dealer needed to know and have to make it successful. (Dodge, Plymouth and the AMC design are registered trademarks of FCA US LLC)*

Chapter 7: The Rapid Transit System Is Born

# The 1970 Rapid Transit System Caravan

The most significant element of the 1970 Plymouth Rapid Transit System program was its well-designed and implemented Caravan promotion. The Rapid Transit System Caravan was essentially a traveling car show that would set up at selected dealers across the country. The Caravan used a combination of regular production and totally custom-built Plymouths to promote the image of performance to the youth market in every city. The caravan included Plymouth race cars and their drivers at selected locations, as they were available. Chrysler went so far as to hire International Car Show Association top promoter Bob Larivee to head up the program. With Larivee's expert leadership the show became more of a traveling commercial for Plymouth and its Rapid Transit System line of performance cars.

In addition to creating and organizing the Caravan, Larivee was given four Plymouths to build and customize into attention-grabbing show cars. Larivee called in some of the best builders in the country to assist him, including Roman's Chariot Shop, the Alexander Brothers, Chuck Miller, and the Sintetex Corporation, who had already built two major Chrysler show cars. Larivee worked closely with Chrysler designers, who had to approve any designs before they were turned into completed cars. Chrysler knew that many young customers and enthusiasts wanted to customize their new Plymouths so they wanted to show them how it was done and give them ideas to follow.

The Caravan was a car show but it was really much more. The Caravan was described by Plymouth as "a customized interpretation of the Rapid Transit System." All of the elements of the program consisted of high-performance cars, special parts on display boards, and the how-to-do-it information for owners who wanted to personalize their cars and make them really individualistic. The caravan included two cut-away performance engines and presented a 27-minute movie on the history of drag racing with highlights of Plymouth's drag racing accomplishments.

The Rapid Transit System dealer kit provided detailed instructions on how the dealer could use the Caravan and advertising materials to attract customers and sell cars with emphasis on high performance. (Dodge, Plymouth, and the AMC design are registered trademarks of FCA US LLC)

### RTS Caravan Launch

The Rapid Transit System Caravan got an early start in the 1970 model year with its highly successful premier event held in New York City. With 73,626 people attending the event, it was soon recognized that the Caravan and the Rapid Transit System program was probably one of the greatest marketing ideas in automotive history. The show included exhibits promoting not only Plymouth high-performance cars, but also parts, accessories, service, racing, and the people associated with them.

The entire show was transported to the events in a big, yellow 44-foot tractor-trailer rig with RTS and "Plymouth Makes It" logos painted on its sides. Three men accompanied the rig just to load and unload the cars and displays and set them up at each location.

Cars displayed in the first show included a stylized version of Don "The Snake" Prudhomme's Hemi-powered 'Cuda Funny Car, a customized 440 'Cuda, a specially designed and built 440-powered 1970 Road Runner, and a highly customized and lowered 340 Duster.

Williams Manufacturing in St. Clair Shores, Michigan, modified and outfitted the custom semi-trailer. The tractor was provided by Dodge, and "tastefully" modified into a Plymouth. The Chrysler-Plymouth display house that George P. Johnson created for the supporting displays traveled with the caravan. All vehicles and displays fit in the trailer.

Included with the dealer information kits for the 1970 Rapid Transit System program were ideas for promoting the RTS Caravan as their own "High-Performance Car Show." The RTS Caravan brought the Plymouth performance show cars and products to the dealership lots. (Dodge, Plymouth, and the AMC design are registered trademarks of FCA US LLC)

## Cars of the RTS Caravan

Cars displayed in the first show included a stylized version of Don "The Snake" Prudhomme's Hemi-powered 'Cuda Funny Car, a customized 440 'Cuda, a specially designed and built 440-powered 1970 Road Runner, and a highly customized and lowered 340 Duster.

## Hemi 'Cuda Funny Car

One of the most spectacular show cars of the 1970 Plymouth Rapid Transit System Caravan was the stylized show version replica of Don "The Snake" Prudhomme's actual Hemi 'Cuda Funny Car. The 'Cuda Funny Car paint work was done by Jack Kampney in Detroit in a basic white pearl with orange, red, and yellow flames on the hood, roof, and rear deck. The 'Cuda was lettered on the sides with the famous Hot Wheels logo, representing the sponsor of the Prudhomme Funny Car. Don Prudhomme's name and "The Snake" were also prominent parts of the panels on the side of the car. Dual parachute packs were attached to the lower rear deck panel and held two 12-foot parachutes to stop the 'Cuda at the end of the track from speeds faster than 225 mph.

The car had a 1,500-hp supercharged 426-ci Chrysler Hemi engine built by Keith Black. The 'Cuda was finished with Cragar chrome wheels and Goodyear racing slicks for an authentic look. The 'Cuda was constructed on a full tube frame, enclosed in a full aluminum floorpan to protect the driver. The 'Cuda body was one-piece fiberglass, hinged at the front so it could be raised for access to the engine and drivetrain. Four individual zoomie headers curbed out from under the body on each side.

## 440 'Cuda

The 1970 RTS show also featured a highly customized 1970 'Cuda 440. This 'Cuda, built by Chuck Miller in Detroit, based on renderings created by designer Harry Bradley in Los Angeles, was the most extensively altered vehicle of the four cars in the Caravan. The stock 'Cuda Shaker hood was

*This highly customized 1970 'Cuda was built by Chuck Miller in Detroit based on a rendering created by designer Harry Bradley in Los Angeles. This 'Cuda was the most extensively altered of the four cars in the RTS Caravan. (Dodge, Plymouth, and the AMC design are registered trademarks of FCA US LLC)*

*Don "The Snake" Prudhomme's Rapid Transit System Caravan Plymouth Barracuda Funny Car. This car was part of the traveling Rapid Transit System Caravan that set up shows at Plymouth dealers around the country. (Dodge, Plymouth, and the AMC design are registered trademarks of FCA US LLC)*

*The Hot Wheels Barracuda Funny Car displayed at the Rapid Transit System Caravan's at Plymouth dealers. Note the distinctive upswept zoomie exhaust pipes and rear wheelie bars to keep the car from flipping over backward at the track. (Dodge, Plymouth, and the AMC design are registered trademarks of FCA US LLC)*

# THE 1970 RAPID TRANSIT SYSTEM CARAVAN

retained but the front end of the car was extended and the entire car was lowered 2½ inches. The customized new grille covered square, concealed Cibie Rallye-type headlamps, and the parking lights were located beneath the front bumper.

The radical 'Cuda had dual side-pipes, and mud deflectors were installed behind each rear wheel. Chrome-plated Cragar rear wheels were 14 inches wide and carried even wider Goodyear racing tires. Rear-end styling was substantially altered to accommodate two wheelie bars and a parachute, which was recessed into the rear lower pan between the bars. The rear window was reinforced with steel braces.

All door handles, rear deck, and hood latches were removed and replaced with electric solenoid openers. The car was equipped with a Stewart-Warner gauge package. The exterior colors were a combination of reds, pinks, oranges, yellows, and whites covered by a final coat of Merano pearlescent for depth.

### 440 Road Runner

The Road Runner built for the 1970 Rapid Transit System Caravan was heavily customized, featuring a wild gold and black Jerry Roman paint job with wide stripes at the lower sides of the car and hood and large white Road Runner images on

*A photo of one of the displays set up for the 1970 sales season. Visitors can be seen checking out the special customized 1970 Plymouth Road Runner built especially for the event.*

**The 1970 Rapid Transit System Road Runner as it appears today in the Steven Juliano collection in California. The rectangular headlights were some of the more unique features of the Road Runner. (Diego Rosenberg Photo)**

**The customized 1970 Road Runner built for the Rapid Transit System traveling Caravan. This car was finished in shades of black and gold with a Road Runner bird on the doors. This Road Runner is now in the Steven Juliano collection. (Dodge, Plymouth, and the AMC design are registered trademarks of FCA US LLC)**

**The passenger-side rear view of the gold and black customized 1970 Road Runner built for the 1970 Rapid Transit System Caravan. The large rear spoiler was one of the more interesting features of the car. (Dodge, Plymouth, and the AMC design are registered trademarks of FCA US LLC)**

each door. The grille was redesigned with four rectangular headlamps and a black mesh background. The rear wheelwells were enlarged to make room for the wide Goodyear drag racing slicks mounted on 14-inch-wide cast-aluminum Cragar wheels. The roof and upper rear of the body was white and the front and rear wheelwells were bordered with bright trim. The rear end of the body carried a molded-in rear spoiler that wrapped around the upper sides of the rear quarters.

## 340 Duster

As with the other RTS show cars, the 1970 340 Duster was highly customized and modified. The body was finished in a striking two-tone bronze and orange metallic with shaded stripes. The front end was completely restyled with a rolled-under front pan and a custom-made thin-line front bumper. The custom-formed grille housed quad Lucas headlights and the parking lights were redesigned and relocated under the front pan. Large block letters spelling "Duster" were added to the front end of the grille.

The entire car was lowered 3 inches and its lowness was accented by chrome-plated molding along the rocker panels. A unique spoiler was built into the rear roofline and the rear pan rolled under to allow the installation of new taillights and rectangular dual exhaust pipes. The Duster had a 340-ci V-8 and a 4-speed manual transmission. The interior was finished in white vinyl and high-back bucket seats.

Harry Bradley designed the Duster and Byron Grenfell of Marquette, Michigan, performed body modifications. Butch Brinza of Milwaukee, Wisconsin, accomplished the custom paint. The large "340" name was spelled out by green cut-out letters at an angle across the flat-black hood. The Duster was also equipped with dual quick-fill racing-type fuel filler inlets.

## Also on Display

Accompanying the cars on display were items to educate and inform potential customers of products available through Chrysler. Among them was a pair of cutaway engines, a 440-6 and 426 Hemi. Spectators could watch as the electrically powered, cutaway engine components simulated their motions at a fraction of their capabilities.

Display boards featuring Hustle Stuff performance parts were also a part of the caravan. Educated staff would inform would-be consumers about the performance benefits of each item on the board, ranging from bell housings to rear gears to headers.

The highly customized 1970 Duster built for the Rapid Transit System Caravan. The Duster's front end was highly modified and featured quad round headlights, differing from the standard Duster design. (Dodge, Plymouth, and the AMC design are registered trademarks of FCA US LLC)

# The 1970 Rapid Transit System Caravan

A spectator, who appears to have biked to the RTS display, gets a close-up view of the 440-6 Plymouth mill.

Craftfully called the "Respiratory System," breathing components such as the carburetors and headers made up a third of the display board of this Hustle Stuff marketing piece.

### Opening Show at Detroit

One of the first auto shows promoting the Plymouth Rapid Transit System was at the November 1969 Detroit Auto Show early in the 1970 model year. The newspaper reported "Performance cars ranging from the all-new Plymouth Road Runner Superbird to the Beep Beep X1 idea car highlighted the Chrysler-Plymouth Division's 42-car exhibit at the Detroit Auto Show." The story stated that the theme of the 26-car Plymouth part of the exhibit was the Rapid Transit System featuring the five muscle cars: 'Cuda, Duster 340, Road runner, GTX, and Sport Fury GTX. The Detroit Plymouth Advertising Association actually gave away a new 1970 Road Runner Superbird to the winner of a drawing who answered Plymouth product questions correctly. The article said that the backdrop and settings would be used for other major shows throughout the country.

Although the auto show schedule began in the fall of 1969, the actual yearlong Rapid Transit System tour did not begin until January 1970. The first was held at Glenwood Motors in Riverside, California, and the tour carried throughout the country. The Rapid Transit System tour moved east from California, across the southern and southeastern United States

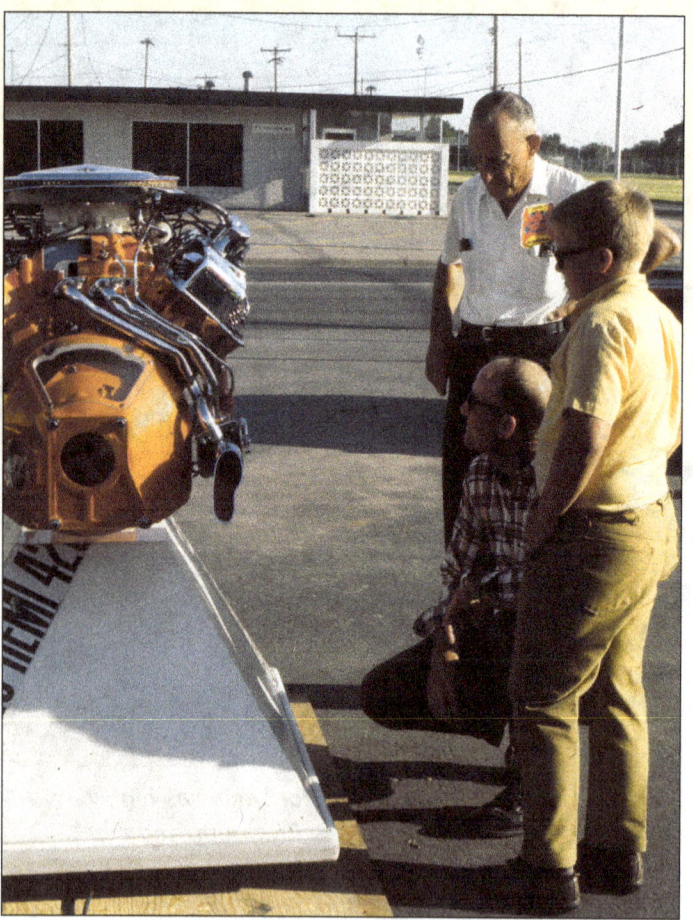

Generations of Mopar fans inspect the RTS Caravan 426 Hemi powerplant on display. The electrically operated Hemi simulated running conditions, albeit at a much, much lower RPM.

*Hustle Stuff performance parts accompanied the RTS cars. Tachometers, hood pins, and drag wheels were just a handful of the parts being shown to prospective buyers.*

through Georgia and Florida, continuing into South Carolina and North Carolina by May 1970.

### Dealer Announcements

To make the most of their creative advertising program, Plymouth made sure that their dealers were made aware of the plan and of their opportunities and responsibilities far ahead of the start early in the 1970 model year. The program's ultimate purpose, of course, was to sell cars and Plymouth marketing made sure that dealers had every tool and every bit of knowledge at their disposal to make the best of their efforts. Like the Sox & Martin and Don Grotheer Supercar Performance Clinics, the Rapid Transit System Caravan did not just happen. Dealers were sent a 15-page information packet that explained the program and what it offered their store. The dealers had to choose which program they were interested in and send in a detailed request form that explained their responsibilities, which included providing and paying for the necessary show space and for the advertising in their local area.

Encouragement for Plymouth dealers to participate in the Rapid Transit System Caravan was important enough for Plymouth Division to require them to sign a "Dealer Sign-Off Form" to verify that they decided not to participate in the program. If they decided to take advantage of the plan, they had to submit another form, which laid out their responsibilities that included supplying a suitable place for the Caravan, prominently displaying the promotional materials provided by Chrysler Corporation, and advertising the Caravan through a specified number of radio and newspaper spots using recorded ads produced by Chrysler. The agreement also noted that the dealer would be responsible for all costs incurred in providing the facilities and advertising. This was a serious and expensive program for everyone involved.

### The RTS Caravan

When the Caravan arrived at the prepared local dealer facility, a well-rehearsed team jumped into action to unload and set up the show cars and displays. Usually, the large tractor-trailer rig with its colorful display signs on the side was the background for the primary parts of the show. The show cars were set up bordering the outer perimeters; the parts and cutaway engines were placed strategically in the center. Dealer-provided new Plymouths surrounded the entire display with sales personnel at the ready throughout the setup.

Local newspaper reporters had been notified ahead of time by the dealer, so it was commonplace for them to be present when the program opened. Newspaper publicity and press release photos and stories in the local press brought even more people to see the show and kept the name of the Plymouth and the Rapid Transit System in the eyes of the public and potential buyers. Local display print ads told the public that "Plymouth's High-Performance Custom Car Show" would be at their local dealership on specified dates in the form of the Rapid Transit System. The ads included descriptions of the show cars, engines, and high-performance parts that would be on display.

# THE 1970 RAPID TRANSIT SYSTEM CARAVAN

Advanced personnel would travel to dealerships to determine if there was adequate space to set up the RTS display. We see here the RTS Duster and 'Cuda with a dealership-provided Superbird populating a vacant lot.

The 1970 Plymouth Rapid Transit System advertising included a new first-of-the-year sales program on TV. The ad featured a red-and-white striped biplane flying above a lineup of the five Plymouths that were part of the Rapid Transit System. The lead slogan was about "Those daring young men in their flying machines," referring to the Plymouth dealers offering special deals at the first of the year. A close-up view of each model showed them speeding down an open highway as the announcer described each one.

Dealerships hung advertisements weeks and months in advance of an upcoming RTS Caravan stop.

Dealerships were advised to sprinkle in their Rapid Transit System cars among the display. Here we see two Barracudas, a GTX, a Duster, and a Superbird mixed in with the RTS cars.

The color cover of a Rapid Transit System information folder sent to Plymouth dealers to promote the program and instruct them on making use of it. (Dodge, Plymouth and the AMC design are registered trademarks of FCA US LLC)

Chapter 7: The Rapid Transit System Is Born 145

# RTS Caravan in Motion
## by Bill Moeller, Director of Sales—Promotions, Inc.

The Rapid Transit System Caravan cars sit under a lit parking lot. It would have been an odd and cool sight driving by at night seeing these modified machines.

The RTS Caravan originated from my meeting (his invitation) with Dick Cook, display & exhibit manager for Chrysler-Plymouth (C-P), in his office on Jefferson Avenue in Detroit, and Joe Schulte of J.R. Thompson Agency. The marketing program for the Rapid Transit System had already been approved but not yet implemented. I was told not to discuss it publicly. Ideas for the Caravan were discussed at the meeting and suggestions were introduced by each of us.

I took the concept back to Bob Larivee, and he gave me approval to proceed. I wrote the plan and estimated the costs, and my secretary typed the many page proposal in multiple carbon copies to present to Dick & Joe. We had established a good relationship with Cook through Plymouth's displays at our indoor shows, collaborating on featured appearances of *Playboy* magazine Playmates and building the customized "Road Runner Probe," which was toured and awarded as an ISCA seasonal Grand Prize. We received approval to proceed with the RTS Caravan. All decisions were made with confirmation from Cook & Schulte.

I was Bob Larivee's second employee at Promotions, Inc., in 1962. I had worked my way up from Show Car Division manager, show manager, assistant general manager, general manager, sales manager, and director of sales before Larivee moved me to SoCal in July of 1971 to establish Pacific

The Rapid Transit System caravan advanced car was a 1970 Plymouth GTX. The car featured yellow and orange hues. The familiar 1969 GTX paint scheme was replicated on the lower portion of the car.

Promotions to produce indoor shows west of the Rockies. At that time, the RTS Caravan was operating smoothly in high gear, and Lee Lasky was hired to manage sales.

John Noga was hired in 1969 to be the advance man for the RTS Caravan and gradually assumed more of the daily management. Noga drove a 1970 GTX that was supplied to him through Chrysler and had its own custom paint work and RTS decals. The GTX was only on display once at our debut show in New York, after that Noga's job was to be on the road weeks and months ahead of the caravan.

Mario Cicone became the lead road manager. Cook & Schulte put us in contact with Don Prudhomme, who referred us to Ronnie Scrima, who provided the Funny Car, which was shown in three different paint schemes over the two years of the RTS Caravan. To dispel a myth, the "Sonic 'Cuda" with the supercharger was never included in the RTS Caravan.

The RTS Caravan was the biggest, most elaborate project ever implemented by Bob Larivee's Promotions, Inc. It was certainly the biggest that I've ever been involved with. I'm extremely proud of the significant contribution that I made.

The following are the employees of Promotions, Inc., who shared a role in the RTS Custom Car Caravan:

*Every Rapid Transit System Caravan display was dictated by the space it was allowed to take up. Here, the RTS cars are shown inside a dealership showroom. A banner hangs behind the cars announcing the Superbird victory in the Daytona 500.*

Bob Larivee
Bill Moeller
John Noga
Mario Cicone
Kathy Gassman Kalm
Jack Kampney
John Greer

Ray Velthuysen
Steve Castl
Chris Davidson
Greg Setterington
Dal Middleton
Lee Lasky

*This shot shows a fairly standard setup for the RTS Caravan display. The two engines, RTS Caravan cars, and factory production models are populating a vacant lot.*

# CHAPTER 8

# RAPID TRANSIT SYSTEM FOR 1971

*"The Rapid Transit System. Or, everything goes."*

The model change for the 1971 Plymouths was dramatic across the B-Body line. The styling of those models was now based on the Satellite, with the Road Runner and GTX appearing only as trim packages on the Satellite. The Duster still continued as the A-Body offering with few alterations to the basic 1970 concept but was no longer listed as a Valiant. The E-Body `Cuda was not changed as much and consisted of only small trim details and increasing the headlights to four.

*An overhead view of a Tor-Red 1971 Plymouth Road Runner shows off the optional reflective roof stripe, flat-black hood graphic, and black rear deck spoiler. (Photo Courtesy Kori Alexander)*

## 1971 Model Overview

Here's a rundown of the details.

### B-Body

Gone was the Belvedere name, and the base for the intermediate B-Body Plymouth models was now called the Satellite. The two-door Satellite was based on a 115-inch-wheelbase platform and fuselage design, much like the larger C-Body cars. The fenders and rear quarter panels had a more rounded appearance, giving the cars a more muscular look. A large loop-type chrome bumper surrounding the grille opening dominated the front end. The roofline was more aerodynamic at the C-pillar, providing a fastback theme to the styling. The cars had a larger and heavier appearance because there was more rear overhang and a shorter front overhang, even though they were actually shorter than the previous year. Engine options were changed for 1971 with a new powerplant for the Road Runner. The four-door and station wagon Satellite models had a longer 117-inch wheelbase and a slightly different styling theme.

*An original, unrestored 1971 'Cuda convertible finished in EV2 Tor-Red with a white top, Rallye wheels, and chrome-plated hood pins. This 'Cuda also has optional fog lights below the front bumper. Note the distinctive bright side louvers used only in 1971.*

*A driver-side rear view of an FJ6 Sassy Grass green 1971 Plymouth GTX with optional black vinyl roof, Rallye wheels, and Goodyear Polyglas raised white-letter tires. This GTX also has an optional black rear deck spoiler. (Photo Courtesy Tim Costello)*

### E-Body

The E-Body Barracuda was changed very little for 1971. The body styling was the same, but the grille now had four round headlights rather than two, as in 1970. The 1971 grille had a series of vertical openings angled back on either side with a peak in the center of the grille opening. The performance-oriented 'Cuda featured four distinctive vertical bright "Gill" louvers added to the upper rear of the front fenders that were not used on the standard Barracuda. The rear panel and taillights with horizontal bright trim were similar to those used on the 1970 model. The performance-minded 'Cuda was available as a two-door hardtop or a two-door convertible.

### A-Body

The A-Body Plymouth Duster 340 was still the 108-inch-wheelbase compact Plymouth performance king of the line for 1971. The Duster's body and styling were much the same as 1970 with subtle changes to the front grille and rear fascia appearance. The Valiant nameplate was dropped from the Duster, giving it a distinct personal identity. The performance-oriented Duster 340 was updated with some engine carburetion improvements to enhance its efficiency and reliability, but the compression ratio was dropped so horsepower remained the same. Twelve new body colors and new stripe options were added to give more choices for a personalized appearance.

### C-Body

The C-Body two-door hardtop Fury and Sport Fury, like the Duster and Barracuda, were changed little with only slight restyling to the grille and rear fascia designs. The Fury line was still based on the same 120-inch-wheelbase C-Body platform as the previous year. The Sport Fury and Sport Fury GT offered the same engine and drivetrain options as the 1970 model, but the TorqueFlite 3-speed automatic was now standard, with the extra cost added to the base price.

## 1971 Road Runner and GTX

The new two-door hardtop Road Runner and GTX were designed on the completely restyled Satellite for 1971. The midsized B-Body platform for 1971 was based on a

*A 1971 Plymouth GTX finished in GK6 Dark Bronze Metallic with an optional 440 Six-Barrel engine, Rallye wheels, and Goodyear Polyglas raised white-letter tires.*

*The three-panel marker light on the driver-side front fender of a Dark Bronze Metallic 1971 Plymouth GTX hardtop. Note the thin black stripe line that follows the full length of the body.*

115-inch-wheelbase unibody design that included a new fuselage-type styling, similar to the larger C-Body Plymouth. No coupes or convertibles were available. The sides and fenders were more rounded than the 1970 models and the body had a longer appearance due to a longer rear overhang and shorter front overhang, giving the body a more massive and muscular appearance. It was actually a little shorter than the 1970 model but wider. The width of the body was increased from 73.4 to 75.9 inches, all adding to the perceived appearance of a much larger car. The GTX and Road Runner shipping weights still ranged from 3,640 to 3,675 pounds, so it was not lighter. The roofline was swept back behind the C-pillar, providing an image of speed and aerodynamic efficiency.

The front ends of both the RM23 Road Runner and RS23 GTX were dominated by a large chrome-plated loop-type inverted B-shaped front bumper surrounding a rectangular black mesh grille insert and quad round headlights. The GTX had a large, bright GTX badge in the center of the grille mesh. The Road Runner grille featured only a small Road Runner bird badge in its center.

An optional Elastomeric color-keyed body color front bumper was available as an option with Sales Code M73. The colored bumpers were created by spraying unchromed steel bumpers with a layer of urethane that was then painted in limited body colors. The GTX and Road Runner colored bumpers were only available in Bright Blue Metallic, Yellow, Avocado, Plum Crazy, Tor-Red, and Red. Each matched coordinated body colors.

Both the Road Runner and the GTX had a standard performance hood that featured twin side-facing simulated scoops with large engine call-outs in their centers. Both the GTX and Road Runner were also available with the optional functional Air Grabber fresh air hood (Sales Code N96), standard when the 426 Hemi engine was ordered. The Air Grabber was mounted in a large power bulge in the center of the hood. An optional flat-black tape panel was available that covered the entire power bulge. Optional chrome-plated hood pins were available with Sales Code J45.

*This is a driver-side rear view of a Tor-Red 1971 Road Runner with an optional black rear deck spoiler, Rallye wheels, Goodyear Polyglas raised white-letter tires, reflective body tape stripe on the roof quarters, and optional urethane painted body color front and rear bumpers. (Photo Courtesy Kori Alexander)*

The 1971 Satellite GTX and Road Runner were available in 24 color schemes, including the extra-cost High-Performance shades of C7 In-Violet, J6 Sassy Grass, V2 Tor-Red, and Y3 Curious Yellow. Standard interior trim in the GTX and optional in the Road Runner consisted of full-foam all-vinyl high-back bucket seats with integral head restraints. A fixed

An overhead front view of a Sassy Grass green 1971 Plymouth GTX with optional sunroof and black vinyl roof, rear deck spoiler, and Rallye wheels. (Photo Courtesy Tim Costello)

center cushion and folding front center armrest were optional at extra cost. The bucket seat interior was available in blue, green, tan, black, gunmetal, white, and gold. The GTX and Road Runner were also available with an optional trim scheme of cloth and vinyl high-back bucket seats with integral head restraints in green, black, and orange/black.

A total of 2,942 GTX and 14,218 Road Runner two-door hardtops were built for the 1971 model year.

Detailed view of the rear deck lid and chrome-plated bumper of a Sassy Grass 1971 GTX two-door hardtop with an optional black rear deck spoiler. (Photo Courtesy Tim Costello)

This Tor-Red 1971 Plymouth Road Runner has the optional urethane painted body color front and rear bumpers, 440 Six-Barrel engine, and Air-Grabber fresh air intake system. It is also equipped with optional Rallye wheels and raised white-letter tires. (Photo Courtesy Kori Alexander)

The rear deck lid of every 1971 GTX has this large red-and-white Plymouth GTX decal. This GTX is finished in Light Blue metallic. (Photo Courtesy Tim Costello)

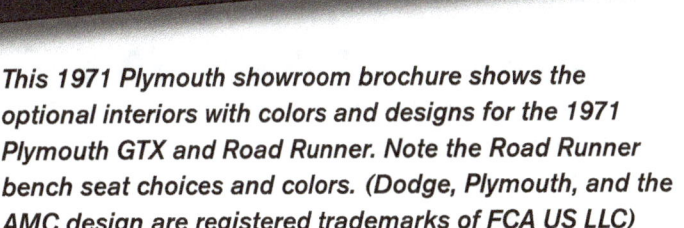

This 1971 Plymouth showroom brochure shows the optional interiors with colors and designs for the 1971 Plymouth GTX and Road Runner. Note the Road Runner bench seat choices and colors. (Dodge, Plymouth, and the AMC design are registered trademarks of FCA US LLC)

Chapter 8: Rapid Transit System for 1971    151

### Engine Options

The standard engine in the 1971 GTX was a 440-ci raised-block 4-barrel V-8 rated at 370 hp at 4,600 rpm and 380 ft-lbs of torque at 3,200 rpm. The 440 4-barrel was equipped with a single Carter AVS 4-barrel carburetor and still had the same 4.32 x 3.75–inch bore and stroke as previous years.

An optional engine for the 1971 GTX was the 440 RB V-8 with three Holley 2-barrel carburetors. The 440 Six-Barrel engine had a 10.2:1 compression ratio and produced 390 hp at 4,700 rpm and 490 ft-lbs of torque at 3,200 rpm.

The second optional engine available in the 1971 GTX was the 426-ci Hemi V-8. This was the last year for the Hemi, which finally succumbed to emissions and fuel mileage concerns. The 1971 version of the Hemi produced 425 hp at 4,600 rpm and 490 ft-lbs of torque at 4,000 with a 10.2:1 compression ratio. The Hemi was still equipped with two Carter AFB 4-barrel carburetors and its iconic wide black crackle-finish valve covers. The Hemi was painted Hemi Orange. Only 30 1971 GTX hardtops were equipped with a 426 Hemi engine in 1971.

Decorative nonfunctional hood louvers and the black-and-white decal on a Light Blue Metallic 1971 GTX show this car has the standard 440 single 4-barrel V-8. (Photo Courtesy Tim Costello)

This is the optional 440 Six-Barrel V-8 engine in a 1971 Plymouth GTX finished in FC7 In Violet. This GTX is equipped with power brakes and power steering. Note the open element air cleaner and black rubber seal for the Air-Grabber fresh air system.

This view shows the standard-equipment 440 Super Commando single 4-barrel V-8 engine in a blue 1971 Plymouth GTX. This GTX has manual brakes and power steering. (Photo Courtesy Tim Costello)

The standard engine in a 1971 Road Runner was the 383 V-8 with a single 4-barrel carburetor developing 300 hp at 4,800 rpm. This Road Runner is equipped with power steering and unassisted manual drum brakes.

The standard engine in a 1971 Road Runner was a 383-ci 4-barrel B-block V-8 with a bore and stroke of 4.25 x 3.75 inches. The 383 4-barrel had a compression ratio of 8.5:1 and produced 300 hp at 4,800 rpm and 410 ft-lbs of torque at 3,400 rpm. The 383 4-barrel had a single 4-barrel carburetor.

The second optional engine in the 1971 Road Runner was the small-block 340-ci V-8. The 340 developed 275 hp and 340 ft-lbs of torque with a 10.3:1 compression ratio. Horsepower ratings changed for the 1971 model year from the previous gross to net horsepower, so they cannot be directly compared. The old gross system measured the engine with no accessories, but the new net system reduced the horsepower ratings by rating the engines with all normal accessories. This change would serve to reduce the insurance surcharges based on horsepower.

The 340 V-8, indicated by an H on the VIN plate and a code of E55 on the fender data plate, had the same 4.04-inch bore and 3.31-inch stroke as the previous year. The 340 was now equipped with a Carter Thermo-Quad 4-barrel carburetor that used a large unsilenced air cleaner like the 1970 version. The air cleaner was finished in black crackle finish with painted metal insert. Only 1,681 Road Runners were built with the 340 V-8 in the 1971 model year.

One of the optional engines for the 1971 Road Runner was the same 440-ci V-8 with three 2-barrel carburetors that was offered in the GTX. Like the GTX version, the Six-Barrel Road Runner had a 10.2:1 compression ratio and produced 390 hp at 4,700 rpm and 490 ft-lbs of torque at 3,200 rpm.

The next engine option for the 1971 Road Runner was the 426 Hemi V-8, producing 425 hp at 4,600 rpm and 490 ft-lbs of torque at 4,000 rpm with a 10.2:1 compression ratio. The Road Runner Hemi had two Carter AFB 4-barrel carburetors and was identical to the engine used in the 1971 GTX. Only 55 Road Runner hardtops were produced with the 426 Hemi option.

## Transmission Options

The 1971 Plymouth Satellite GTX had a standard cast-aluminum case A727 3-speed TorqueFlite automatic transmission when equipped with the 440 V-8 engines. The TorqueFlite was operated with either a column- or console-mounted chrome shift lever, depending on the interior options. The standard transmission with the 1971 Road Runner with the 383 4-barrel V-8 only was the less expensive cast-iron case 3-speed manual transmission. The 3-speed was fully synchronized in all forward speeds, so you could downshift to low gear while the car was still moving. The 3-speed manual was available column-mounted, floor-mounted, and console-mounted, depending on the model and interior trim. The A727 TorqueFlite was optional with the Road Runner 383 V-8. A special small-diameter (11-inch) high-stall-speed torque converter was standard with the Road Runner.

*This is the P6X9 black vinyl bucket seat interior of an FJ6 Sassy Grass 1971 Plymouth RS23 GTX two-door hardtop. This GTX has the optional 4-speed transmission with Hurst pistol grip shifter and full-length center console. It also has the optional tape player. (Photo Courtesy Tim Costello)*

A cast-iron case A833 4-speed manual transmission with a 2.44:1 low gear was standard with the 426 Hemi and 440 and optional with a 2.47:1 low gear with the 383. The 4-speed used a Hurst shifter, which for the first time used a unique walnut-grain pistol grip design on a wide, flat Hurst chrome-plated handle. The chrome console-mounted shifter handle was curved to the left and back, as in the previous year, while the floor-mounted version was curved back and up. Original handles had a distinct taper in thickness toward the top. Both shifters used a pleated black rubber boot. The Hemi was available with an optional TorqueFlite automatic transmission.

## Rear Axle Options

The standard rear axle with the 1971 GTX with a 383, 440, or 426 Hemi engine and TorqueFlite automatic transmission was the Chrysler 8¾-inch banjo-type, which was available in ratios from 2.94:1 to 3.91:1, with 3.23:1 being standard. A 1⁷⁄₈-inch pinion stem differential used a carrier with Casting Number 2881489. A special Performance Axle Group option (Sales Code 358) was available that provided a 3.55:1 rear axle gear ratio, special slip-drive fan, and an extra-wide high-performance radiator fan shroud. When a 4-speed transmission was ordered with the 440 or 426 Hemi engine, a 9¾-inch ring gear Dana 60 heavy-duty rear axle with a 3.54:1 gear ratio was used, with an optional 4.10:1 ratio provided when the Super Track Pak or Super Performance Axle Packages were ordered. Single-piston power front disc brakes with floating calipers were optional. Both axles were supported with Chrysler-designed heavy-duty longitudinal parallel leaf springs.

### Wheel and Tire Options

The 1971 GTX was equipped with standard 14 x 6–inch stamped-steel wheels, which could be equipped with either a small hubcap or one of two new optional styled wheel covers. Optional 14-inch Magnum 500 styled Rallye road wheels with chrome trim rings were available. All-new 15-inch Rallye wheels with F60x15 Wide Oval tires were available as an option if heavy-duty brakes and Rallye Suspension were ordered.

Standard tires on the 383-powered Road Runner were F70 x 14–inch white sidewall tires that were only available with the heavy-duty suspension and power disc brakes that came with the Road Runner. Standard wheels were 14x6 painted pressed steel.

### Advertising and Publicity

Few magazine ads were produced for the 1971 GTX and Road Runner, but one of the first pieces was a two-page spread in the October 1970 issue of *Motor Trend*. The left page of the ad featured the front fascia of a red 1971 Road Runner placed on a desert background. The picture showed the distinctive Road Runner hood with the side-facing scoops and 383-engine callout. The large legend at the top of the page read, "It still goes Beep Beep," referring to the fact that although very different in appearance from the previous model, it was still a Road Runner.

The right page of the ad showed the rest of the car and alongside it, a very large image of the two feet of a Road Runner bird placed firmly on the ground. At the top of the page, a light area contained text that detailed the standard features of the Road Runner, plus the wider rear track and shorter wheelbase. At the bottom of the text, the rest of the 1971 Rapid Transit System was detailed, including the GTX, `Cuda, Duster 340, and Sport Fury GT. At the end of the small text, the last line in large black letters read, "The Rapid Transit System. Coming through."

Plymouth showroom brochures featured a few images of the 1971 GTX and Road Runner but not to the extent they were shown in previous years. One such brochure showed a

*A passenger-side front close-up view of the optional Rallye wheel and Goodyear Polyglas raised white-letter G60x15 tire on a Sassy Grass 1971 Plymouth GTX. Note the iconic Mopar gold Pentastar badge that was only on the passenger-side fender. (Photo Courtesy Tim Costello)*

*This two-page 1971 Plymouth Road Runner ad was published in a number of enthusiast magazines. It shows a red 1971 Road Runner with a 383 engine posed with the feet of a very large Road Runner bird. (Dodge, Plymouth, and the AMC design are registered trademarks of FCA US LLC)*

A page from a 1971 Plymouth dealer showroom brochure shows images of a red Road Runner and gold GTX along with text explaining the equipment and features of both models. Richard Petty's blue race car is in the background image. (Dodge, Plymouth, and the AMC design are registered trademarks of FCA US LLC)

two-page spread of a green Road Runner with a black strobe stripe over the C-pillar and Magnum 500 Styled wheels. A vertical white panel to its right detailed all of the standard features. Another page featured a yellow GTX shown from the passenger's side. The car had a black dual racing stripe across the front fenders and had steel Rallye wheels. Like the Road Runner pages, a vertical white panel to the right listed all of the standard features and equipment of the 1971 GTX. Additional pages had a table that listed all of the standard and optional equipment and specifications of both models.

### Performance

As expected, a number of enthusiast magazines such as *Car Life*, *Road & Track*, and *Motor Trend* published stories and road test reports on the new offerings from the Plymouth Rapid Transit System. The 1971 GTX with the 440 V-8 recorded a 0-60–mph run in 6.5 seconds, and a trip down the quarter-mile took 15.2 seconds at a trap speed of 92 mph. When equipped with the 426 Hemi engine, 0–60 mph came in at 5 seconds and the quarter-mile was 13.5 seconds at 105 mph. A similar 1971 Plymouth Road Runner with the 426 Hemi was estimated to run a 0-60–mph time of 5.6 seconds. The Hemi Road Runner was estimated to lap the quarter-mile at 13.49 seconds at 106 mph. All very capable performance numbers for the time. Performance differences between the GTX and Road Runner could be attributed to the variations in weight and options on each car.

Additional advertising opportunities came with the colorful brochures produced for the Supercar Clinics, presented by

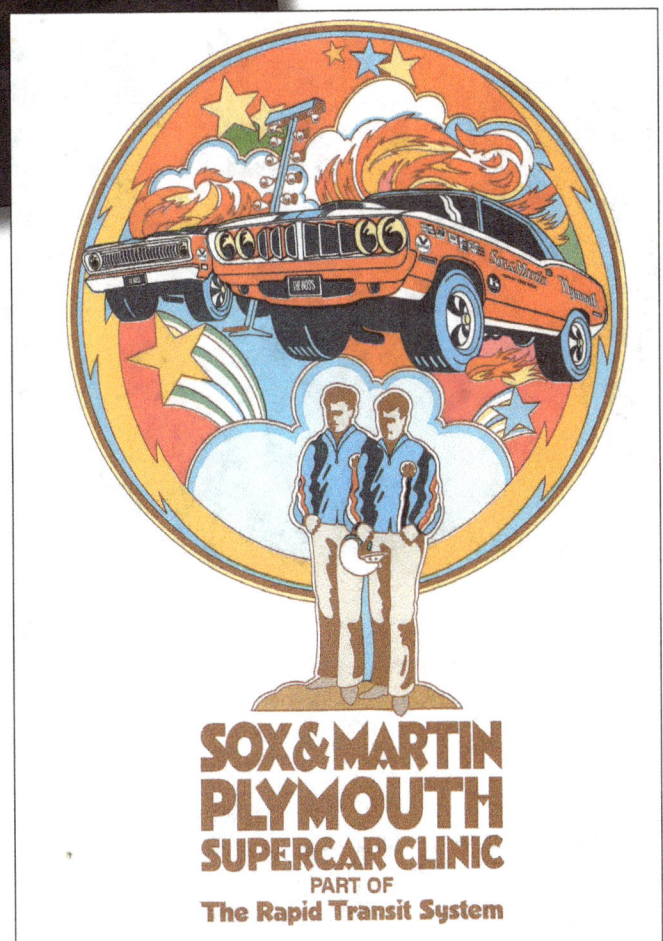

The back cover of one of the publications distributed for the Sox & Martin Supercar Clinics held at dealerships and racetracks around the country in 1971. It includes the iconic psychedelic artwork and a reference to the Rapid Transit System program. (Dodge, Plymouth, and the AMC design are registered trademarks of FCA US LLC)

Plymouth drag racing stars Don Grotheer and Sox & Martin. These illustrations were also used in showroom posters at the dealers presenting the programs. Both versions made it clear that these drag racing events were a part of the Rapid Transit

Don Grotheer was a prominent Super Stock and Pro Stock racer from the Midwest who ran Supercar Clinics and promoted the Rapid Transit System around his part of the country. This cover from one of his publications connects him to the RTS with this colorful image. (Dodge, Plymouth, and the AMC design are registered trademarks of FCA US LLC)

divider. Each panel had nine bright horizontal bars. The basic body design was the same, but a row of four vertical fake louvers decorated the upper rear of the front fenders. The rear fascia was redesigned by making the taillights and backup lights with horizontal passenger-side trim separate, rather than mounted in a single unit as in 1970.

The Barracuda and `Cuda were still offered in two-door hardtop and two-door convertible configurations, still on the same 108-inch-wheelbase unibody chassis. The 1971 `Cuda was offered in 17 body colors, including the five high-impact colors of Curious Yellow, Tor-Red, Sassy Grass, In Violet, and Lemon Twist. The 17 interior trim combinations accented the body color schemes. The standard `Cuda interior had full-foam all-vinyl high-back bucket seats with integrated backs. Production of the 1971 `Cuda showed 6,228 BS23 two-door hardtops and 374 BS27 two-door convertibles, including seven Hemi `Cuda convertibles for domestic sales and four more for Canada and foreign sales.

System program. None of the drag racers actually used RTS logos or decals prominently on their cars.

### 1971 `Cuda

The E-Body `Cuda for 1971 was much the same as the 1970 and did not offer the dramatic styling changes that identified the B-Body platform. The most noticeable update to the Barracuda and `Cuda was the change to four headlights and the accompanying redesign of the grille. The 1971 `Cuda grille featured six distinctive grille panels separated by a vertical center

#### `Cuda Engine Options

The standard engine in a 1971 `Cuda was a 383-ci B-block V-8 with a single 4-barrel carburetor, a bore and stroke of 4.25 x 3.38 inches, and a compression ratio of 8.5:1, producing 250 hp (net) at 4,800 rpm. The 383 was equipped with an unsilenced air cleaner and dual exhaust, making 325 ft-lbs (net) of torque at 3,400 rpm. Most significant was the special high-performance camshaft used only in the 383 V-8. This camshaft had a lift of .450 inch on the intake and .465 inch on the exhaust valve. Intake and exhaust duration was 268 degrees for the intake and 284 degrees for the exhaust, with 46 degrees of overlap. The 383 V-8 used in the 1971 `Cuda was also equipped

This GA4 Winchester Gray Metallic 1971 Hemi `Cuda convertible represents the ideal in second-year styling and performance of the E-Body design. Only seven 1971 Hemi `Cuda convertibles were built domestically, and this is one of only two with a 4-speed transmission. Note the chrome "gills" on the fenders and quad headlights.

*The engine compartment of a 1971 'Cuda with the optional 340-ci V-8 engine. This 'Cuda has optional power brakes. Note the black crackle-finish air cleaner and engine identity plate.*

with heavier valve springs, a standard windage tray, and dual exhaust. The 383 V-8 had a single Holley 4160 carburetor with vacuum-operated secondaries. Most 383 high-performance engines in 1971 were painted Chrysler Performance Orange, but some 1971 engines may have been finished in Chrysler Engine Medium Blue.

The first optional engine in the 1971 'Cuda was the LA-series V-8 with 340 ci that developed 235 hp and 310 ft-lbs of torque. Horsepower ratings changed for the 1971 model year from the previous gross to net horsepower, so they cannot be directly compared. The old standard BHP system measured the engine with no accessories, but the new net system reduced the horsepower ratings by rating the engines with all normal accessories. This change would serve to reduce the insurance surcharges based on horsepower.

The 340 V-8, indicated by an H on the VIN plate and a code of E55 on the fender data plate, had the same 4.04-inch bore and 3.31-inch stroke as the previous year. The 340 was equipped with a Carter Thermo-Quad 4-barrel carburetor that used a large unsilenced air cleaner like the 1970 version. The air cleaner was finished in black crackle finish with painted metal insert that read "340 4-barrel." The 340 engine was painted Street Hemi Orange until April 1971, when the finish was changed to Chrysler Engine Blue.

The second engine option in the 1971 'Cuda was the 440-ci RB-based V-8 with three 2300 series 2-barrel Holley carburetors mounted on a Chrysler cast-iron intake manifold. This engine was identified with a V-code on the VIN and E87 on the body code plate. The 440 Six-Barrel engine had a 10.3:1 compression ratio and was now rated at 330 hp (net) at 4,700 rpm and 410 ft-lbs (net) of torque at 3,200 rpm. The 440 Six-Barrel was indicated by a V in the VIN and a sales code of E87 on the fender data plate. A limited number of 440 4-barrel equipped 'Cudas may have been built, but they were special order and not a regular option.

The third engine option available with the 1971 'Cuda was the 426 Hemi V-8 rated at 425 gross hp at 5,000 rpm and 490 ft-lbs of gross torque at 4,000 rpm. The new net horsepower was rated at 350 at 5,000 rpm with net torque at 390 at 5,000 rpm. The two Carter AFB 4-barrel-equipped Hemis had a bore and stroke of 4.25 x 3.75 inches and a compression ratio of 10.3:1. The Hemi cast-iron and heads and cast-aluminum intake manifold were finished in Late Street Hemi Orange with a black crackle-finish air cleaner. The large, wide Hemi valvecovers were black crackle finish. An R on the VIN and E74 on the body code plate indicated the Hemi. This was the final year for the Hemi.

### Transmissions Options

The A230 Synchro-Silent 3-speed manual transmission was standard with the 383 and 340 engines. The 3-speed had a cast-iron case and aluminum extension.

*The black vinyl pleated bucket seat interior of a Sassy Grass 1971 'Cuda hardtop. This 'Cuda has a console-mounted shifter for the TorqueFlite 3-speed automatic transmission.*

Chapter 8: Rapid Transit System for 1971

The 1971 Plymouth 'Cuda was equipped with the 440 and 426 Hemi engines and had a standard cast-aluminum case A727 3-speed TorqueFlite automatic transmission when equipped with the 440 V-8 engines. The TorqueFlite was optional with all engines. The TorqueFlite was operated with either a column- or console-mounted chrome shift lever, depending on the interior options. A cast-iron case A833 4-speed manual transmission with a 2.44:1 low gear was standard with the 426 Hemi and optional with the 440. The 4-speed used a Hurst shifter with a unique walnut-grain pistol grip design on a wide, flat Hurst chrome-plated handle. The chrome-plated console-mounted shifter handle was curved to the left and back, as in the previous year, while the floor-mounted version was curved back and up. Original handles had a distinct taper in thickness toward the top. Both shifters used a pleated black rubber boot. The Hemi was available with an optional TorqueFlite automatic transmission.

### Rear Axle Options

The standard rear axle with the 1971 'Cuda equipped with a 440 or 426 Hemi engine and TorqueFlite automatic transmission was the Chrysler 8¾-inch banjo-type, which was available in ratios from 2.76:1 to 3.91:1, with 3.23:1 being standard. A 1⁷⁄₈-inch pinion stem was used on all 1971 models, so they will have a differential carrier with Casting Number 2881489. A special Performance Axle Group option (Sales Code 358) was available that provided a 3.55:1 rear axle gear ratio, special slip-drive fan, and an extra-wide high-performance radiator fan shroud. When a 4-speed transmission was ordered with the 440 or 426 Hemi engine, a 9¾-inch ring gear Dana 60 heavy-duty rear axle with a 3.54:1 gear ratio was used. An optional 4.10:1 ratio was provided when the Super Track Pak or Super Performance Axle Packages were ordered. Single-piston power front disc brakes with floating calipers were optional.

### Wheel and Tire Options

The 1971 'Cuda had standard 14 x 6–inch stamped-steel wheels, which could be equipped with either a small hubcap or one of two new optional styled wheel covers. Optional 14-inch Magnum 500 styled road wheels with chrome-plated trim rings were available. Because of the redesigned standard wheels, 15-inch wheels were no longer required for the 426 Hemi. All-new 15-inch Rallye wheels with F60x15 Wide Oval tires were available as an option if heavy-duty brakes and Rallye Suspension were ordered. All steel wheels were restyled for 1971 and featured a flat surface at the lug nut–mounting area.

### Production Numbers

The 1971 model year 'Cuda production included 6,228 BS23 'Cuda hardtops and 374 BS27 'Cuda convertibles.

### 'Cuda Advertising and Publicity

A pair of nearly identical 71 'Cudas adorned a Rapid Transit System advertisement in the fall of 1970. Both cars wore a shade of red with matching billboard stripes and black vinyl roofs. The main difference was on and under the hood. On the left, a 340-equipped machine sat underneath the standard hood. On the right, a 426 Hemi lay underneath a shaker assembly.

The 340 (left) and 426 (right) powered 'Cudas showed off their muscular appearance in front of the now-defunct Motor City Dragway grandstands. Although visually similar, the 86-cube difference left little doubt as to which one would win should they tackle the quarter-mile. (Dodge, Plymouth, and the AMC design are registered trademarks of FCA US LLC)

### 1971 Plymouth Duster 340

The 1971 Plymouth Duster was still based on the same 108-inch-wheelbase unibody platform as the Valiant. The Duster was available as only a two-door hardtop coupe in two different models. The Duster model destined for the Plymouth Rapid Transit System program was the VS29 Duster 340, which was equipped with a standard 275-hp 340-ci LA-series V-8. The 340 Duster had a shipping weight of 3,110 pounds, which gave it a power-to-weight ratio offering the potential for performance-level acceleration and handling. Like the previous 1970 model, quarter-mile times into the 14-second ET bracket were a prerequisite for the Rapid Transit System team, and the 340 Duster made the grade.

The 1971 Duster 340 was available in seven standard body colors and eight interior trim schemes, with an optional vinyl roof available in complementary colors. The 1971 model was similar to the 1970, but the grille was redesigned and the Valiant badge no longer appeared on the nameplate. The interior was available with a standard bench seat or optional bucket seat and center console configuration. A pistol-grip floor shifter accompanied the optional 4-speed transmission and an optional 8,000-rpm tachometer was available with the center console. A 3-speed manual transmission was standard with a 3-speed TorqueFlite automatic optional. The Duster was equipped with standard front disc brakes and E70x14 tires mounted on 14 x 5–1.2 Rallye wheels. A total of 12,886 Duster 340s were built for the 1971 model year.

### Engine Specifications

The standard engine in the 1971 Duster 340 was the LA-series V-8 with 340 ci that developed 235 hp and 310 ft-lbs of torque. Horsepower ratings changed for the 1971 model year from the previous gross to net horsepower, so they cannot be directly compared. The old standard brake horsepower system measured the engine with no accessories, but the new net system reduced the advertised horsepower by rating the engines with all normal accessories. This change would serve to reduce the insurance surcharges based on horsepower.

The 340 V-8, indicated by an H on the VIN plate and a code of E55 on the fender data plate, had a 4.04-inch bore and 3.31-inch stroke. The 340 had a 10.3:1 compression ratio and had a new Carter Thermo-Quad 4-barrel carburetor that used a large unsilenced air cleaner. Of course, premium fuel was required. The air cleaner was finished in black crackle finish with painted metal insert that read "340 4-barrel." The 340 engine was painted Street Hemi Orange until April 1971, when the finish was changed to Chrysler Engine Blue. Dual exhaust was standard with the Demon 340. Standard brakes were 10 x 2¼–inch front and 10 x 1³⁄₂–inch rear brake drums. Power brakes and power disc brakes were optional on the Demon 340.

### Transmission Options

The 1971 Plymouth Duster 340 was equipped with a standard fully synchronized 3-speed manual shift transmission with a floor-shift. An A-833 cast-iron case 4-speed manual transmission with a floor-mounted shifter was optional. An A727 TorqueFlite 3-speed automatic transmission was also optional in the Duster 340.

### Rear Axle Options

The standard rear axle was a Chrysler 8¾-inch ring gear with a number of optional gear ratios. A 3.23:1 ratio was standard, with 3.55:1 and 3.91:1 optional. The standard Rallye suspension was supported with heavy-duty front torsion bars, Firm-Ride shock absorbers, anti-sway bar, and heavy-duty rear longitudinal parallel leaf springs.

### Wheel and Tire Options

Standard tires were E70x14 Fiberglass-belted mounted on 14x5.5J steel wheels. Rallye and styled road wheels were available as options.

### Advertising and Publicity

Like that of other Plymouth models, advertising for the 1971 Duster 340 and Twister was limited. One of the more common two-page magazine layouts featured two cars, a Duster 340 and a Twister, both in bright green, facing the reader. Each had special options to attract the attention of

**One of the pages that was used in the showroom brochure and in a number of magazine ads. It shows the 1971 Duster Twister and Duster 340. The Twister has optional twin simulated hood scoops. (Dodge, Plymouth, and the AMC design are registered trademarks of FCA US LLC)**

### Duster 340 and Duster

Dusters, coming through and lookin' good. And in comparison with other economy cars they look even better. Big difference between the Duster and the Duster 340 is the size of the engine. And since that's a pretty big difference, we also gave the Duster 340 cloth-and-vinyl seats with a bucket-seat appearance, and special tape stripes. Standard.

*A green 1971 Plymouth Duster 340 is featured on this page from a dealer showroom brochure. This Duster has the white special tape stripe, standard on the Duster 340. (Dodge, Plymouth, and the AMC design are registered trademarks of FCA US LLC)*

readers and potential buyers, such as the twin hood scoops, Rallye wheels, and body stripes.

A rear view of a bright green Duster 340 was also shown prominently in a factory showroom brochure for 1971. The image showed a young couple gazing at a Duster 340 in the foreground; in the background, another couple seemed to be looking over at the green car while they were examining an orange Duster.

### 1971 Sport Fury GT

The Plymouth Sport Fury GT continued as the largest and most expensive car in the Rapid Transit System stable. The 1971 Sport Fury GT styling was much the same as the 1970 model and still rested on a long 120-inch-wheelbase chassis.

The high-performance model of the Fury line was the 1971 Sport Fury with the GT package. The PP23 1971 Sport Fury GT was the ideal candidate for the Rapid Transit System with a standard 370-hp 440-ci wedge V-8. The Sport Fury GT was also available with an optional 390-hp 440 Six-Barrel V-8 with three Holley 2-barrel carburetors.

Sport Fury GT suspension was heavy-duty and included .98-inch-diameter torsion bars, heavy-duty shock absorbers, a .94-inch-diameter front anti-sway bar, and heavy-duty six-leaf rear springs. Standard brakes were 11-inch drums with self-adjusting 3-inch-wide

*The sweeping and flowing lines of the 1971 Sport Fury GT present an image of definite power, even in this large and heavy car. The 440-ci V-8 with three 2-barrel carburetors provides the proof. (Curtiss Lichty Photo)*

*The 1971 Plymouth Sport Fury GT was arguably the most unusual of the Rapid Transit System cars. The large C-Body was not generally thought of as a high-performance vehicle, but the promotional materials and shows strongly presented that image to the buying public. (Curtiss Lichty Photo)*

*One of the distinctive features of the 1971 Plymouth Sport Fury GT was the large graphic stripes and logo on the hood. The letters GT and 440 logo left no doubt that this was something special. (Curtiss Lichty Photo)*

shoes in the front and 2½-inch-wide shoes in the rear. Power disc front brakes with full-floating calipers were optional.

To identify the Sport Fury GT, the hood had dual power bulges with bright 440 engine badges and pinstripes on both sides of the hood, in addition to special stripes on the body sides. Only 375 Sport Fury GTs were produced for the 1971 model year.

### Engine Options

The standard powerplant of the 1971 Plymouth Sport Fury GT was the 440-ci Commando V-8 based on the RB wedge combustion chamber design. The 440 Commando engine had a single 4-barrel carburetor and a 9.7:1 compression ratio that produced 370 hp at 4,600 rpm and 480 ft-lbs of torque at 2,800 rpm. The horsepower and torque at lower RPMs than the higher-performance versions of the 440 were needed to move the heavier Fury down the road with vigor. The 440 V-8 had a bore of 4.32 inches and a stroke of 3.75 inches. The air cleaner was a dual snorkel design that provided more efficient airflow for the large displacement engine. The 440 V-8 in the Fury required premium fuel to prevent knock.

### Transmission Options

The 1971 Plymouth Fury GT standard equipment transmission was a "High-Upshift" A727 TorqueFlite 3-speed automatic. There were no optional transmissions available. The driveshaft was attached to an extra-heavy-duty Dana built 9¾-inch ring gear rear axle by a 3.25-inch-diameter driveshaft with heavy-duty 7290 universal joints. The standard rear axle gear ratio was 3.23:1, with 2.76:1 optional.

### Wheel and Tire Options

Standard wheels for the 1971 Sport Fury GT were 15 x 6–inch steel with H-70x15 Polyglas-belted tires. Styled steel 15-inch Rallye wheels with bright trim rings were optional on the Sport Fury GT.

### Advertising and Publicity

There was little print advertising for the new 1971 Sport Fury GT, but it was featured prominently in the factory showroom brochures alongside the other Fury models. The limited market for a large C-Body high-performance car meant that Plymouth Division would not put too much into any promotional programs directed toward the buying public. One colorful brochure page showed a red 1971 Sport Fury GT with the black graphic "GT" on its hood. A bright yellow Road Runner GTX was posed in the background.

*An option in the 1971 Sport Fury GT was the 440 Super Commando V-8 that developed 370 hp at 4,600 rpm. This black Sport Fury is also equipped with air conditioning and power disc front brakes. (Curtiss Lichty Photo)*

*A 1971 Plymouth showroom brochure page shows a red Sport Fury GT and a Yellow GTX with special black stripe package, both members of the Rapid Transit System for 1971. (Dodge, Plymouth, and the AMC design are registered trademarks of FCA US LLC)*

*A dealer showroom brochure page features a red 1971 Sport Fury GT with a standard equipment 440 4-barrel V-8 engine. The Sport Fury had a "look of restrained elegance" and was considered a Super Luxury car. (Dodge, Plymouth, and the AMC design are registered trademarks of FCA US LLC)*

# THE 1971 RAPID TRANSIT SYSTEM CARAVA

The Rapid Transit System production cars and the national RTS Caravan continued well into 1971 with similar model offerings and momentum from 1970. The biggest and most obvious changes were in the styling and construction of the 1971 B-Body lineup of performance cars available for sale. From the production plants to the dealer lots, 1971 was the most significant model change in many years. Much like the Dodge Charger, the midsized Plymouth model lineup was changed for 1971, and the styling of the cars took an entirely new direction.

### Duster

The momentum of the 1970 RTS Caravan was not lost to the 1971 model change, and the excitement and interest of the

*This is a Plymouth publicity image of the RTS Duster as it looked in 1971 with changes in the paint and graphics. The 340 graphic on the hood was a major update. (Dodge, Plymouth, and the AMC design are registered trademarks of FCA US LLC)*

*This passenger-side rear view shows more of the modifications made to the custom Duster for the 1971 Rapid Transit System Caravan tours. Note the updated multiple exhaust setup. (Dodge, Plymouth, and the AMC design are registered trademarks of FCA US LLC)*

The green 1971 Duster as it looks today in the fabulous Steven Juliano collection in California. The updated Duster now received the same hood callout numbering as seen on the production models, sans the "WEDGE" wording. Steve has almost every piece of Scat Pack and Rapid Transit System material and cars. (Diego Rosenberg Photo)

Left front shot of the green custom 1971 Duster shows exactly how the car appears today and how it was when last shown at the RTS Caravans. (Diego Rosenberg Photo)

A passenger-side rear detailed view of the custom green 1971 Duster shows the level of workmanship used in the modifications of these cars. The custom-fabricated rectangular exhaust tips were fitted into matching openings in the rear fascia. (Diego Rosenberg Photo)

A detailed view of the passenger-side front end and special round European-style headlights of the green custom 1971 Duster used in the Rapid Transit System Caravans in 1971. (Diego Rosenberg Photo)

public at those dealer events continued to feed sales. The four Caravan cars remained much the same, except for the Duster and a new Road Runner. The Duster was significantly restyled. In place of the wild two-tone bronze and orange metallic finish on the 1970 version, the 1971 Duster was updated and repainted with a bright multi-hued high-impact green with a darker side panel over a lighter base body shade.

### Road Runner

The 1971 RTS Road Runner Caravan concept car was based on the entirely new body design and had a front fascia that was swept forward at the tops and carried dual rectangular headlights of each side, stacked one on top of the other. The paint finish was a bright orange with a wide white panel that wrapped around the perimeter of the body and across the top of the front fascia. On top of the hood were two wide, longitudinal scoops, inset at the rear of the hood panel with horizontal air intake screens. The deck lid sloped down at the rear and a wide spoiler was placed across the deck between the fenders. The rear deck panel was white and carried two horizontal rectangular taillight assemblies. The wheels were extra-wide Magnum-type with bright deep trim rings.

Chapter 8: Rapid Transit System for 1971     163

This is a driver-side front quarter view of the fully customized 1971 Road Runner built for the 1971 Rapid Transit System traveling Caravan. This is a Plymouth publicity shot. (Dodge, Plymouth, and the AMC design are registered trademarks of FCA US LLC)

A passenger-side rear image of the custom 1971 Plymouth Road Runner built to display at the 1971 Rapid Transit System shows around the country. (Dodge, Plymouth, and the AMC design are registered trademarks of FCA US LLC)

The 1971 Rapid Transit System Caravan featured specially built custom Plymouths, including a 1971 Road Runner emblazoned with wild paint schemes, colors, and graphics to attract the interest of potential young buyers. Little of the Road Runner remained stock. (Diego Rosenberg Photo)

A photo of the highly modified 1971 Road Runner on display at one of the Rapid Transit System shows on a Plymouth dealer's lot. All of the display materials were brought to the location in a larger tractor-trailer rig with advertising on the sides. (Dodge, Plymouth, and the AMC design are registered trademarks of FCA US LLC)

The Rapid Transit System customized 1971 Road Runner on display in Steve Juliano's collection. The Road Runner showroom memorabilia are very appropriate display items to accompany the car. (Diego Rosenberg Photo)

*Very little changed aesthetically from the 1970 rendition. The front fascia, mirrors, shaker assembly and sidepipes returned for 1971. One clear addition was a dash-mounted tachometer. (Photo Courtesy Promotions, Inc.)*

## `Cuda

In addition to the updated Duster and new Road Runner, the 1971 Caravan included two cars carried over from the 1970 program. The Don Prudhomme `Cuda Funny Car was kept much as it was shown on the 1971 Caravan, but the `Cuda 440 was updated.

The 1971 `Cuda show car was the same car used in the 1970 Caravan, but because the production `Cuda received design changes, those needed to be applied to the show car edition. The dual headlight arrangement in 1970 was changed to quad headlights so the show car would represent the current model. Stylists decided that the distinctive chin spoiler and front-end extension and Shaker hood scoop were important and would remain identical to 1970. The side of the `Cuda kept the impressive sides pipes for a look of power. With changes to the front fascia most important, the rear of the `Cuda remained much the same with its parachute, wheelie bars, and rear window braces. The overall look of the car was changed dramatically for 1971 by the addition of red, yellow, and white panels coated with Merano Pearlescent to give it a depth of color.

*Year two of the RTS 'Cuda saw a repaint to an orange and white scheme. Simulated wheelie bars and a parachute cap off the rear of the car. (Photo Courtesy Promotions, Inc.)*

Chapter 8: Rapid Transit System for 1971     165

# CHAPTER 9
# RAPID TRANSIT SYSTEM FOR 1972

*"Whether you become a member of the System. Or a not-so-distant cousin."*

The last official year for the Plymouth Rapid Transit System program and cars was 1972. By this time, insurance surcharges and government regulations had marked the end of the American high-performance automobile enthusiasm of the time. Compression ratios were down, horsepower was down, and the American automobile manufacturer's taste for performance seemed to dwindle. Gone was the 426 Hemi V-8, Dodge and Plymouth's leader in high-performance image. Now it seemed that fuel mileage, emissions, and safety were pushed to the front of the line and made the priority. None of this stopped Plymouth from continuing to promote and make the most of their highly successful Rapid Transit System advertising and marketing program.

### 1972 Rapid Transit System Lineup

The basic lineup was the same, except that along with the 426 Hemi, the GTX and the Sport Fury GT were gone. A new 400-ci B-block V-8 replaced the old 383, but horsepower and compression ratio overall was lower across the lineup. The 440 Six-Barrel option still existed in the brochures and catalogs, but horsepower was reduced to 385. It's currently known that only a couple of 1972 Plymouths were built.

Very few print ads were produced mentioning the 1972 Rapid Transit System and they were directed at pointing out that the standard line of cars had almost the same features as

**One of very few ads representing the 1972 Rapid Transit System line of cars from Plymouth. The ad shows a GTX, Satellite, Duster 340, Twister, Barracuda, and 'Cuda. The ad is illustrating how the non-RTS cars are similar to the RTS stable. (Dodge, Plymouth, and the AMC design are registered trademarks of FCA US LLC)**

166    Dodge Scat Pack and Plymouth Rapid Transit System

the performance-oriented Rapid Transit System choices. One ad was a two-page full color piece with RTS models on the left and standard models on the right in an outdoor setting. The headline said, "The Rapid Transit System and friends." The point was that you might not need what those performance cars offered and the others would be good enough. The Sport Fury was not shown at all.

Another 1972 color print ad showed twin images of a blue 1972 Satellite compared with a blue 1972 Road Runner. The headline simply said, "There's even a stronger resemblance." The text to the right explained that both cars have the same kind of guts and engineering, giving one the same choice without spending more money. Not really a performance encouragement for a new car buyer. Beyond that, the showroom brochures and print ads pretty much ignored the RTS entirely, concentrating on the basic features of each model.

### 1972 Road Runner

As in 1971, the RM23 Road Runner was based on the Satellite line and was available only as a two-door hardtop model. The Road Runner was based on the same body as the 1971 models with only small changes in sidelights, rear bumper, and taillights, a restyled grille with a vertical center peak, and some new tape stripe choices. The Road Runner still had a standard equipment Performance Hood with the side-facing scoops. The GTX was no longer offered, but if the Road Runner was ordered with the 440 engine it was called a Road Runner GTX and added GTX grille and deck lid badges. The Road Runner was available in 14 body colors and 13 interior trim combinations.

The sweeping lines of the body of a 1972 Road Runner two-door hardtop are clear in this rear view. This Road Runner has an optional sunroof with black vinyl roof, and Rallye wheels and white-letter tires, one of two known with the 440 Six-Barrel V-8. (Photo Courtesy Tim Costello)

### Engine Options

The standard powerplant in the 1972 Plymouth Road Runner was the new 400-ci B-block V-8, replacing the 383. The 400 block was identical to the 383, except that it had a larger 4.34-inch bore. The 1972 Road Runner 400 had an 8.2:1 compression ratio and developed 255 hp at 4,800 rpm and 340 ft-lbs of torque at 3,200 rpm. The 400 V-8 in the Road Runner was equipped with a single 4-barrel carburetor.

An EV2 Tor-Red 1972 Plymouth Road Runner with an optional black vinyl roof, Air Grabber fresh air intake system, and Rallye wheels with Goodyear Polyglas raised white-letter tires. This Road Runner also has an optional sunroof and rare 440 Six-Barrel V-8 engine. (Photo Courtesy Tim Costello)

The 280-hp 440 single 4-barrel V-8 was optional with the 1972 Plymouth Road Runner two-door hardtop. This original unrestored 1972 Road Runner GTX has the optional vacuum-operated Air-Grabber fresh air intake system.

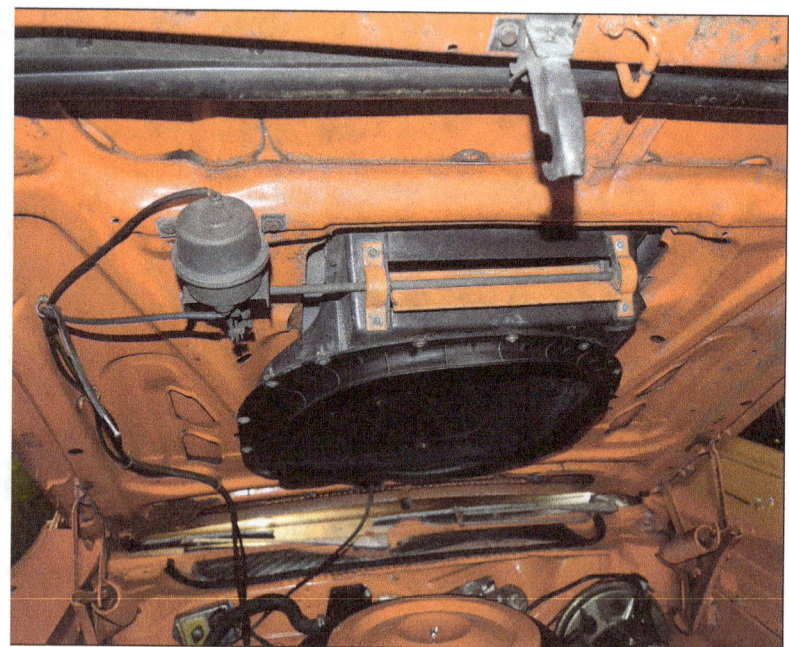

*The optional N96 Air-Grabber fresh-air intake system was a $71 addition to the price of a new 1972 Road Runner GTX. A switch on the instrument panel manually operated the Air-Grabber door on the hood.*

Optional in the 1972 Road Runner was a small-block 340-ci V-8 with a single 4-barrel carburetor and 8.5:1 compression ratio that developed 240 hp at 4,800 rpm and 290 ft-lbs of torque at 3,600 rpm. A total of 2,168 1972 Road Runners were built with the 340 V-9.

*The 440 V-8 with three 2-barrel Holley carburetors was a rare option in the 1972 Road Runner GTX. Only three were built. This restored 440 engine has the correct orange oval-shaped air-cleaner with the distinctive 440 Six-Barrel decal. (Photo Courtesy Tim Costello)*

The second optional engine was the 440 ci RB-block-based V-8 with a single 4-barrel carburetor and an 8.2:1 compression ratio. The Road Runner GTX 440 developed 280 hp at 4,800 rpm and 380 ft-lbs of torque at 3,200 rpm. A total of only 672 Road Runners came with the 440 4-barrel engine in the 1972 model year.

The 1972 Road Runner drivetrain options were much the same as the 1971 models. When equipped with the 440 engines, the 1972 Road Runner was badged as a Road Runner GTX.

In addition to the 440 single 4-barrel V-8, one 1972 Road Runner exists to date with the 440 Six-Barrel option that was not originally supposed to be built due to increased EPA restrictions and requirements.

### Transmission Options

A fully synchronized 3-speed manual transmission was standard with the 1972 Road Runner with the 340- or 400-ci V-8. A 3-speed TorqueFlite 727 automatic was optional with the 340 and 400 and standard when equipped with either of the two 440 V-8 engines. A 4-speed manual transmission was optional with all engines.

*This shows the P6X9 black vinyl bucket seat interior trim of a Tor-Red 1972 Plymouth Road Runner. This Road Runner is equipped with the optional tape player and center console with shifter for the TorqueFlite automatic transmission. (Photo Courtesy Tim Costello)*

### Rear Axle Options

The standard rear axle with the 1972 Road Runner with a 400, 440, or 340 engine and TorqueFlite automatic transmission was the Chrysler 8¾-inch banjo-type, which was available in ratios from 2.94:1 to 3.91:1, with 3.23:1 being standard. A 1⅞-inch pinion stem differential used a carrier with Casting Number 2881489. A special Performance Axle Group option (Sales Code 358) was available that provided a 3.55:1 rear axle gear ratio, special slip-drive fan, and an extra-wide high-performance radiator fan shroud. When a 4-speed transmission was ordered with the 440 engine, a 9¾-inch ring gear Dana 60 heavy-duty rear axle with a 3.54:1 gear ratio was used, with an optional 4.10:1 ratio provided when the Super Track Pak or Super Performance Axle Packages were ordered. Single-piston power front disc brakes with floating calipers were optional. Both axles were supported with Chrysler-designed heavy-duty longitudinal parallel leaf springs.

### Wheel and Tire Options

Standard tires on a 1972 Plymouth Road Runner were F70x14–inch white sidewall. F70x14, G70x14 and G60x15-inch raised white-letter tires were optional.

*This 1971 magazine ad is emphasizing the strong resemblance between the performance Plymouths of the Rapid Transit System and the cheaper non-performance models. This clearly shows the end of the high-performance era of that time. (Dodge, Plymouth, and the AMC design are registered trademarks of FCA US LLC)*

*This detailed shot shows the optional 15-inch Rallye wheels with G60x15 Goodyear Polyglas raised white-letter tires on the rear of a Tor-Red 1971 Road Runner. (Photo Courtesy Tim Costello)*

### Production Numbers

A total of 7,628 Plymouth Road Runners were built for the 1972 model year. A total of 2,168 of them were equipped with the 340 V-8 and 672 with the 440 single 4-barrel engine.

### Advertising and Publicity

The 1972 Road Runner was shown in only a couple of ads. One of the more commonly found in a number of magazines is a double-page presentation showing three RTS Plymouths on the left in a rocky, desert setting balanced with images of three nonperformance but similar cars on the right. The ad featured a Duster 340, a Road Runner, and a `Cuda, compared to their economical cousins on the right side of the picture. The message of the text was that although the RTS cars on the left have more performance and less luxury, you might be well satisfied with those on the right. The idea was to try to de-emphasize the importance of the performance image and encourage you to buy something else instead.

A similar-themed ad was also published in 1972 that directly compared a blue Road Runner on the left with an upside-down identical-appearing blue Satellite on the right. The text said that you might be happy with the Road Runner's not-so-distant cousin.

### 1972 Plymouth `Cuda

The 1972 Barracuda and V-8 powered `Cuda used the same basic unitized body shell and subframe but were treated

*The 1972 Plymouth `Cuda Sport Coupe styling was changed little from 1971 with only a modified grille design and the loss of the iconic "gills" that identified the 1971 model. This TX9 black `Cuda shows the standard 14-inch steel wheels and small hubcaps.*

to styling changes and reverted to the two-headlight configuration used in 1970 but with an entirely new grille design. The lower deck panel of the Barracuda also received a new look with two pairs of round taillights. Both models were now available only as a base two-door hardtop. The chrome front bumper with standard guards was continued from 1971 with optional M85 rubber inserts. The `Cuda featured a standard steel Sport Hood with standard scoops that was also available as an option on any standard Barracuda.

### Exterior Options

The 1972 `Cuda was available in 15 body colors, including two high-impact colors in EV2 Tor-Red and FY1 Lemon Twist. At this time, however, wild colors had begun to lose their appeal as more buyers opted for mundane colors.

### Interior Options

The 1972 `Cuda had full-foam all-vinyl high-back bucket seats as standard equipment. The seats featured a pattern with plain, smooth skirts, bolsters, and back side, and 10 longitudinal pleats on each cushion and back. The interior was available in 10 color schemes.

### `Cuda Engine Options

The standard engine for the 1972 `Cuda was now the LA-based 318-ci V-8 with a single 2-barrel carburetor that developed 150 hp at 4,000 rpm.

**The 340 V-8 engine in a 1972 `Cuda was painted Chrysler Engine Blue and topped with an orange air cleaner and 340 4-barrel decal. A standard electronic ignition module was located on the passenger side of the firewall. This 340 is equipped with optional air-conditioning.**

The only optional engine offered in the 1972 Plymouth `Cuda was the LA-based 340 V-8. The 340 was changed for 1972 and now had the same cylinder heads as the Chrysler 360 V-8 with smaller intake valves and a compression ratio of 8.5:1. The 1972 340 had a single 4-barrel carburetor and produced 240 hp at 4,800 rpm and 290 ft-lbs of torque at 3,800 rpm. A new electronic ignition system was made standard on 340 engines after September 1972 and featured a control box mounted on the passenger-side firewall. The electronic ignition distributor eliminated the breaker points and condenser, increasing reliability. The electronic ignition system was optional on the 318 V-8.

### Transmission Options

The standard transmission on the 1972 `Cuda was the Synchro-Silent A-230 3-speed manual. The A-833 4-speed was an extra-cost option with the 340 4-barrel only. The Hurst floor shift was the same type used on the 1970–1971, using the iconic pistol-grip handle. Two versions of the TorqueFlite 3-speed automatic were available, depending upon which engine was ordered. The Slant Six and 318 V-8 used the A-904G or L version, while the 340 V-8 used the A-727A. Both had a natural finish aluminum case and unfinished steel oil pan.

### Rear Axle Options

Standard rear axle on a 318-equipped 1972 `Cuda was a 7¼-inch ring gear with removable rear inspection plate, with the 8¾-inch Chrysler banjo-type unit optional. Standard gear ratios were 2.76:1, with optional ratios up to 3.55:1 available. The optional 3.55:1 axle ratio was available only with the A36 Performance Axle Package that included the Sure Grip differential, heavy-duty 26-inch radiator with fan shroud, and power steering oil cooler (if power steering was ordered). This package was available only with the 340 engine.

### Wheel and Tire Options

Standard tires for the 1972 `Cuda were F70x14 bias-belted Wide Oval white sidewall. All models were available with any optional tires, including the F70x14 bias-belted Wide Oval with raised white-letters, but heavy-duty suspension was required. The F70x14 RWL tires were a no-cost option with the `Cuda.

### Production Numbers

A total of 5,864 340 `Cudas were built for the 1972 model year, as pony cars in general all saw slumping sales.

### Advertising and Publicity

Paired with the pedestrian Barracuda two-door hardtop, the 1972 `Cuda in the ad seemed to be driving away from its muscle car persona as the Barracuda "6 or V-8" took center stage. With the big-block off the menu, the 'Cuda began the slow slide into oblivion and wouldn't last past the 1974 model year.

### 1972 Plymouth Duster 340

The 1972 Plymouth Duster 340 was much the same as the 1971, with few changes. The engine now featured the new electronic ignition system for more reliable running. The interior had new thin-back buckets seats with three different interior trim choices, including a standard split-back bench seat.

#### Engine Options

The Duster 340 was available in 10 body colors and four vinyl roof colors. The only engine available was the 240 hp single 4-barrel 340 V-8, identical to the one used in the 1972 'Cuda.

#### Transmission Options

The 1972 Plymouth Duster 340 had a standard fully synchronized 3-speed manual shift transmission with a floor-shift. An A-833 cast-iron case 4-speed manual transmission with a floor-mounted shifter was optional. An A727 TorqueFlite 3-speed automatic transmission was also optional in the Duster 340.

*The Chrysler Engine Blue 340 engine in a 1972 Duster was topped with an orange snorkel-type air cleaner housing covering the Carter Thermoquad 4-barrel carburetor. The 340 developed 240 hp at 4,800 rpm.*

#### Rear Axle Options

The standard rear axle was a Chrysler 8¾-inch ring gear with a number of optional gear ratios. A 3.23:1 ratio was standard, with 3.55:1 and 3.91:1 optional. The standard Rallye suspension was supported with heavy-duty front torsion bars, Firm-Ride shock absorbers, anti-sway bar, and heavy-duty rear longitudinal parallel leaf springs.

#### Wheel and Tire Options

Standard tires on a 1972 Plymouth Duster were E70x14 Fiberglass-belted mounted on 14x5.5J steel wheels. Rallye and styled road wheels were available as options.

*By 1972 the emphasis was on standard models rather than high performance, so the 'Cuda 340 was pushed to the back of factory showroom brochure pages. Even this blue 'Cuda 340 coupe "Charter member of the Rapid Transit System" was turned away and to the rear. (Dodge, Plymouth and the AMC design are registered trademarks of FCA US LLC)*

### Production Numbers

A total of 15,681 HV2 Duster 340 two-door Sport Coupes were built for the 1972 model year.

### Advertising and Publicity

As the sun set on the muscle car era, Plymouth took the approach that it would need to pair its performance cars with their economy variants. This was evident in the Duster advertisements. Instead of using high-impact colors, the company settled for a pair of mundane Tan cars.

#### The End of the High-Performance Era

By the end of the 1972 model year, much of the excitement of the short run of the first version of American high-performance and muscle cars was over. Much of Chrysler's and Plymouth's advertising and promotional material after 1972 was concentrated on fuel economy, emissions, and low prices. Instead of "Rapid Transit System. Coming through," their slogan changed to "Coming through with the kind of car American wants." By the 1973 model year, all references to performance, speed, and power seem to have vanished from the scene. Marketing was directed more to higher fuel economy and fresh, young, modern styling. The hood scoops, wide tires, and big, powerful engines of the past few years were gone, and as far as the buying public knew, they were gone forever. It was about this time that the term "musclecar" was invented to describe the cars of the past.

*Like much of the Chrysler advertising in 1972, the message was directed toward convincing the buying public that the nonperformance Duster looked as good as the performance model but was less expensive. The 1972 Duster 340 kept its individuality by using a unique grille design and optional body stripes. (Dodge, Plymouth, and the AMC design are registered trademarks of FCA US LLC)*

## CHAPTER 10

# 2014 AND BEYOND

## SCAT PACK VERSION 2.0

*"If History has taught us anything, it's to respect those that came before us and to never forget where we came from."*

Most high-performance enthusiasts believed that the muscle car and performance era was over, but by the time the new millennia began, manufacturers realized that the new engines with sophisticated computers, electronic fuel injection, and improved suspension and transmission technology allowed them to start building real American cars again that would stir the hearts of the young and the not-so-young driver. The second generation of the muscle car had been born.

### The Hemi Returns

As always, Chrysler, and especially Dodge, was at the top of the heap when it came to being well prepared for the new performance rally. The third-generation Hemi was introduced in 2002, and from that grew an exciting new opportunity for manufacturers and fans to enjoy that feeling of power. Although many said that the Generation III Hemi was not a real Hemi, its obvious performance capabilities and reliabilities made that concern a non-issue very quickly.

The new 5.7-liter Hemi was first made available in the 2003 Ram truck, but by the 2005 model year it had expanded into the Chrysler 300, Dodge Durango, Dodge Magnum R/T, and Jeep Grand Cherokee. In 2006 the Hemi became available in the Charger R/T, and when the Challenger was introduced in 2009 the Hemi was standard in the Challenger R/T with a 6.1-liter version offered in the Challenger SRT8, Chrysler 300 SRT8, Jeep Grand Cherokee SRT8, and Charger SRT8 models.

*The 2015 Challenger R/T was available with the 392 engine and Shaker hood scoop. This Challenger also has an optional black stripe package and sunroof. The green Challenger in the center is another Challenger R/T Shaker and the blue one at the rear is a Challenger R/T. (Dodge, Plymouth, and the AMC design are registered trademarks of FCA US LLC)*

## 2014: Chrysler Markets Directly to the Muscle Car Era

The success of the Chrysler and Dodge high-performance models prompted Dodge to look back on its history to find the highly successful Scat Pack Programs of 1968 to 1971 and apply that same idea to the new Challenger R/T, Charger R/T, and Dart performance lines. The first clues that Scat Pack was being born again appeared at the November 2013 SEMA (Specialty Equipment Manufacturers) Show in Las Vegas, the popular forum for releasing new ideas and concepts to the public and the industry.

Mopar wowed the crowds at the 2013 SEMA Show with a trio consisting of 2014 Challenger, Charger, and Dart GT performance models. What Chrysler was calling their "Moparized" cars represented what would become the new Scat Pack option packages for the 2014 model year. Each showed the performance improvement parts and modifications that were available for each of the three performance-oriented model lines. Dodge brand President and CEO Tim Kuniskis championed the resurrection of the Scat Pack name since taking over Dodge in April 2013.

### SEMA Scat Pack Challenger

The 2014 Challenger exhibited at the SEMA Show was finished in dark metallic red accented with a gloss-black hood

This specially prepared 2014 Challenger was used to present and promote Dodge's new Scat Pack Stage packages. The dark-red and gloss-black Challenger is shown here on a dragstrip at the introduction. (Dodge, Plymouth, and the AMC design are registered trademarks of FCA US LLC)

and roof. The Challenger rolled on 20-inch black "Classic II" forged aluminum wheels. The concept Challenger also had black hood pins, a black fuel filler door, and a black rear spoiler. A short, black variable side exhaust pipe exited just in front of the rear wheel opening. The interior featured black leather with Dodge stripes on the doors and a red Challenger logo on the seat backs.

### SEMA Scat Pack Charger

The Concept Dodge Charger was finished similarly to the Challenger in dark metallic red with 20 x 9–inch lightweight

The special 2014 Challenger built to present and promote the new Scat Pack Stage program for Dodge. The dark-red and gloss-black finish and other additions were shared across the three cars used at this introduction of Scat Pack. (Dodge, Plymouth, and the AMC design are registered trademarks of FCA US LLC)

A special full-color window badge was included when the new Scat Pack 3 kit was purchased and installed on any 2014 or earlier Challenger or Charger. (Dodge, Plymouth, and the AMC design are registered trademarks of FCA US LLC)

This is the specially prepared 2014 Charger with dark-red and gloss-black finish used to present and demonstrate the new Scat Pack Stage kits to the public. (Dodge, Plymouth and the AMC design are registered trademarks of FCA, US LLC)

A driver-side rear of the specially prepared and finished 2014 Challenger used to present the new Scat Pack programs to the public. It was one of three cars finished in similar styling and colors. (Dodge, Plymouth, and the AMC design are registered trademarks of FCA US LLC)

### SEMA Dart GT

The Dart GT was also finished in dark metallic red and black with black 19-inch wheels and a three-piece rear deck spoiler for downforce at speed. The SEMA Dart was also equipped with a dual-vented aluminum hood and the aero package was used with the 2013 Dart.

This Mopar Performance front end brace, cold-air system, and high-flow air cleaner were part of the new Scat Pack Stage kits offered for 2014 and earlier Dodges. This is the engine compartment of a 2014 Charger with a 5.7 L Hemi V-8. (Dodge, Plymouth, and the AMC design are registered trademarks of FCA US LLC)

Even the smaller 2014 Dodge Dart offered available Scat pack kits to improve its performance and handling. This Dart was finished in the same dark-red and gloss-black theme as the other two demonstration cars shown at the end of 2013 SEMA Show in Las Vegas. (Dodge, Plymouth, and the AMC design are registered trademarks of FCA US LLC)

aluminum wheels. The hood and roof were also finished in gloss black and a black rear spoiler sat at the edge of the rear deck. The interior of the charger was also trimmed much like the Challenger in black leather with red accents and logos. A black variable exhaust pipe was placed in front of the rear wheel openings like the ones on the Challenger.

### 2014 Detroit Auto Show

The next important showing of Dodge's new Scat Pack program was at the Detroit Auto Show that opened at Cobo Hall in January 2014. This exhibit featured more details, such as exhibits of the packages offered and applicable models of the programs, and Dodge was ready with real sales materials to begin taking orders. As in 1968, Dodge presented the new Scat Pack program accompanied by Dodge spokesmodels, called "Dodge Scat Pack Product Specialists." Taylor and Sarah, the modern-day spokesmodels, made their debut at the North American International Auto Show in Detroit and gave showgoers the scoop on the new 2014 Challenger, modified with Scat Pack upgrade kits. As a link to the past, the duo was outfitted in updated versions of the fashions worn by their predecessors, complete with white skirts emblazoned with the Scat Pack logo and matching white go-go boots. The Scat Pack name was chosen to coordinate with the 45th anniversary of the announcement of the original Dodge Scat Pack cars and Scat Pack Club of 1968. Dodge even created a new Scat Pack Club with a website for owners and enthusiasts to learn about and purchase the new parts and Scat kits for their car.

### Digging Up Bones

The announcement of Dodge's new Scat Pack program dug up an old legal dispute that began while the first Scat Pack program was being promoted. Chrysler Group was being sued by a California aftermarket company for infringing on its nearly 50-year-old "Scat" trademark on the Dodge Challenger and other vehicles. The lawsuit, filed in the U.S. District Court in California in October 2014, revived a trademark dispute between Scat Enterprises Inc. and Chrysler that dates back to 1968.

Chrysler vowed to defend its use of the "Scat Pack" name. In a written statement, Chrysler said Scat Enterprises' lawsuit was "a meritless and opportunistic attempt to hold Chrysler hostage just days before the upcoming SEMA show. Chrysler vowed that it would vigorously defend itself against this attack and look to enforce its own rights."

Scat Enterprises is a 51-year-old performance parts maker in Redondo Beach, California, that makes crankshafts, seats, and other parts for Dodge and other brand vehicles. Scat's lawsuit alleged that Chrysler infringed on its long-held trademarked name in 2013, when the brand revived its Scat Pack name for the Dodge Challenger.

In 1968, Dodge first used a Scat Pack name on the Charger R/T, Coronet R/T, Dart GTS, and the Coronet Super Bee. That year, Scat Enterprises sent a cease-and-desist letter to the automaker attempting to defend its trademark, the lawsuit contends. Dodge stopped using the Scat Pack name in 1971. Subsequently, by the 1980s Scat sold and marketed its products, including crankshafts, connecting rods, and other performance parts directly to Chrysler for use in Chrysler's vehicles for testing and sale to the public.

### Trademark Battle

In August 2013, Chrysler applied to the U.S. Patent and Trademark Office to revive the Scat Pack name, three months before it revealed its first Scat Pack Challenger at the 2013 Specialty Equipment Market Association Show in Las Vegas. Chrysler's request was denied by the USPTO, but they proceeded with the program anyway. Scat's argument was that Chrysler had ceased to use and thereby abandoned its claim, if any, to the Scat name over the prior 40 years and no longer had any claim to it. U.S. Trademark laws state that a trademark must be used continuously in interstate commerce in a particular category and be renewed frequently to remain valid. The lawsuit said negotiations between Scat Enterprises and Chrysler Group to resolve the current dispute have been unsuccessful.

### The New Scat Pack

The Dodge high-performance lineup for the 2014 model was already formidable without any extra help. The new 116.2-inch-wheelbase Challenger looked much the same as the 2009 model but performance capabilities had increased significantly due to continuing upgrades. The new cylinder heads released for the 2009 model 5.7 Hemi V-8 engines brought horsepower levels from their original and respectable 350, when first introduced in the Ram truck, to 375 at 5,800 rpm (with manual transmission) and 410 ft-lbs of torque in the new 2014 Challenger R/T. The highly successful and strong ZF-designed TorqueFlite 8-speed transmission was now standard. The Challenger was available as an R/T, R/T Plus, and R/T Classic.

The 120.2-inch-wheelbase four-door 2014 Dodge Charger R/T was equally powerful with a standard 370-hp, 395 ft-lbs of torque version of the 5.7 Hemi V-8, and TorqueFlite 8-speed transmission. The 2014 Charger was available as an R/T, R/T Plus, R/T Road & Track, and R/T Max, each with varying trim equipment.

The smallest member of Dodge's 2014 Performance team was the Dart. The 2014 Dodge Dart was built on a 106.4-inch-wheelbase platform. Although considered a compact, the Dart was advertised as having the interior room and comfort of a midsized car. The base Dart engine was a 2-liter inline 4-cylinder dual overhead-cam Tigershark that developed 160 hp. The performance-oriented Dart GT engine was a 2.4-liter single overhead-cam inline 4-cylinder Tigershark that developed 184 hp and 175 ft-lbs of torque. The power was connected by either a standard 6-speed manual or PowerTech automatic transmission.

The Scat Pack program for the 2014 model year was not about special cars but more about the special "Stage" kits developed so that owners could modify and improve their new already powerful Dodges using an organized assembly of parts directly from Dodge and Mopar Performance. Separate Stage kits were offered for the Challenger, Charger, and Dart GT, each with different enthusiast requirements and engine and drivetrain equipment. Although the Challenger and Charger were intended more for the street and dragstrip, the smaller 4-cylinder-powered Dart GT would be more interesting to those younger drivers looking for handling and road course efficiency. Dodge Scat Pack kits for 2014 would satisfy all of their needs. Dodge Brand CEO Tim Kuniskis said, "Bringing back factory stage kits allows Dodge enthusiasts to extract the maximum performance from their vehicles without the fear and guesswork typically associated with modifying late-model vehicles."

### Challenger and Charger R/T Stage Kits

The Stage 1 kit for the Challenger and Charger R/T included a cold air intake and filter, a full Cat Back exhaust system, and an engine calibration designed to optimize the power output of the 5.7 Hemi with those items. Stage 2 added a special Mopar Performance camshaft package and another new engine calibration. Stage 3 had added CNC-ported and polished cylinder heads, along with high-flowing exhaust headers and yet another engine tune to take advantage of the improvements. To top it all off, each of the stage kits for the Scat Pack–equipped Charger R/T and Challenger R/T featured a hard window badge depicting the sporty little Scat Pack Bee with a red number indicating the level of stage chosen. The Stage 2 and 3 kit modifications did not meet Federal emission standards so were listed as being for off-road use only or for the limited areas where those laws did not apply.

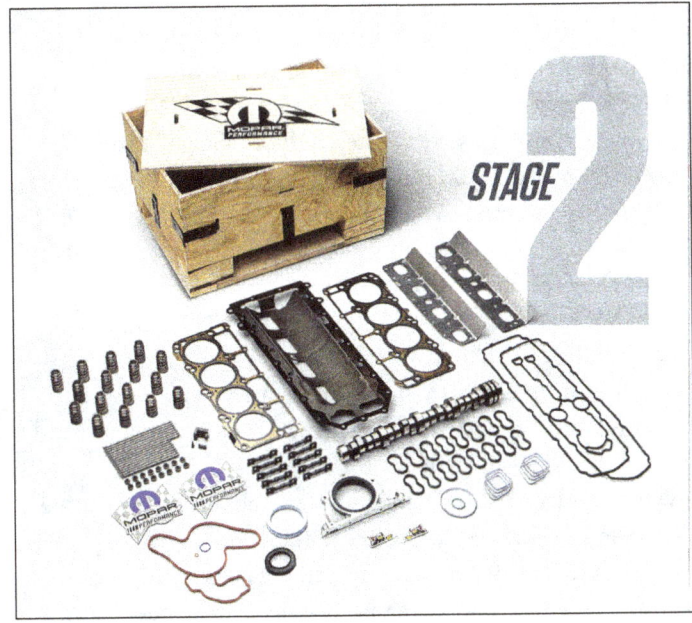

*These are the parts included in the Stage 2 Scat Pack kit for 2014 and earlier Challengers and Chargers equipped with the 5.7 L Hemi engine. (Dodge, Plymouth, and the AMC design are registered trademarks of FCA US LLC)*

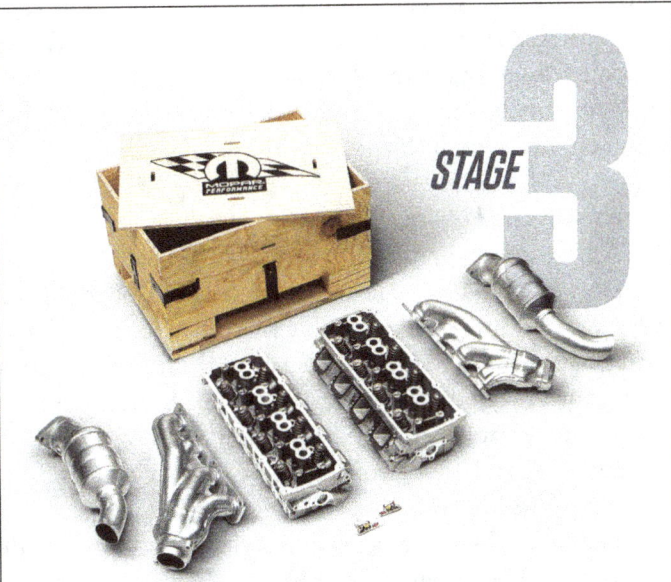

*These additional components, including new cylinder heads and high-flow exhaust headers, were included in the Stage 3 Scat Pack kit that was intended for the Stage 1 and Stage 2 kits. (Dodge, Plymouth, and the AMC design are registered trademarks of FCA US LLC)*

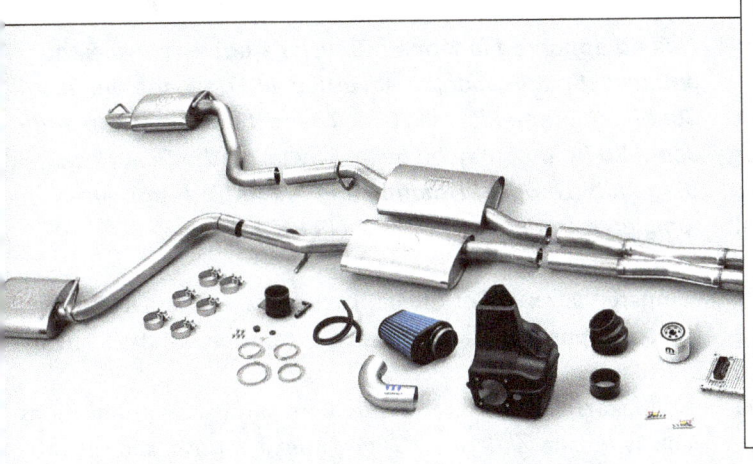

*In late 2013, the Mopar Performance catalog featured this Stage 1 performance kit to upgrade the horsepower of any 5.7-liter Hemi-equipped Dodge Charger or Challenger. The kit consisted of new exhaust system, mufflers, resonators, and a high-flow cold-air system. (Dodge, Plymouth, and the AMC design are registered trademarks of FCA US LLC)*

### Chrysler 300 Stage Kits

A lesser-known application of the Scat Pack Stage kits was for the 5.7 Hemi-powered 2014 Chrysler 300. The same power and performance increasing parts and modifications were available through the 2014 Mopar Performance Parts Catalog for the Chrysler 300, so luxury sedan owners could enjoy the same high-performance action as Challenger and Charger owners. The kits were listed only as "Stage" kits rather than Scat Pack, but the same restrictions and 8- to 63-hp increases were offered.

### 2014 Dart GT Stage Kits

The Stage kits for the 2014 Dodge Dart GT with the 4-cylinder 184-hp 2.4 L Tigershark engine took a slightly different path and concentrated more on handling than dragstrip performance. The Stage 1 kit for the Dart provided a Mopar cold-air-intake system, a Mopar short-throw shifter, and a Mopar Performance brake package that featured slotted rotors and high-friction brake pads. The Stage 2 kit added a Cat Back exhaust system and a special engine tune that allowed the engine to make the most use of the other changes to the airflow. Stage 3 replaced most of the brake systems with a Mopar big brake package that included pads, rotors, and calipers. Stage 3 also added an adjustable performance suspension package, including upgraded front and rear sway bars. Of course, an appropriately numbered Scat Pack hard badge was part of each of the kits.

### Advertising and Publicity

Advertising and public relations in 2013 and 2014 was not what it was in the 1960s and 1970s, so much of Dodge's efforts were directed at television, the Internet, and YouTube, rather than magazines and newspapers. Some of the first professional video YouTube spots shown in late 2013 featured the three red Scat Pack cars from the SEMA show and noted automotive authority and TV personality Steve Magnante and host of Velocity TV's *All Girls Garage* show Cristy Lee.

The first spot was a general overview of all three of the 2014 Scat Pack offerings set up at Milan Dragway near Detroit. Steve and Cristy explained all three Scat Pack kits and the Challenger, Charger, and Dart that served as the recipients of this power increase program. The second spot showed and explained the installation of a Scat Pack 3 kit on a new Challenger by Magnante in the shop, along with a description of the components. The third video showed two Challengers back at Milan with Magnante and Lee driving them in a drag race to compare the results of the improvements. Of course, the Scat Pack–equipped Challenger easily outran the standard one by a strong lead.

Magazine ads were featured in enthusiast publications such as *Mopar Collector's Guide*, *Mopar Muscle*, and the official *Mopar* magazine, published on behalf of Chrysler LLC, for dealers and subscribed enthusiasts. A full-page color ad in the number-5 issue of *Mopar* in 2015 featured the Scat Pack Bee at the top of the page and large red type that read: "Run with the Pack" in the center of the page. Images of the red-and-black 2014 Charger and Challenger with the Scat Pack kits and posed on a dragstrip finished the bottom of the page.

*This ad appeared in* Mopar, *Chrysler's dealer service and enthusiast publication, to advertise and describe the new Scat Pack Stage kits for 2014. The text describes the additional 20 hp that may be gained by using the Scat Pack Stage kit. (Dodge, Plymouth, and the AMC design are registered trademarks of FCA US LLC)*

## 2015 Dodge Scat Pack

For the 2015 model year, Dodge Brand changed its marketing direction and introduced a new line of models that used the Scat Pack name in their description and badging. The separate Scat Pack kits were still offered through Mopar Performance Parts, but now a new car buyer could order a 2015 Challenger or a Charger already equipped for performance and a Scat Pack image. When the new 2015 models were announced in the fall of 2014, the Challenger line now included the addition of an R/T Scat Pack equipped with a 392 Hemi V-8 and a 392 Hemi Scat Pack Shaker. The 2015 Charger line also added an R/T Scat Pack.

### Challenger R/T Scat Pack

The Challenger was based on the 116.2-inch-wheelbase two-door hardtop unibody platform first introduced in 2008. Body styling was much the same and changes to the original design were few and subtle. The base Challenger SXT had a standard 3.6-liter DOHC Pentastar V-6 rated at a respectable 305 hp. As the models progressed, the standard features increased and the Challenger R/T's engine power was changed to the 5.7-liter V-8. The Standard 18-inch Satin Carbon aluminum wheels on the SXT were enlarged to 20-inch across the R/T line, which consisted of the R/T Plus, R/T Shaker, R/T Plus Shaker, and R/T Classic.

The two special Challenger R/T Scat Pack models were based on the R/T and added a number of performance and appearance items to the list of standard features. First and foremost, both Scat Pack Challenger models were equipped with a standard 392-ci (6.4 liter) SRT V-8 that produced 485 hp and 475 ft-lbs of torque. Either a TorqueFlite 8 automatic or Tremec 6-speed manual transmission was available. When equipped with the TorqueFlite automatic, the Hemi also had Fuel Saver Technology that seamlessly deactivated four of its cylinders when not needed. Active exhaust was included with the Scat Pack equipment to make the Hemi's presence known on the street. Scat Pack wheels were 20 x 9-inch polished aluminum with black pockets and satin finish shod with all-season performance 245/45ZR20 tires. Standard Scat Pack styling upgrades included performance front splitter, Scat Pack badging, Satin Black rear spoiler, gloss-black Brembo four-piston power disc brakes, and high-performance premium cloth seats.

### Challenger 392 Hemi Scat Pack Shaker

The second Challenger Scat Pack model added a number of distinctive features to the basic R/T Scat Pack model, most important, the Shaker Hood. The iconic Mopar Shaker Hood was first used on the 1970 E-Body Challenger and 'Cuda. The Shaker was an engine-mounted air cleaner assembly that stuck

This Shaker hood scoop was an available option for later 392 Hemi Challengers and was also available through Mopar Performance for installation on cars not delivered with it.

The engine compartment of this 2015 Challenger equipped with a 392 Hemi engine, optional Shaker hood scoop, and Scat Pack fresh air system and high-flow filter. (Dodge, Plymouth, and the AMC design are registered trademarks of FCA US LLC)

out through an opening in the center of the hood and moved with the engine when it accelerated, creating an impressive and attention-getting image to anyone seeing it in action. The new version of the Challenger R/T Shaker was first introduced for the 2014 model year and was touted by Dodge as "a unique factory-designed foundation to maximize the three all-new Dodge Scat Packs, enabling customers to unleash even more power from their Challenger R/T Shaker." The new Challenger Scat Pack functional Shaker Hood and cold-air intake

Challenger owners wasted no time in taking advantage of the new Scat Pack kits and other components available to increase the appearance and performance of their already-impressive cars. This Challenger has a Mopar Shaker hood, special strips, and a 392 Hemi badge.

This silver 2015 Challenger R/T Scat Pack with Shaker hood scoop was prominently featured in the 2015 Challenger showroom brochure and online Dodge promotional materials. (Dodge, Plymouth, and the AMC design are registered trademarks of FCA US LLC)

A rear view is of a 2015 Challenger R/T Scat Pack Shaker equipped with optional black roof stripes. Note the twin bright oval exhaust-pipe tips. (Dodge, Plymouth, and the AMC design are registered trademarks of FCA US LLC)

This silver 2015 Challenger 392 Hemi Scat Pack Shaker was one of the Challengers chosen for display at important new auto shows for the 2015 model year. (Dodge, Plymouth, and the AMC design are registered trademarks of FCA US LLC)

and an iconic popular shade from the past called B5 Blue. The colors could be accented with a choice of a Scat Pack Bumblebee stripe or Shaker center stripe in contrasting or complementary colors. Unique to the two Scat Pack models was a choice of an optional $1,195 Scat Pack Appearance Group, consisting of 20 x 9–inch Matte Black lightweight forged aluminum wheels, Scat Pack Bumblebee tail stripe, HID headlamps, Hectic mesh interior accents, Performance cloth seats with Scat Pack logo, Scat Pack premium floor mats, black grille, back fuel-filler door, and leather-wrapped performance steering wheel. The group also came with a 506-watt Alpine premium audio system with premium speakers and subwoofer.

reproduced the same image as the earlier version, although it was mounted to the electronic fuel-injection intake rather than a 4-barrel carburetor.

In addition to the obvious Shaker Hood, the Challenger 392 Hemi Scat Pack Shaker added a gloss-black grille surround, Scat Pack fender, and 392 Shaker hood scoop badging, Satin Black fuel filler door, spoiler, and Shaker graphics. The interior was upgraded with heated and ventilated front seats trimmed in high-performance Nappa leather with graduated plow-through inserts and Shaker logo. Also standard was a leather-covered Dodge Performance steering wheel with power tilt/telescoping steering column. The package included a Shaker dash plaque and startup splash screen.

### Challenger R/T Scat Pack Options

Both 2015 Challenger R/T Scat Pack models were offered in eleven distinctive body colors, including five shades of pearl

### Charger R/T Scat Pack

The Charger was redesigned for 2015, creating what Dodge called a new and more dramatic impact. A new crosshair design in the piano-black R/T grille, projector headlamps, and LED lighting emphasized the styling in the front end. The long profile with new door scallops and more pronounced flying buttress capped with what Dodge called a "tighter end" and a more advanced execution of the seamless signature racetrack tail lamp and a new three-piece spoiler completed the look.

Charger's contribution to the Dodge Scat Pack family in 2015 was the Charger R/T Scat Pack. Equipped with the same SRT 6.4-liter (392-ci) Hemi V-8 as the Charger SRT 392, the Scat Pack version had a few less extra amenities to lower the base price by about $7,390. The body of the Scat Pack Charger was almost identical to that of the SRT 392 and featured a black honeycomb grid-pattern grille with Scat Pack badge and body-color manual folding outside mirrors. The most identifying feature was the large center-mounted integral hood scoop. The scoop allowed fresh air to enter the engine compartment but was not connected directly to the intake system that would make it fully functional. The R/T Scat Pack changed the SRT body-color spoiler for a matte-black rear spoiler.

The 2015 Charger R/T Scat Pack was equipped with standard 20 x 9–inch polished aluminum spoke wheels mounted with 245/45ZR20 Goodyear RS-A all-season, with Goodyear F1 Supercar rubber optional. Standard brakes were Brembo

This is one of the 20 x 9–inch polished aluminum spoke wheels with painted lack pockets and 245/45ZR20 performance tires included with the 2015 Challenger R/T Scat Pack 392 Hemi Shaker. (Dodge, Plymouth, and the AMC design are registered trademarks of FCA US LLC)

The passenger-side front view of a blue 2015 Charger R/T 392 Hemi Scat Pack from Charger's online brochure and information site. The Scat Pack Charger has 20 x 9–inch forged-aluminum wheels and performance tires and a hood scoop. (Dodge, Plymouth, and the AMC design are registered trademarks of FCA US LLC)

A passenger-side view of a blue 2015 Charger R/T 392 Hemi Scat Pack. The Charger has standard 20x9 forged-aluminum wheels and 245/45ZR20 performance tires and other equipment. (Dodge, Plymouth, and the AMC design are registered trademarks of FCA US LLC)

The rear view of a blue 2015 Dodge Charger R/T 392 Scat Pack four-door sedan shows the spoiler and rear deck with R/T logo. A hood scoop and this R/T badge on the rear deck lid are the only identifying items that tell the public this is a high-performance sedan. (Dodge, Plymouth, and the AMC design are registered trademarks of FCA US LLC)

*The center console and shifter for the 2015 Charger R/T 392 Scat Pack sedan separates the front bucket seats for a sporty appearance. Note the reference to the Dodge Brothers in the soft tray next to the shifter. (Dodge, Plymouth, and the AMC design are registered trademarks of FCA US LLC)*

*This large display screen with performance information and choices is part of the included instrument package in a 2015 Charger R/T 392 Hemi Scat Pack. The driver can choose a number of performance options for the transmission and suspension. (Photo Courtesy David Zatz, Allpar.com)*

four-piston high-performance power discs at all four corners. Charger R/T Scat Pack suspension was high-performance with Bilstein shock absorbers and was identical to that of the SRT 392. The 6.4-liter Hemi V-8 produced 485 hp and 475 ft-lbs of torque and drove the rear wheels through a state-of-the-art ZF-designed 8-speed TorqueFlite 8 automatic transmission.

The heavy-duty rear axle had a 3.09:1 ratio and standard anti-spin differential.

The Charger R/T Scat Pack was available in 10 body colors, including five shades of pearl and a retro-look Sublime Green. Heritage-inspired B5 Blue and Tor-Red were two of the bold colors to choose from. The interior was available in a standard Sedoso/Ballistic Performance cloth and optional Nappa leather trim with Alcantara suede bolsters, Ruby Red accent stitching, and Alcantara perforated-suede inserts with embroidered Scat Pack logo in Black/Ruby Red or black.

The 2015 Charger R/T Scat Pack did not have an optional Scat Pack Appearance Group, as did the Challenger, so there were fewer choices for an owner to personalize his car. The most important option was the Technology Group. The Technology Group consisted of rain-sensing windshield wipers, LaneSense lane departure warning, and Lane Keep assist, Auto High-Beam headlight control, Full Speed forward collision warning with active braking, adaptive cruise control with stop, power tilt/telescoping steering column, and power adjustable pedals. The Technology Group also required the Plus Group that included Sport leather-trimmed heat and ventilated seats and much more.

### Advertising and Publicity

Like the 2014 introduction, most advertising and publicity efforts for the 2015 model year were directed toward the Internet and YouTube videos. Magazine exposure was concentrated mainly on reviews and road tests, with only a few large market print ads in major publications. The separate Scat Pack kits were still being advertised in Mopar enthusiast publications and listed in the Mopar Performance Parts Catalog.

### 2016 Scat Pack Lineup

The 2016 Scat Pack Program was much like the 2015, and Challenger and Charger model identification remained the same. Dodge advertising material emphasized the more than 45 years of muscle-car heritage and more than 100 years of Dodge production as a base for success. The Challenger was available in 10 models, including the base SXT and SXT Plus to the R/T, R/T Shaker, R/T Plus, R/T Plus Shaker, R/T Scat Pack, 392 Hemi Scat Pack Shaker, SRT 392, and the SRT Hellcat. Engine choices ranged from the 3.6 Pentastar V-6 to the 5.7 and 392 Hemi V-8 to the 6.4-liter supercharged 707-hp Challenger SRT Hellcat.

The 2016 Dodge Charger models included the base SE to the SXT, R/T, R/T Road & Track, R/T Scat Pack, SRT 392, SRT Hellcat, SE AWD, and SXT AWD. Like the Challenger, Charger engines ranged from the 3.6-liter V-6 to the 5.7 and 392 Hemi V-8 to the 6.4-liter 707-hp Charger SRT Hellcat.

### Challenger R/T Scat Pack

The 2016 Challenger R/T Scat Pack was based on the same 116.2-inch-wheelbase unibody LC platform used since 2008. Styling changes were subtle and few, and the basic look of the Challenger remained identical to earlier models. The R/T Scat Pack was distinguished externally from the base and intermediate models by the use of larger wheels and tires and the addition of front and rear spoilers and stripe trim. The R/T Scat Pack also had a standard double-bulge hood with functional vents that allowed fresh air into the engine compartment. The R/T Scat Pack also had a standard R/T grille badge on the left side of the gloss-black split rectangular mesh grille.

The 2016 Challenger R/T Scat Pack had a standard 392-ci (6.4-liter) SRT Hemi V-8 that produced 485 hp and 475 ft-lbs of torque and connected to a Tremec 6-speed manual transmission. The 8-speed TorqueFlite was optional, and when the TorqueFlite was ordered, the Hemi engine had added Fuel Saver Technology that seamlessly deactivated four of the cylinders when they were not needed. The heavy-duty rear axle was equipped with 3.90:1 ratio with the manual transmission and a 3.09:1 ratio when equipped with the optional automatic. Both had a standard anti-spin differential.

The 2016 Challenger R/T Scat Pack was equipped with 245/45ZR20 All-Season Performance BSW tires mounted

The driver-side rear quarter of a Redline Red Tri-Coat Pearl 2016 Challenger R/T 392 Hemi Scat Pack with a black rear quarter Bumblebee stripe and black finish fuel filler cap. This Challenger is equipped with a black rear deck spoiler, standard with this model.

The full-color Scat Pack Bee badge is used on the front fenders of a black 2016 Dodge Challenger 392 Hemi Scat Pack two-door hardtop.

A driver-side front of a 2016 Challenger R/T 392 Hemi Scat Pack finished in Redline Red Tri-Coat pearl with black Bumblebee tail stripe. The custom black finish and lettering on the hood is an owner custom application.

This shows a lightweight forged-aluminum 20x9 aluminum wheel and high-performance 245/45ZR20 tire standard on the 2016 Challenger R/T 392 Hemi Scat Pack.

on 20 x 9–inch polished aluminum spoke wheels with black pockets and satin finish. The Super Track Pak package was a mandatory option and included high-performance steering, Performance Suspension, and anti-lock four-wheel high-performance power disc brakes.

The 2016 Challenger R/T Scat Pack interior included power seats for the passenger and driver, along with a 60/40 split-folding rear bench seat with armrest and two cup holders. The standard R/T interior trim was Sedoso/Houndstooth Premium cloth sport in black but also available in Sedoso/Tungsten Torque cloth and Black/Tungsten.

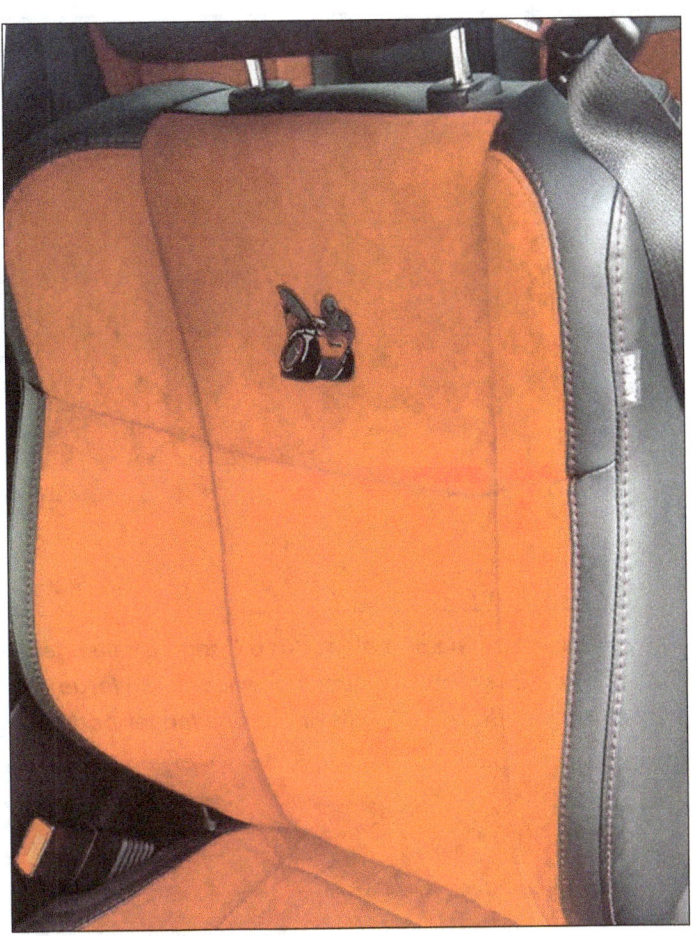

The Scat Pack Bee logo on the Ruby Red suede and black Nappa leather interior trim on a 2016 Challenger R/T 392 Hemi Scat Pack is part of the optional interior trim option.

The optional interior trim of a black 2016 Challenger R/T 392 Hemi Scat Pack. Note the Ruby Red suede inserts and black Nappa leather trim.

The passenger's side of a black 2016 Dodge Challenger R/T 392 Scat Pack with 20 x 9 black finish forged aluminum wheels. The large diameter wheels actually fit very nicely into the wheel wells of the Challenger body design.

The passenger-side rear quarter of a black 2016 Challenger R/T 392 Hemi Scat Pack shows the red Bumblebee stripes and standard rear deck spoiler.

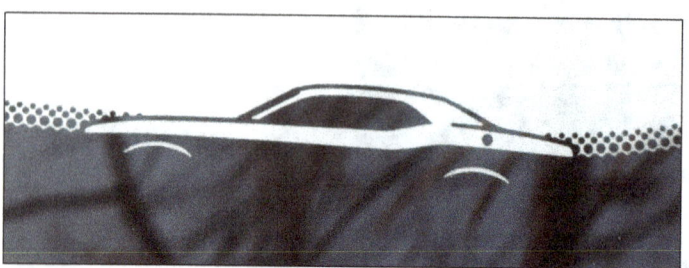

This is one of the small details that make a 2016 Challenger Scat Pack special. The standard windshield has a black silhouette of a Challenger printed into the lower driver-side windshield glass.

### Challenger 392 Hemi Scat Pack Shaker

The 392 Hemi Scat Pack Shaker had all of the same standard features as the R/T Scat Pack but added a distinctive functional Shaker hood scoop assembly that poked out through an opening in the center of the Challenger hood as it did in the same 2015 model. The Shaker moved as the engine revved, grabbing the immediate attention of anyone watching. The Shaker included a Mopar conical air filter and cold-air intake.

The Scat Pack Shaker optional wheels were 20 x 9–inch lightweight forged aluminum spoke with 245/45ZR20 Performance BSW tires. The standard interior on the 392 Hemi Scat Pack Shaker was Nappa leather trim with Ruby Red accent stitching and Nappa Axis II perforated inserts with graduated plow-through performance seats. The interior was also available in black.

As in 2015, the R/T Scat Pack and 392 Hemi Scat Pack Shaker were available with the optional Scat Pack Appearance Group, which included a black grille surround, Scat Pack Bumblebee rear stripe, high-intensity discharge headlamps, Scat Pack logo embroidered seats, performance steering wheel, and premium floor mats.

### Charger R/T Scat Pack

The 2016 Charger R/T Scat Pack was much the same as the 2015 model and included a standard 392-ci Hemi V-8 with Fuel Saver Technology. The 392 Hemi produced 485 hp and 475 ft-lbs of torque. The Hemi was connected to a standard TorqueFlite 8 automatic transmission and a 3.09:1 rear axle with anti-spin. The Charger R/T Scat Pack hood featured a large center inlet and scoop that transferred gulps of fresh air beneath the hood to cool the engine compartment. The Charger R/T Scat Pack included a standard black rear spoiler and a black mesh grille with a Scat Pack badge on its left side. The standard wheels were 20 x 9–inch polished aluminum with black pockets and Satin finish mounted with 245/45R20 BSW All-Season performance tires.

The 2016 Charger was available in twelve body colors, including three in pearl and retro-themed high-impact colors of Plum Crazy, Tor-Red, B5 Blue, and Go Mango. The standard interior of the Charger R/T Scat Pack was Sedoso/Ballistic Performance cloth with embroidered Scat Pack

The 2016 Charger R/T Scat Pack advertised its ancestry with a distinctive Scat Pack badge on the driver-side front grille. A Scat Pack badge was also mounted at the rear side of both front fenders. (Dodge, Plymouth, and the AMC design are registered trademarks of FCA US LLC)

A Granite Crystal Metallic Charger R/T Scat Pack was featured in a full-page display in the 2016 and 2017 Charger showroom brochure. The scalloped panels on the sides of the car were reminders of the similar design on Chargers from past years. (Dodge, Plymouth, and the AMC design are registered trademarks of FCA US LLC)

### Advertising and Publicity

As it was in the previous years of the program, print advertising was limited, but a few full-page ads appeared in Mopar enthusiasts' publications such as *Mopar Collector's Guide*. The last page of the March 2016 issue featured a full-page ad with the Scat Pack Bee at the top of the page and the headline: "Get Stung" in large bold red type just below. The ad was not for the Scat Pack car models but for the still popular Scat Pack Kits offered through Mopar Performance Parts for the 2011–2015 Challenger and Charger with the 5.7 Hemi V-8 engine.

The Scat Pack 1 Performance Package included a cold-air intake, Cat-Back exhaust system, oil filter, powertrain control module, and two Scat pack badges. This kit produced an increase of 20 hp and 23 ft-lbs of torque over the stock configuration. Scat Pack 2, which required the Kit 1 pack, added a camshaft, valve springs, tie bar kit, heavy-duty push rods, upper and lower gasket set, and two Scat Pack badges, adding 56 hp and 30 ft-lbs of torque. Scat Pack Kit 3 added CNC-ported high-flow cylinder heads, gasket set, 6.4-liter Apache SRT exhaust manifold and catalyst, mounting brackets, and Scat Pack 3 badges. This package, of course, required the 1 and 2 kits and added 75 hp and 44 ft-lbs of torque. A silver Challenger and red Charger were displayed at the bottom of the page.

logo and Tungsten accent stitching in black. An optional Nappa leather interior trim was available with Alcantara suede bolsters, Ruby red accent stitching, and Alcantara perforated-suede inserts with embroidered Scat Pack logo in black/Ruby Red.

This is a full-page ad that appeared in *Mopar* and other commercial enthusiast *Mopar* publications to promote the Scat Pack Stage Kits for the 2016 model year. These kits were available from Mopar Performance dealers and could be used on any Hemi-powered Challenger or Charger.

**2017 Scat Pack Program**

For the 2017 model year, Dodge's new marketing slogan was "Domestic. Not Domesticated." This, of course, referred to the new 2018 Dodge Challenger Demon that was announced early in the 2017 calendar year. This new and exciting super-high-performance Dodge surpassed the Hellcat, introduced in 2015 as the most powerful, quickest, and fastest passenger automobile available. With a potential of 840 hp, the Demon was developed as a drag-racing street car and definitely not for everyone. However, its image and great publicity campaign put Dodge's performance image to the front of the line and brought notice to the other Dodge choices such as the Hellcat Challenger and Charger, the Charger Daytona, and the R/T Challenger and Charger Scat Pack models.

The 2017 Scat Pack models included the Challenger R/T Scat Pack and 392 Hemi Scat Pack Shaker and the Charger R/T Scat Pack. All three models were still equipped with the 392-ci (6.4-liter) Hemi V-8 that made 485 hp and 475 ft-lbs of torque.

The 2017 Scat Pack Program was much like the 2015 and 2016, and Challenger and Charger model identification remained the same. Dodge advertising material emphasized the more than 45 years of muscle-car heritage and more than 100 years of Dodge production as a base for success. The Challenger was available in 10 models, including the base SXT and SXT Plus to the R/T, R/T Shaker, R/T Plus, R/T Plus Shaker, R/T Scat Pack, 392 Hemi Scat Pack Shaker, SRT 392, and the SRT Hellcat. Engine choices ranged from the 3.6-liter Pentastar V-6 to the 5.7 and 392 Hemi V-8 to the 6.4-liter supercharged 707-hp Challenger SRT Hellcat.

The 2017 Dodge Charger models included the base SE to the SXT, R/T, R/T Road & Track, R/T Scat Pack, SRT 392, SRT Hellcat, SE AWD, and SXT AWD. Like the Challenger, Charger engines ranged from the 3.6-liter V-6 to the 5.7 and 392 Hemi V-8 to the 6.4-liter 707-hp Charger SRT Hellcat.

### Challenger R/T Scat Pack

The 2017 Challenger R/T Scat Pack was based on the same 116.2-inch-wheelbase unibody LC platform used since 2008. Styling changes were subtle and few, and the basic look of the Challenger remained identical to earlier models. The R/T Scat

Pack was distinguished externally from the base and intermediate models by the use of larger wheels and tires and the addition of front and rear spoilers and stripe trim. The R/T Scat also had a standard double-bulge hood with functional vents that allowed fresh air into the engine compartment. The R/T Scat Pack also had a standard R/T grille badge on the left side of the gloss-black split rectangular mesh grille.

The 2017 Challenger R/T Scat Pack had a standard 392-ci (6.4-liter) SRT Hemi V-8 that produced 485 hp and 475 ft-lbs of torque and connected to a Tremec 6-speed manual transmission. The 8-speed TorqueFlite was optional, and when the TorqueFlite was ordered the Hemi engine had added Fuel Saver Technology that seamlessly deactivated four of the cylinders when they were not needed. The heavy-duty rear axle had 3.90:1 ratio with the manual transmission and a 3.09:1 ratio when equipped with the optional automatic. Both had a standard anti-spin differential.

The 2017 Challenger R/T Scat Pack was equipped with 245/45ZR20 All-Season Performance BSW tires mounted on 20 x 9–inch polished aluminum spoke wheels with black pockets and satin finish. The Super Track Pak package was a mandatory option and included high-performance steering, Performance Suspension, and anti-lock four-wheel high-performance power disc brakes.

The 2017 Challenger R/T Scat Pack interior included power seats for the passenger and driver, along with a 60/40-split folding rear bench seat with armrest and two cup holders. The standard R/T interior trim was Sedoso/Houndstooth Premium cloth sport in black but also available in Sedoso/Tungsten Torque cloth and Black/Tungsten.

### Challenger 392 Hemi Scat Pack Shaker

The 392 Hemi Scat Pack Shaker had all of the same standard features as the R/T Scat Pack but added a distinctive functional Shaker hood scoop assembly that poked out through an opening in the center of the Challenger hood as it did in the same 2015 model. The Shaker moved as the engine revved, grabbing the immediate attention of anyone watching. The Shaker included a Mopar conical air filter and cold-air intake.

The Scat Pack Shaker optional wheels were 20 x 9–inch lightweight forged aluminum spoke with 245/45ZR20 Performance BSW tires. The standard interior on the 392 Hemi Scat Pack Shaker was Nappa leather trim with Ruby Red accent stitching and Nappa Axis II perforated inserts with graduated plow-through Performance seats. The interior was also available in black.

As in 2015 and 2016, the R/T Scat Pack and 392 Hemi Scat Pack Shaker were available with the optional Scat Pack Appearance Group, which included a black grille surround, Scat Pack Bumblebee rear stripe, high intensity discharge headlamps, Scat Pack logo embroidered seats, performance steering wheel, and premium floor mats.

### Charger R/T Scat Pack

The 2017 Charger R/T Scat Pack was much the same as the 2015 and 2016 model and included a standard 392-ci Hemi V-8 with Fuel Saver Technology. The 392 Hemi produced 485 hp and 475 ft-lbs of torque. The Hemi was connected to a standard TorqueFlite 8 automatic transmission and a 3.09:1 rear axle with anti-spin. The Charger R/T Scat Pack hood featured a large center inlet and scoop that transferred gulps of fresh air beneath the hood to cool the engine compartment. The Charger R/T Scat Pack included a standard black rear spoiler and a black mesh grille with a Scat Pack badge on its left side. The standard wheels were 20 x 9–inch polished aluminum with black pockets and Satin finish mounted with 245/45R20 BSW All-Season performance tires.

*Go-Mango is one of the new high-impact body colors available on the 2016 and 2017 Charger R/T Scat Pack. These exciting shades are reminiscent of the colors first introduced on Dodge and Plymouth performance cars in 1970. (Dodge, Plymouth, and the AMC design are registered trademarks of FCA US LLC)*

The 2017 Charger was available in twelve body colors, including three in pearl and retro-themed high-impact colors of Plum Crazy, Tor-Red, B5 Blue, and Go Mango. The standard interior of the Charger R/T Scat Pack was Sedoso/Ballistic Performance cloth with embroidered Scat Pack logo and Tungsten accent stitching in black. An optional Nappa leather interior trim was available with Alcantara suede bolsters, Ruby red accent stitching and Alcantara perforated suede inserts with embroidered Scat Pack logo in black/Ruby Red.

*This image of the passenger-side front of a 2017 Charger R/T 392 Hemi Scat Pack was used in Dodge brochures and online publicity materials. The pictures actually used existing images of the 2015 cars. (Dodge, Plymouth, and the AMC design are registered trademarks of FCA US LLC)*

*This is a passenger-side view of a purple 2017 Charger R/T 392 Hemi Scat Pack four-door sedan used in showroom brochures and online advertising and publicity material. The 392 Hemi badge is visible on the front fender. (Dodge, Plymouth, and the AMC design are registered trademarks of FCA US LLC)*

*A rear view of a 2017 Charger R/T 392 Hemi Scat Pack four-door sedan. The small red R/T badge appeared only on the passenger's side of the deck lid. (Dodge, Plymouth, and the AMC design are registered trademarks of FCA US LLC)*

*This is one of the standard black forged aluminum 20 x 9 wheels and 245/45ZR20 performance tires on a new 2017 Charger R/T 392 Hemi Scat Pack. The brakes are the standard four-piston Brembo discs with electronic stability control and Advanced Brake Assist.*

### 2018 Scat Pack Program

As of the end of the 2017 model year the Dodge Scat Pack program showed no sign of letting up and the design and production of innovative high-performance automobiles is still a significant part of Dodge's model line and image. The 2018 models, announced in October 2017 made it clear that this successful program is not letting up just yet. The 2018 model lineup is essentially identical to the previous years with little more than minor changes. The styling of the 2016 and 2017 models was well accepted and kept the same for 2018 with changes rumored only for the 2019 model year and beyond. The Scat Pack Challengers and Chargers based on the powerful Generation III 392 Hemi and the American Automobile industry's most powerful automobiles such as the 2009 to 2015 Drag Pack Challengers, the new 2018 475 horsepower Durango SRT and 2015 to 2018 Hellcats and Demons will keep FCA and Dodge at the forefront of American high performance.

*This is the backrest of the driver's front bucket seat Sedoso/Ballistic Performance cloth with embroidered Scat Pack logo and Tungsten accent stitching in black.*

### Advertising and Publicity

The 2017 marketing and advertising program continued much like the previous year. Limited full-page ads were published in Mopar enthusiast publications with additional video presentations on YouTube. As always, Dodge's dealer publication, Mopar, usually carried ads and feature articles on the new cars.

# Additional books that may interest you...

**HOW TO BUILD NEW HEMI PERFORMANCE ON THE DYNO** by *Richard Holdener* Fitted with the right high-performance parts, these powerful New Hemi engines can produce far more horsepower and torque than stock. Selecting the ideal parts for the engine and application is essential. Veteran author and dyno testing expert Richard Holdener has done the research, gathered the data, and provided a detailed analysis of the results. Heads and camshafts, headers and exhaust, intakes, throttle bodies, manifolds, electronic engine controls, forced-air induction, and nitrous oxide are all tested. Softbound, 8.5 x 11 inches, 144 pages, 400 color photos. **Item # SA418**

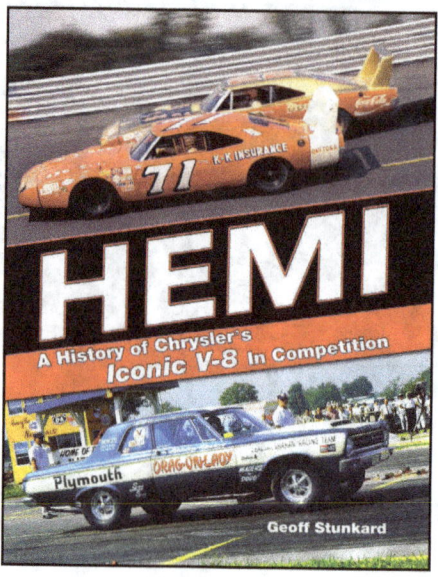

**HEMI: A History of Chrysler's Iconic V-8 In Competition** by *Geoff Stunkard* In the pages of this comprehensive Hemi history, the author goes behind the scenes and reveals how the engine was designed, built, tested, and eventually raced. He follows the engine as it rewrote racing history, became a highly sought-after engine in street cars, and redefined V-8 performance. Whether the Hemi was installed in a Charger, Super Bee, Baracuda, Superbird, or other car, it dominated in NHRA, NASCAR, and other forms of competition. The racing triumphs of Richard Petty, David Pearson, Dick Landy, Don Garlits, and countless others are brought back to life. Hardbound, 8.5 x 11 inches, 192 pages, 400 color photos. **Item # CT537**

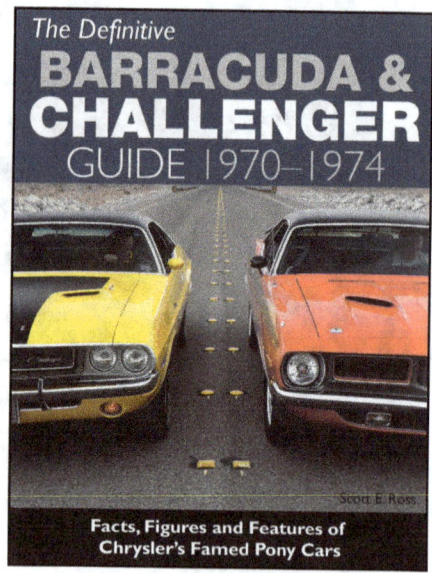

**THE DEFINITIVE BARRACUDA AND CHALLENGER GUIDE: 1970–1974** by *Scott Ross* If you have been searching for the comprehensive story and vital option information for these classic Mopar muscle cars, you don't need to look any further. Seasoned journalist Scott Ross has unearthed new information from the key personnel involved in designing, engineering, and building these brash muscle cars. He provides comprehensive engine, transmission, and interior options as well as essential trim package and color code information. Hardbound, 8.5 x 11 inches, 192 pages, 350 color photos. **Item # CT558**

**DODGE DAYTONA AND PLYMOUTH SUPERBIRD: Design, Development, Production and Competition** by *Steve Lehto* In the fiercely competitive world of NASCAR, every manufacturer was looking for a competitive edge. Ford and Chrysler turned their attention to the aerodynamics of their race cars, resulting in a brief era affectionately called the Aero Wars. During the height of this competition, Chrysler and Ford produced, among other things, cars with radically altered grilles and tail sections. These exotic beasts became some of the most costly, creative, and collectible machines ever assembled in Detroit, whether in race trim or in stock street trim. Author Steve Lehto gives a thorough and detailed account of this battle that culminated with the final wars between the Ford Talladega/Mercury Cyclone and the Dodge Daytona/Plymouth Superbird. Hardbound, 10 x 10 inches, 204 pages, 360 photos. **Item # CT543**

Check out our website:

## CarTechBooks.com

✓ Find our newest books before anyone else

✓ Get weekly tech tips from our experts

✓ Featuring a new deal each week!

**Exclusive Promotions and Giveaways at www.CarTechBooks.com!**

## www.cartechbooks.com or 1-800-551-4754

www.ingramcontent.com/pod-product-compliance
Lightning Source LLC
Chambersburg PA
CBHW081445070526
44586CB00019B/2232